Bought in Norwich
when on hols with Louise.
July 2015,

C. S. Lewis and His Circle

C. S. Lewis
and His Circle

*Essays and Memoirs from
the Oxford C. S. Lewis Society*

Edited by

ROGER WHITE

JUDITH WOLFE

AND BRENDAN N. WOLFE

OXFORD
UNIVERSITY PRESS

OXFORD

UNIVERSITY PRESS

Oxford University Press is a department of the University of Oxford.
It furthers the University's objective of excellence in research, scholarship,
and education by publishing worldwide.

Oxford   New York
Auckland   Cape Town   Dar es Salaam   Hong Kong   Karachi
Kuala Lumpur   Madrid   Melbourne   Mexico City   Nairobi
New Delhi   Shanghai   Taipei   Toronto

With offices in
Argentina   Austria   Brazil   Chile   Czech Republic   France   Greece
Guatemala   Hungary   Italy   Japan   Poland   Portugal   Singapore
South Korea   Switzerland   Thailand   Turkey   Ukraine   Vietnam

Oxford is a registered trade mark of Oxford University Press
in the UK and certain other countries.

Published in the United States of America by
Oxford University Press
198 Madison Avenue, New York, NY 10016

© Oxford University Press 2015

Library of Congress Cataloging-in-Publication Data
C. S. Lewis and his circle : essays and memoirs from the Oxford C. S. Lewis Society / edited
by Roger White, Judith Wolfe and Brendan N. Wolfe.
    p.   cm.
Includes index.
ISBN 978–0–19–021434–0 (cloth : alk. paper) 1. Lewis, C. S. (Clive Staples), 1898–1963—
Criticism and interpretation. 2. Oxford University C. S. Lewis Society. I. White, Roger, 1957–
editor. II. Wolfe, J. E. (Judith Elisabeth), 1979– editor. III. Wolfe, B. N. (Brendan N.) editor.
PR6023.E926Z5963 2015
823'.912—dc23

2014036236

1   3   5   7   9   8   6   4   2

Printed in the United States of America on acid-free paper

Contents

Foreword

IN MICHAELMAS TERM of 1981, the beginning of the academic year at Oxford University, the two of us kept meeting at the seemingly innumerable sherry parties that bring new students and their dons together.

We were both reading English Language and Literature at Mansfield College. Greg had arrived from the United States with an undergraduate degree under his belt, seeking at Oxford to deepen his literary education, while Suzanne had come from Loreto Convent School in Manchester. Almost instantly, as the saying goes, 'sparks flew' between us.

Early on we found points of connection through our shared love of C. S. Lewis and J. R. R. Tolkien. Suzanne's first gift to Greg was a single-volume paperback edition of *The Lord of the Rings*.

As we walked through the gorgeous halls of the Examination Schools at the 'Freshers' Fair'—the annual event where all the Oxford University student societies set up booths and recruit new members—we came to the room with various religious clubs. Most appeared to be strongly focused on either spirituality alone or on social justice and political action.

Later, as we reflected on what we'd seen, we felt that something was missing. Why wasn't there a society that grappled with the rich relationship between Christianity, culture, and the imagination, including literature?

Pondering the idea that we could found such a society, we were immediately struck with a question: What would it be called? What would the focal point be? If we named it 'The Theology and Culture Club', the result would be too abstract and academic. We wanted a serious discussion of ideas, to be sure, but we also hoped for lively conversation, wit, laughter, and a vibrant sense that literature, faith, and daily life might be deeply entwined.

Then it occurred to us: C. S. Lewis would be the ideal patron. He was not only a great 'talker', a towering literary and theological figure and former Oxford don, but above all a writer who was passionate to introduce his readers to *other* great writers and thinkers.

That's why the picture Suzanne drew to illustrate our first term card of scheduled meetings was of books whose spines showed the names of the Inklings and related figures, including G. K. Chesterton and Dorothy L. Sayers. We hoped that this sense of Lewis not only in his own right but also as a 'gateway' figure would also combat the tendency—which Greg felt was especially strong in the United States—to turn Lewis into a plaster saint, rendering every statement about him into hagiography.

With the generous aid of Walter Hooper we founded the Oxford University C. S. Lewis Society in Hilary term, 1982. Looking back over the past three decades—and in particular at the distinguished and substantial essays and memoirs that comprise this volume—we are filled with gratitude for all those who have made the Society's history so stimulating and generative.

Suzanne M. Wolfe and Gregory Wolfe

Preface

CONTEXTUALIZATION IS A common theme in the academic work of C. S. Lewis and J. R. R. Tolkien. Lewis's expositions of mediaeval cultures and outlooks remain highly regarded today; equally important are the determined arguments about the nature of *Beowulf* made by Tolkien. Lewis's denunciation of what he called the personal heresy, the desire to look through a work of art to the state of mind that produced it, is occasionally equated with disdain for any biographical investigation, but to do so is to miss the point entirely. Providing the context of a work of literature or philosophy was the essential task of the teacher for Lewis and Tolkien.

This collection of essays and memoirs originates from the Oxford C. S. Lewis Society and arises from the same intellectual and university community that formed and sustained C. S. Lewis, J. R. R. Tolkien, Charles Williams, Owen Barfield, and other members of the Inklings. The talks offered here in written form were first presented at meetings of the Society, which has convened continuously at the University of Oxford for over thirty years, only steps away from where the Inklings regularly met. The first audience for many of these papers included friends and colleagues of the Inklings, but also their successors as students and teachers at the university.

In the tradition of previous volumes of essays and memoirs, such as *Light on C. S. Lewis* (1965) and *C. S. Lewis at the Breakfast Table* (1979), this collection offers firsthand accounts and analyses from family, friends, colleagues, and acquaintances to provide a fuller picture of Lewis and his circle. We thought we had seen the last of these primary source anthologies and the exclusive context they bring because the voices within and directly linked to this group are disappearing. But the archived recordings of talks delivered at the Oxford C. S. Lewis Society still bear the living voices of Owen Barfield, John Tolkien, Elizabeth Anscombe, John Wain, and others. Some of the Society talks have since been published, but until now, many had remained only on audiotapes in the Society archives.

This endeavour unfolded through a series of phases, beginning with a review of the entire archive of over 200 talks. Those believed to contain unique content of particular interest to Lewis and Inklings scholars and devotees were selected for digitization and transcription. Collaboration with living authors and literary estates yielded authorized versions of the selected titles. The project was offered to Oxford University Press; the US branch in New York enthusiastically took up the mantle. The final product is a collection of essays and memoirs from a range of contributors representing scholars, family members, students, and friends from within the circle of those who crossed paths (and sometimes wits) with this great man. In the written versions we have retained UK spellings and punctuation. All notes are by the editors unless otherwise indicated.

A project of this duration and magnitude involves the time, toil, and treasure of many others, all of whom it would be impossible to include for sake of space. However, we would like to express our gratitude to several key collaborators on the project. Andrew Smith recorded many of the talks. Long-time Oxford C. S. Lewis Society members Peter Cousin, Richard Jeffery, Peter Miller, Timothy Bartel, and Jennifer Swift gave early advice on selection criteria for the collection. Laura C. Schmidt, Archivist at Wheaton College's Marion E. Wade Center, provided assistance in retrieving and digitizing some of the taped recordings; Joe Fortey helped decode some of the most inaudible selections. Transcription costs were partially funded by a grant from the Azusa Pacific University Faculty Research Council. Azusa Pacific University Provost Michael Whyte and Dean of the Libraries Paul Gray were gracious and generous in approving the time Roger needed to dedicate to the project. Michael Ward's knowledge, expertise, and advice were invaluable all along the way.

We extend particular thanks to those responsible for the literary estates of late authors, for their generosity, encouragement, and collaboration: Mary Geach and Luke Gormally (without whom parts of Elizabeth Anscombe's talk would have remained near-indecipherable), Owen A. Barfield (grandson of Inklings member Owen Barfield), Penelope Bide, Margaret Sayer, and Will Wain. Thanks and gratitude go to Cynthia Read and Glenn Ramirez at Oxford University Press in New York for their commitment, vision, energy, efficiency, and invariable good humour in seeing the project through to completion and marketing. Roger would like to especially thank his wife, Theresa Tisdale, for her loving support, wise counsel, and editorial input.

Roger White
Judith and Brendan N. Wolfe
September 2014

Author Biographies

Stella Aldwinckle (1907–1989) studied theology at Oxford and subsequently served as chaplain of the Oxford Pastorate. In 1941, she founded the Oxford Socratic Club, of which C. S. Lewis was President from 1942 to 1954.

Elizabeth Anscombe (1919–2001) was Professor of Philosophy at the University of Cambridge from 1970 to 1986. She was a student, editor, and translator of Wittgenstein, and is among the important philosophers of the twentieth century. Her 1948 debate with Lewis at the Oxford Socratic Club is often cited as his only outright intellectual defeat.

Owen Barfield (1898–1997) was a prolific writer and philosopher. Beginning in 1919, Barfield and Lewis maintained a life-long literary and intellectual friendship. From 1922 to 1930 the two engaged in an intense debate concerning imagination and truth, their 'Great War', as a result of which Barfield was instrumental in converting Lewis to theism. Barfield was a founding father of the 'Anthroposophical Society' and a visiting professor in North America. Lewis was godfather to Barfield's daughter Lucy; he dedicated and wrote the first Narnia book for her. Barfield was also Lewis's lawyer, adviser, and then trustee.

Peter Bide (1912–2003) studied English at Oxford before serving as a Royal Marines officer during the 1939–1945 war and then working at the Foreign Office. In 1949, he was ordained as a priest in the Church of England. After many years of parish ministry, he returned to Oxford as chaplain and tutor in Theology at Lady Margaret Hall in 1977, and remained there until his retirement in 1980. He officiated the marriage of C. S. Lewis and Joy Davidman Gresham.

Paul S. Fiddes holds the title of Professor of Systematic Theology in the University of Oxford, and is Director of Research at Regent's Park College, Oxford, having been Principal of the College from 1989 to 2007. His research interests include work on the interface between modern theology, literature, and continental philosophy. Among his many publications are *The Creative Suffering of God* (1988), *Past Event and Present Salvation: The Christian Idea of Atonement* (1989), *Freedom and Limit: A Dialogue between Literature and Christian Doctrine* (1991), *The Promised End: Eschatology in Theology and Literature* (2000), *Participating in God: A*

Pastoral Doctrine of the Trinity (2000), *Seeing the World and Knowing God: Hebrew Wisdom and Christian Doctrine in a Late-Modern Context* (2013).

Malcolm Guite is the Chaplain of Girton College. He also teaches for the Divinity Faculty in Cambridge and for the Cambridge Theological Federation, and lectures widely in England and North America on theology and literature. He is the author of *What Do Christians Believe?* (2006), *Faith Hope and Poetry* (2010), *Sounding the Seasons: Seventy Sonnets for the Christian Year* (2012), and *The Singing Bowl: Collected Poems* (2013). He contributed the chapter on Lewis as a poet to the *Cambridge Companion to C. S. Lewis* (2010). His blog can be found at www.malcolmguite.com.

Ronald Head, Rev. Canon, (1919–1991) was Vicar of Holy Trinity Church, Headington Quarry—the church C. S. Lewis and his household attended—from 1956 to 1990.

Walter Hooper was C. S. Lewis's personal secretary, friend, literary executor, and editor, and remains the foremost expert on Lewis in the world. Works by Lewis that he has edited include the *Complete Poems* (1964), the *Collected Letters* (2000–2006), and numerous essay collections. His own books include *Past Watchful Dragons* (1979), *War in Deep Heaven: The Space Trilogy of C. S. Lewis* (1987), and *C. S. Lewis: A Companion and Guide* (1996).

Stephen Logan is a musician and poet, who works also as a psychotherapist and lecturer in English. As lecturer, he has held senior appointments in Oxford, Cardiff, and Cambridge, where he is currently Principal Supervisor in English at Clare College. He has written several books of poetry, a monograph on Wordsworth, and has published widely in the national press. He has recently edited Peter Lomas's last book, *Natural Psychotherapy*, and has released a new album of original songs, 'Signs and Wonders'. His website is www.stevelogan.co.uk.

Alister McGrath was born in Belfast in 1953. Originally an atheist, he discovered Christianity while a student at Oxford University. McGrath served as Professor of Historical Theology at Oxford (1999–2008), and Professor of Theology, Ministry, and Education at King's College London (2008–2014). He is now the Andreas Idreos Professor of Science and Religion at Oxford University. He has written extensively on Lewis, and published two works to mark the fiftieth anniversary of Lewis's death: *C. S. Lewis—A Life: Eccentric Genius, Reluctant Prophet* (2013), and *The Intellectual World of C. S. Lewis* (2013).

Joan Murphy (née Lewis) was born in 1926 in Belfast and is first cousin, once removed to C. S. Lewis (her grandfather and C. S. Lewis's father were brothers). She studied History and Political Science at Trinity College Dublin with a research interest in the social world of Jane Austen. For many years she was a school librarian with an expertise in children's literature at the Church of England upper school in Oxford and an editor for *The School Librarian*. In retirement she trained as a Blue Badge Guide for the city of Oxford and specialized in C. S. Lewis related tours.

Michael Piret studied English Literature at the State University College at Fredonia, New York, then at the University of Michigan and Merton College, Oxford. He was Fulford Junior Research Fellow at St Anne's College, Oxford, before training for ordination in the Scottish Episcopal Church. After a curacy at Inverness Cathedral, he returned to Oxford to serve as Dean of Divinity (Chaplain) at Magdalen College.

George Sayer (1914–2005) studied English at Magdalen College, Oxford, where he was tutored by C. S. Lewis. He went on to teach at Malvern College, and remained a friend of J. R. R. Tolkien and C. S. Lewis, whose first biography he wrote.

Tom Shippey was an undergraduate at Cambridge (1961–1964), and attended Lewis's last set of lectures there. Since then he has taught at three British universities (Birmingham, Oxford, and Leeds) and three American ones (Harvard, Texas, and St Louis). He has published widely on mediaeval studies and mediaevalism, and has written three books on Tolkien. Now retired, he writes regularly for the *Wall Street Journal*.

John Wain C.B.E. (1925–1994), poet, author, and critic, was born in the Potteries and educated at St John's College, Oxford, in which city he spent most of his life. He served the University as Professor of Poetry from 1973 to 1978. His publications include thirteen novels and an acclaimed biography of Samuel Johnson (1974). The website of his Literary Estate is www.johnwain.com/wordpress.

Michael Ward is Senior Research Fellow at Blackfriars Hall in the University of Oxford and Professor of Apologetics at Houston Baptist University, Texas. A former warden of Lewis's home, The Kilns, he is the author of *Planet Narnia: The Seven Heavens in the Imagination of C. S. Lewis* (OUP 2008) and co-editor of *The Cambridge Companion to C. S. Lewis* (2010).

Kallistos Ware is an English bishop within the Eastern Orthodox Church under the Ecumenical Patriarchate of Constantinople, and one of the best-known contemporary Eastern Orthodox theologians. He holds the Titular Metropolitan Bishopric of Diokleia. From 1966 to 2001, Ware was Spalding Lecturer of Eastern Orthodox Studies at the University of Oxford. He has authored many books and articles pertaining to the Orthodox Christian faith, including *The Orthodox Church* (rev. ed. 1993).

Roger White is Curator of the Inklings Special Collection for the University Libraries as well as Professor of Ministry for the Seminary at Azusa Pacific University in Azusa, California. He has presented in Oxford and the U.S. on the personal library of C. S. Lewis and on Lewis's views of education. White is a co-author of *Mapping Out Curriculum in Your Church: Cartography for Christian Pilgrims* (2012).

Rowan Williams, Baron Williams of Oystermouth PC FBA FRSL FLSW, is an Anglican theologian. He was Lady Margaret Professor of Divinity at the University of Oxford before being appointed first Bishop of Monmouth and then Archbishop of Wales. From 2002 to 2012, he was the 104th Archbishop of Canterbury. After his resignation, he took up the Mastership of Magdalene College, Cambridge, where C. S. Lewis was a professor. Lord Williams has written numerous books of theology, literary criticism, and poetry, and is one of the most influential religious thinkers of the present.

Brendan N. Wolfe is, like J. R. R. Tolkien, a Germanic Philologist at Oxford, where in addition to the Gothic seminars and Old Saxon reading groups, he has for seven years taught Tolkien and Lewis to visiting students. He is Executive Editor of the *Journal of Inklings Studies*, and past President and Secretary of the C. S. Lewis Society of Oxford University. With Judith Wolfe, he has edited two other collections on C. S. Lewis: *C. S. Lewis and the Church* (2009) and *C. S. Lewis's Perelandra: Reshaping the Image of the Cosmos* (2013).

Gregory Wolfe is the founder and editor of *Image* journal. He serves as director of the low-residency MFA in Creative Writing program at Seattle Pacific University. His books include *Beauty Will Save the World, Intruding Upon the Timeless,* and *Malcolm Muggeridge: A Biography.*

Judith Wolfe teaches theology and the arts at the University of St Andrews, Scotland. She is the founding General Editor of the *Journal of Inklings Studies*, and has coedited two other collections on C. S. Lewis: *C. S. Lewis and the Church* (2009) and *C. S. Lewis's Perelandra: Reshaping the Image of the Cosmos* (2013). She also publishes on theology, literature, and philosophy more widely, most recently in the books *Heidegger's Eschatology* (OUP 2013) and *Heidegger and Theology* (2014).

Suzanne M. Wolfe, writer in residence at Seattle Pacific University, is a novelist whose books include *Unveiling* and the forthcoming *Augustine's Concubine.*

C. S. Lewis and His Circle

PART I

Essays

Philosophy and Theology

I

C. S. Lewis, Defender of the Faith

Alister McGrath

IT IS A very great pleasure to be able to speak to you tonight on the subject of C. S. Lewis as a defender of the Christian faith.[1] It is often said that the most original people are those who are most indebted to others, and there is certainly a sense in which this is true of Lewis. As we read his writings, we are bombarded with ideas and arguments drawn from throughout the rich heritage of the Christian church, and Western literature. Lewis's approach to defending the Christian faith rests on a very deep knowledge of a number of classic texts, including those of the great patristic theologian Augustine of Hippo (354–430).

Let me begin by introducing Clive Staples Lewis—'Jack' to his friends. Lewis was born in the city of Belfast on 29 November 1898. His father was a successful solicitor, who was doing well enough to allow the family to move to a large house ('Little Lea') on the outskirts of Belfast in 1905. Shortly afterwards, Lewis's mother died, leaving his father to look after Lewis and his elder brother Warren. The two brothers spent hours alone in the vast attic of the old house, inhabiting imaginary worlds of their own making.

If Lewis ever had any Christian faith to start with, he seems to have lost it in his teens. After a period serving in the British Army during the First World War, Lewis went up to Oxford. He was a student at University College in the period 1919–23, taking first class honours in Greats (classics and philosophy) in 1922, and first class honours in English the following year. After a period during which his future seemed uncertain, he was elected a fellow of Magdalen College in 1925. He would remain at the college until 1954, when he was invited to take up the newly-created chair of mediaeval and Renaissance English at the University of Cambridge, which carried with it a fellowship at Magdalene College. Lewis died at his Oxford home at 5.30 p.m. on 22 November 1963, a few hours before the world was shocked by the news of the assassination of President John F. Kennedy at Dallas, Texas.

During the 1920s, Lewis had time to reconsider his attitude to Christianity. The story of his gradual return to the faith he abandoned as a boy is described in great detail in his autobiography, *Surprised by Joy*. After wrestling with the clues concerning God he found in human reason and experience, he eventually decided that intellectual honesty compelled him to believe and trust in God. He did not want to; he felt, however, that he had no choice. The passage describing this great moment of decision has become well known:

> You must picture me alone in that room in Magdalen, night after night, feeling, whenever my mind lifted even for a second from my work, the steady, unrelenting approach of Him whom I so earnestly desired not to meet. That which I greatly feared had at last come upon me. In the Trinity Term of 1929 I gave in, and admitted that God was God, and knelt and prayed: perhaps, that night, the most dejected and reluctant convert in all England. I did not then see what is now the most shining and obvious thing; the Divine humility which will accept a convert even on such terms. The Prodigal Son at least walked home on his own feet. But who can duly adore that Love which will open the high gates to a prodigal who is brought in kicking, struggling, resentful, and darting his eyes in every direction for a chance of escape?[2]

After his conversion, Lewis began to establish his reputation as a leading authority on mediaeval and Renaissance English literature. *The Allegory of Love*, published in 1936, is still regarded as a masterpiece, as is his later *Preface to Paradise Lost*. It is a tribute to their excellence that both are still in print. Alongside his scholarly writings, however, Lewis began to write books of a very different character. Aiming at clarity and conviction, Lewis produced a series of works aimed at communicating the reasonableness of Christianity to his own generation. The works brought him popular acclaim, but seemed to some to destroy his scholarly reputation. In 1946, he was famously passed over for the Merton professorship of English Literature at Oxford. Someone who writes popular books, it was whispered, couldn't be a *real* academic.

Lewis's first popular book was *The Pilgrim's Regress*, based loosely on John Bunyan's classic work *Pilgrim's Progress*. It was not a commercial success. Nevertheless, Lewis continued writing at a popular level. *The Problem of Pain* appeared in 1940. It was well received, and, on the basis of its clarity and intelligence of its argument, Lewis was invited to give a series of radio talks by the British Broadcasting Corporation. In 1942, these were published as *The Case for Christianity*. Such was their success that Lewis combined them with two other short works—*Christian Behaviour* (1943) and *Beyond Personality*

(1944)—to yield *Mere Christianity*. 1942 also saw the publication of *The Screwtape Letters*, whose wit, insight, and sheer originality firmly established Lewis's reputation as a leading popular defender of the Christian faith.

That reputation was consolidated by further works, including *Miracles* (1947) and *The Four Loves* (1960). Outspokenly critical of 'Christianity-and-water' (as he dubbed liberal versions of Christianity), Lewis struck a deep chord of sympathy with his readers. The critics were furious. The Anglo-American journalist Alistair Cooke described him as a 'very unremarkable minor prophet', who would soon be forgotten once the Second World War had ended—a prediction in which Cooke showed himself to be both a very unremarkable and incompetent minor prophet.

Professional theologians were also irritated at Lewis's success, and accused him of grossly simplifying complicated things, best left to the professionals such as themselves. Lewis responded graciously, suggesting that if professional theologians had done their job properly there would be no need for lay theologians such as himself. For Lewis, one of the reasons for his own success (and the comparative lack of impact of professional theologians on a lay readership) was his ability and willingness to learn and speak the language of his audience, rather than making unwise and unrealistic assumptions about their abilities.

> We must learn the language of our audience. And let me say at the outset that it is no use laying down *a priori* what the 'plain man' does or does not understand. You have to find out by experience. . . . You must translate every bit of your theology into the vernacular. This is very troublesome . . . but it is essential. It is also of the greatest service to your own thought. I have come to the conviction that if you cannot translate your thoughts into uneducated language, then your thoughts were confused. Power to translate is the test of having really understood one's own meaning.[3]

Lewis's death in 1963 did nothing to stem the growing tide of interest in his writings. In April 1980, *Time* magazine reported that Lewis was unquestionably 'this century's most-read apologist for God.' Even after his death, his influence lives on; thousands who never knew Lewis in the flesh attribute their discovery of, or return to, Christianity to the influence of his writings.

So what is it about those writings which possesses such an appeal to so many? Unquestionably, part of the answer lies in Lewis's intelligent and persuasive approach to Christianity. For Lewis, Christianity makes sense. It commends itself by its reasonableness. Believing in God makes more sense,

Lewis argued, than not believing in him. *Mere Christianity* is perhaps as outstanding an example of a lucid and intelligent presentation of the rational and moral case for Christian belief as we are ever likely to see.

Yet there is more to Lewis than this. Alongside Lewis the cool-headed thinker we find a very different style of thinker—a man who is aware of the power of the human imagination, and the implications of this power for our understanding of reality. Perhaps one of the most original aspects of Lewis's writing is his persistent and powerful appeal to the religious imagination. Lewis was aware of certain deep human emotions which pointed to a dimension of our existence beyond time and space. There is, Lewis suggested, a deep and intense feeling of longing within human beings, which no earthly object or experience can satisfy. Lewis terms this sense 'joy', and argues that it points to God as its source and goal (hence the title of his autobiography). It is a powerful idea, with a long history of use and application in the Christian tradition. We find it in the famous prayer of Augustine of Hippo: 'You have made us for yourself, and our heart is restless until it finds its rest in you.' For Lewis, the apologist must speak to this restless human heart, and help it find its way home to its source and goal—the living and loving God.

To understand Lewis at this point, the idea of 'joy' needs to be explained in some detail. From the windows of his home in Belfast, the young Lewis could see the distant Castlereagh Hills. These far-off hills seemed to symbolize something which lay beyond his reach. A sense of intense longing arose as he contemplated them. He could not say exactly what it was that he longed for; merely that there was a sense of emptiness within him, which the mysterious hills seemed to heighten, without satisfying. In *The Pilgrim's Regress*, these hills appear as a symbol of the heart's unknown desire—something that nothing created or finite seems able to satisfy. We find much the same idea in Pascal's *Pensées*, in which Pascal develops the theme of an 'abyss' in human nature which is divinely created and can only be divinely satisfied. Lewis speaks of a sense of emptiness, a yearning for something indefinable, a deep conviction that there is something beyond our grasp which calls to us from the ends of the world, summoning us to something deeper and greater that presently lies beyond our reach.

Lewis describes this experience in his autobiography. He relates how, as a young child, he was standing by a flowering currant bush, when—for some unexplained reason—a memory was triggered off.

> There suddenly arose in me without warning, and as if from a depth
> not of years but of centuries, the memory of that earlier morning at the
> Old House when my brother had brought his toy garden into the

nursery. It is difficult to find words strong enough for the sensation which came over me; Milton's "enormous bliss" of Eden . . . comes somewhere near it. It was a sensation, of course, of desire; but desire for what? not, certainly, for a biscuit tin filled with moss, nor even (though that came into it) for my own past. . . . and before I knew what I desired, the desire itself was gone, the whole glimpse withdrawn, the world turned commonplace again, or only stirred by a longing for the longing that had just ceased. It had taken only a moment of time; and in a certain sense everything else that had ever happened to me was insignificant in comparison.[4]

Lewis here describes a brief moment of insight, a devastating moment of feeling caught up in something which goes far beyond the realms of everyday experience. But what did it mean? What, if anything, did it point to?

Lewis addressed this question in a remarkable sermon entitled 'The Weight of Glory', preached on 8 June 1941. Lewis spoke of 'a desire which no natural happiness will satisfy', 'a desire, still wandering and uncertain of its object and still largely unable to see that object in the direction where it really lies'. There is something self-defeating about human desire, in that what is desired, when achieved, seems to leave the desire unsatisfied. Lewis illustrates this from the age-old human quest for beauty. For Lewis, the quest for beauty is not so much for something that we merely see. We long 'to be united with the beauty we see, to pass into it, to receive it into ourselves, to bathe in it, to become part of it'. Yet we fail in our quest, because we fail to grasp where that beauty is situated.

The books or the music in which we thought the beauty was located will betray us if we trust to them; it was not *in* them, it only came *through* them, and what came through them was longing. These things—the beauty, the memory of our own past—are good images of what we really desire; but if they are mistaken for the thing itself they turn into dumb idols, breaking the hearts of their worshippers. For they are not the thing itself; they are only the scent of a flower we have not found, the echo of a tune we have not heard, news from a country we have never yet visited.[5]

Human desire, the deep and bittersweet longing for something that will satisfy us, points beyond finite objects and finite persons (who seem able to fulfil this desire, yet eventually prove incapable of doing so); it points *through* these objects and persons towards their real goal and fulfilment in God himself.

A similar pattern is observed with human personal relationships. In love, perhaps the deepest human relationship of all, we encounter the strange longing to lose ourselves in another—to enter into a relationship which paradoxically simultaneously heightens and obliterates our own identity. Yet even love, which seems to offer all, delivers less than it seems to promise. Somehow in personal relationships there is to be found a bittersweet longing— something which comes through the relationship, but is not actually in that relationship. Evelyn Waugh's novel *Brideshead Revisited* also speaks of the frustration of so much personal experience, whether in the quest for love or the quest for beauty. Somehow, that quest always fails to find its object. Even when the search seems close to its end, we find we have yet another corner to turn. Whatever it is that we are pursuing remains elusively ahead of us, evading our grasp.

For Lewis, human love seems to point to something beyond it, as a parable. The paradox of hedonism—the simple, yet stultifying, fact that pleasure cannot satisfy—is another instance of this curious phenomenon. Pleasure, beauty, personal relationships: all seem to promise so much, and yet when we grasp them, we find that what we were seeking was not located in them, but lies beyond them. There is a 'divine dissatisfaction' within human experience, which prompts us to ask whether there is anything which may satisfy the human quest to fulfil the desires of the human heart.

Lewis argues that there is. Hunger, he suggests, is an excellent example of a human sensation which corresponds to a real physical need. This need points to the existence of food by which it may be met. Thirst is an example of a human longing pointing to a human need, which in turn points to its fulfilment in drinking. Any human longing, he argues, points to a genuine human need, which in turn points to a real object corresponding to that need. And so, Lewis suggests, it is reasonable to suggest that the deep human sense of infinite longing which cannot be satisfied by any physical or finite object or person must point to a real human need which can, in some way, be met.

Lewis argues that this sense of longing points to its origin and its fulfilment in God himself. 'As the deer pants for streams of water, so my soul pants for you, O God. My soul thirsts for God, the living God' (Psalm 42:1). Lewis here echoes a great theme of traditional Christian thinking about the origin and goal of human nature. We are made by God, and we experience a deep sense of longing for him, which only he can satisfy. Lewis suggests that the pursuit of the clues offered by human desire only makes sense if there is a fourth dimension to human existence, served by the human imagination. The 'watchful dragon' of human reason is hesitant to allow us to speak of anything which goes beyond experience.

But is this transcendent object of desire real? Critics of Christianity such as Ludwig Feuerbach and Sigmund Freud argue that God is simply the projection of human desires and longings. We invent God to meet our deepest needs and longings. As Freud puts it, God is nothing more than a 'wish-fulfilment'. So how does Lewis respond to such arguments?

To deal with this question, Lewis turns to Plato's famous analogy of the cave. As Plato uses the analogy, we are asked to think of a group of men who are confined to a cave. A fire is burning, and they see shadows thrown onto the wall of the cave. The cave is the only world they have ever experienced, and so they naturally assume that it is the real world—the *only* world. The shadows they see are all that there is to reality. Then one of the men escapes from the cave, and discovers the great world outside; he returns to tell the others, who cannot believe him. Can there really be another world, which transcends the one they know from experience?

In Lewis's hands, this familiar image is transformed into a persuasive and powerful tool for relating the world of experience and the world that lies beyond it and through it—which Lewis identifies with God. Lewis uses this analogy in *The Silver Chair*, the sixth of the seven Chronicles of Narnia, which is based on two separate realms: the 'Overworld'—the real world of everyday experience—and a dark underground world, known as the 'Underworld'. A Narnian finds himself in the Underworld, where he is confronted by a witch who attempts to persuade him that the underground kingdom is the real world. There is no other reality outside this underground kingdom. The Narnian is not impressed. Knowing that she is wrong, however, he has to persuade her to enlarge her mental horizons. His argument is telling.

> Suppose we *have* only dreamed, or made up, all those things—trees and grass and sun and moon and stars and Aslan himself. Suppose we have. Then all I can say is that, in that case, the made-up things seem a good deal more important than the real ones. Suppose this black pit of a kingdom of yours *is* the only world. Well, it strikes me as a pretty poor one. And that's a funny thing, when you come to think of it. We're just babies making up a game, if you're right. But four babies playing a game can make a play-world which licks your real world hollow.[6]

The argument here is a classic, having its origins in the Greek fathers, and finding its mature expression in Thomas Aquinas: if certain ideas in our minds cannot be accounted for on the basis of our experience of the world, they must be accounted for in terms of something beyond that world. The apparently 'real' world must be supplemented by another world, an 'imagined world'—not in the sense of an *invented* world, but a *real* world into which we must enter by our imagination.

We see here a reflection of Lewis's own journey to faith. As a young man, Lewis found himself yearning for a world of passion, beauty, and meaning which he had come to believe did not and could not exist. His imagination told him there was a better world; his reason told him that this was nonsense. He therefore believed that he had no option other than to confront the bleakness of a senseless world and his pointless existence—until his discovery of the 'joy' of God.

Yet Lewis has not quite dealt with the objection we noted earlier. There remains the possibility that this 'imagined world' is an invented world. The reality, it might be argued, lies in the present world; the analogous idea is imaginary. Human fathers are real; God the father is a human invention. Lewis deals with this question head-on in a highly imaginative manner a few pages earlier in *The Silver Chair*. In her debate with the Narnian prince, the witch challenges him to tell her about what he calls 'the sun'. There is no equivalent in the underworld to which she belongs. The prince replies by constructing an analogy: the sun is like a lamp.

> 'You see that lamp. It is round and yellow and gives light to the whole room; and hangeth moreover from the roof. Now that thing which we call the sun is like the lamp, only far greater and brighter. It giveth light to the whole Overworld and hangeth in the sky.'
>
> 'Hangeth from what, my lord?', asked the Witch; and then, while they were all still thinking how to answer her, she added, with another of her soft, silver laughs: 'You see? When you try to think out clearly what this *sun* must be, you cannot tell me. You can only tell me that it is like the lamp. Your *sun* is a dream; and there is nothing in that dream that was not copied from the lamp. The lamp is the real thing; the *sun* is but a tale, a children's story'.[7]

In other words, the sun is an imagined and invented notion, which is based on a real object—a lamp.

Knowing that his readers are perfectly aware that the sun really exists, Lewis is thus able to demonstrate the superficial sophistication of the witch's argument: it seems clever and persuasive, but is actually seriously wrong. God is not just based on human figures (such as a shepherd, ruler, or father), but is an independent existence in his own right. Human figures are able to mirror him to some extent; this analogy, however, does not imply God's nonexistence! Throughout his writings, Lewis stresses the correspondence between human longings and their satisfaction through an encounter with the living God.

Lewis's remarkable genius lies partly in his taking some core Augustinian ideas, and re-crafting them in a way that's suitable for our own period. The Augustinian idea that God has created us for Himself, and therefore that we will always be dissatisfied and restless until we relate to God, is clearly seminal to Lewis. Likewise, Lewis also draws on Augustine's argument that it is easy for a desire for God to become falsely attached to transient, finite, and created objects. For Lewis, that can only lead to sadness and frustration. This divinely-created dissatisfaction is designed to make us ask where there is anything or anyone that is finally able to satisfy this emptiness. For Lewis this could only happen by God's grace and through God's presence.

So why was Lewis so successful as an apologist? A close friend of Lewis, the Oxford scholar Austin Farrer, pointed out how Lewis recognized that the rationality of faith was important for its broader cultural acceptance.

> For though argument does not create conviction, the lack of it destroys belief. What seems to be proved may not be embraced; but what no one shows the ability to defend is quickly abandoned. Rational argument does not create belief, but it maintains a climate in which belief may flourish.[8]

Yet Lewis did not limit the appeal of the Christian faith to its patterns of rationality. Lewis's success, Farrer argued, reflected his ability to offer 'a positive exhibition of the force of Christian ideas, morally, imaginatively, and rationally'.[9]

Perhaps we may learn something from Farrer's assessment of Lewis. Yet we most certainly can learn much about how best to present the Christian faith to an increasingly secular culture by reading Lewis himself. Lewis helps us to understand how the imagination retains both its hold on human nature and its capacity to break through the barriers of both secularism and rationalism. It is not simply Lewis's ideas that we must treasure, but the means by which he expresses them—above all, a well-told story.

Notes

1. This talk was given on 3 February 1998.
2. C. S Lewis, *Surprised by Joy* (London: HarperCollins, 2002), 228–229. For reflections on the nature and date of this conversion, see Alister McGrath, *C. S.*

Lewis—A Life: Reluctant Genius, Eccentric Prophet (London: Hodder & Stoughton, 2013), 135–59.

3. C. S. Lewis, *God in the Dock* (Grand Rapids, MI: Eerdmans, 1970), 96–98.

4. Lewis, *Surprised by Joy*, 16.

5. C. S. Lewis, *The Weight of Glory* (New York: HarperCollins, 2001), 30–31.

6. C. S. Lewis, *The Silver Chair* (London: Collins, 1993), 145.

7. Lewis, *The Silver Chair*, 141–142.

8. Austin Farrer, 'The Christian Apologist', in *Light on C. S. Lewis*, ed. Jocelyn Gibb, (London: Geoffrey Bles, 1965), 23–43; quote at p. 26.

9. Farrer, 'The Christian Apologist', 26.

2

C. S. Lewis's Rewrite of Chapter III
of Miracles

Elizabeth Anscombe

[PROFESSOR ANSCOMBE BEGAN by saying that she did not intend to discuss Chapter III of the first edition of *Miracles,* an argument within which she had criticised in a paper she gave to the Socratic Club in 1947.[1] Those interested in the earlier argument and criticism would need to refer to the first edition of *Miracles* and to the original publication of her criticism in the *Socratic Digest* or its reprinting in the second volume of her *Collected Philosophical Papers.*[2]]

What I want to talk about today is the argument of Chapter III of the second and later editions. The first edition chapter was called 'The Self-Contradiction of the Naturalist' and the second edition Chapter III was called 'The Cardinal Difficulty of Naturalism'. The first page or two are the same as in Chapter III of the first edition; after that it is quite different and is longer.

I said I wouldn't be saying anything about the original argument, but there is one thing that I will say, which is that there is a quotation by J. B. S. Haldane which occurs in both chapters, both in the Chapter III of the first edition, and he kept it in the second edition, though the quotation is embedded in a different paragraph. The quotation runs like this: 'If my mental processes are determined wholly by the motions of atoms in my brain, I have no reason to suppose that my beliefs are true . . . and hence I have no reason for supposing my brain to be composed of atoms.'[3]

Now I am going to consider this quotation on its own. Lewis says in 'The Cardinal Difficulty of Naturalism'—which is the only chapter I am going to be considering this evening—that he thinks what he calls Naturalism, even if not purely materialistic, seems to him to involve the same difficulty, though in a rather less obvious form.[4] That is the difficulty of having a certain self-inconsistency about the considered view of things, materialism being what J. B. S. Haldane was considering. That is to say, he says that a strict materialism refutes itself for the reason given by Haldane, for the reasons in the quotation I've just read to you.[5]

Now I want to consider that quotation all by itself. Let us suppose that it makes sense to say that mental processes—and this means everything they are inclined to call mental processes—are determined, determined wholly, by the motions of atoms in one's brain. That is, let us forget about the difficulties that might be raised about this, I mean the difficulties of talking about mental processes and when they are supposed to be determined.

In order to keep any such difficulties out of view, let us construct an analogous supposition, namely that it makes sense to say that linguistic marks—that is, marks that are parts of a language as they occur in a printed book—are wholly determined by the machinery that printed the book. Well, it might be a book. I don't think this book [in my hand] got any pencil notes in it or anything that might be linguistic matter that isn't printed.

This analogue has the advantage of certainly making sense, that is, that the linguistic marks occurring in this book are wholly determined by the machinery that printed the book. And indeed, it's got the advantage of not just certainly making sense, but of being true. Only we wouldn't dream of saying: *if* that is true, we have no reason to suppose that any of the things said in the book are true or are false, or anything like that.

Well, this illustrates the way in which a thought—a thought that somebody puts forward—trades on a mysteriousness about its objects. In the case of Haldane's remark, the mysterious objects are 'mental processes'; 'if every bit of every mental process is determined by motions of atoms, then I have no reason to suppose that my beliefs are true'. If we change the example to something lacking the mysteriousness of 'mental processes', for example to the existence of the print in a printed book, as I have in my analogue, then we observe two things. First, that the supposition that this is wholly determined by the machinery, the printing machinery, is true. And second, that that has no bearing whatever on whether anything said in the book is true, or whether we have reason or no reason to think so.

I'm taking 'wholly determined' to mean 'every bit of it is determined'; this is why I said I don't think that there are any words scribbled in the margin, that certainly weren't produced by printing machinery. This book [in my hand] is just a printed book that I haven't annotated, put any marks in, nor has anybody else. Every bit of it, every bit of the printed text, is determined. There aren't any bits of the text to be found in the book that aren't determined by the printing process. But of course 'it's wholly determined' might mean everything about it is determined by the machinery. And with that we'd be after all plunged into mystery and vagueness. Or, 'it's wholly determined' might mean its total and ultimate explanation is the motions of the machinery; there is no further or other causation involved.

Actually we wouldn't believe either of these propositions, so they wouldn't lure us into talking nonsense about whether there can be reason to believe a printed sentence.

Most of what I am going to say about Chapter III concerns just one spread, if I may call this a spread, of two pages, which in fact lie face to face, pages 20 to 21 in the paperback edition of the second edition.

In this chapter Lewis distinguishes between a cause-effect 'because',— 'Grandfather is ill . . . *because* he ate lobster yesterday',[6] and a ground-consequent 'because',—'Grandfather must be ill . . . *because* he hasn't got up yet (and we know he is an invariably early riser when he is well).'[7]

I'm going to divide the argumentation in this spread into A, B, C, D, E, and F.

A. 'Now', says Lewis, 'a train of reasoning has no value as a means of finding truth unless each step in it is connected with what went before in the Ground-Consequent relation.'[8] Each step in the train of reasoning must be connected with what went before in the Ground-Consequent relation *if* the train of reasoning is to have value as a means of finding truth. On the other hand, acts of thinking are events and 'every event in Nature must be connected with previous events in the Cause and Effect relation'.[9]

B. This presents him with a problem. If our conclusion is not the logical consequent of a ground, it is worthless, true only by accident, but it is true. Now 'unless it is the effect of a cause, it can't occur at all'.[10] So it looks as if, 'for a train of thought to have any value, these two systems of connection must apply simultaneously to the same series of mental acts'.[11]

C. 'But . . . the two systems are wholly distinct'; that's his expression, *'are wholly distinct'*. Being caused isn't being proved. Being caused raises a presumption of being groundless in belief. 'If causes fully account for a belief, then, since causes work inevitably, the belief would have had to arise whether it had grounds or not'.[12] We don't have to consider the grounds for something that can be fully explained without them.[13]

D. 'Even if grounds do exist', he goes on, 'what have they got to do with the actual occurrence of the belief as a psychological event?'[14] It must be caused if it is an event. If caused, it had to happen. It is just a link in a causal chain going back to the beginning of time. 'How could such a trifle as lack of logical grounds prevent the belief's occurrence or how could the existence of grounds promote it?'[15]

E. Faced with this problem, Lewis suggests that one way that a mental event can cause a subsequent mental event is 'simply by being a ground for it. For then being a cause and being a proof would coincide.'[16] However, he says this won't yet do. Thoughts don't 'necessarily cause all, or even any, of the thoughts which logically stand to it as Consequents to Ground. We should be in a pretty pickle', he says, 'if we could never think "This is glass" without drawing all the inferences which could be drawn. It is impossible to draw them all.'[17]

F. So he has reformulated the suggested law and says 'one thought can cause another not by *being*, but by being *seen to be*, a ground for it'.[18]

Let me pause in my exposition now in order to comment.

On my [A]: 'acts of thinking are events'. Well, it seems to me that a belief is not the same thing as an act of thinking. Nor need a belief even involve an act of thinking.

This may be unimportant to Lewis, however; he might say that the belief is usually a long-term state of mind and that, as such, beliefs must have causes too, like lasting temperatures. And anyway, he might say, a conclusion is an event and must therefore have a cause. Indeed he does say this in [B]. And it is fair enough that he should concentrate on thoughts that are conclusions, as what he is interested in is Reason, and so reasoning or inference. We may say to him: 'drawing a conclusion may be an event', even though it doesn't actually have to be one, it *can* be an event—'but a conclusion is not an event'.

However, that brings us nearer to his problem. If a conclusion isn't an event, as we've just said, what has something *being* a conclusion got to do with one's *coming* to believe it? And coming to believe is *surely* an event!

And so we can go on to consider [C]: being caused is utterly different from being proved, and what is caused is inevitable. 'Causes work inevitably',[19] he said. So there is, so to speak, no room for reasons or grounds to play any part.

Lewis sees, all right, that being a logical ground is not the same thing as operating in someone's mind as a logical ground. And equally, we can say, being a logical conclusion is not the same thing as being drawn as a logical conclusion. And so we can say one problem that he has is 'what *is* operating in someone's mind as a logical ground?' And that is a serious question. It is I think *the* serious question that he is asking in this chapter. It is confusingly combined in his text with the inevitability with which causes work. This, given the necessity of an event's having a cause, seems to leave reasons, logical grounds, out of the picture of natural processes.

Lewis's philosophical education had imbued him with such a conviction of determinism about events that he says he can't believe that modern physicists believe what they say—I think he's talking about indeterministic physics—he can't believe that they believe what they say.[20] He can *hardly* believe it.

Now, he's wrong about determinism and all causes necessitating their effects. But if we eliminated this part of his considerations, we'd be left with the problem which we have reached. It is just intensified by Lewis: causes aren't grounds, causes are necessary, causes necessitate their effect, so [D], where do grounds come into the possible explanation of human thoughts?

It is natural enough, however, that as that is the course his thinking takes here, he goes on to try and say—this is my [E]—that being caused and being a ground can coincide when the effect is a thought. But he sees an immediate consequence, given his conception of causes as working inevitably: we'd always have to draw all the conclusions of anything we believed and this we manifestly do not do. Hence he concludes that the cause of a 'rational' thought, that is to say, one which we do not have as a datum of sense experience or as any sort of mental record of a datum of sense experience, is *seeing* the logical implications of some other thought which will have had the same origin, unless it is itself an expression of sensation. For it was also part of Lewis's philosophical convictions that knowledge is all obtained by inference from sense experience and, as he sometimes adds, axioms, but I think he doesn't mention them here. It's in some other writing of his. Here he is saying 'knowledge is all obtained by inference and sense experience.'

Well, it is false that our knowledge is all inference from sensations (that's his term, by the way, rather than sense experience, *inference* from sensations)[21]: it is false that all causes necessitate their effects; it is even false that seeing that something is a logical consequence of something you already believe inevitably causes you to believe the new thing.

However, all these things are really side issues. We can leave them on one side and concentrate on the problem—the problem that Lewis is grappling with and which is not a problem for him just because he has some of those opinions. So let's return to it: What *is* operating in someone's mind as a logical ground? What is it for something—which *is* a logical ground—to operate in someone's mind as that?

Lewis gives nice expression to this problem when he says, 'Even if grounds do exist, what exactly have they got to do with the actual occurrence of the belief as a psychological event?'[22] He also says, 'acts of inference can, and must, be considered in two different lights. On the one hand they are subjective events, items in somebody's psychological history. On the other hand, they are insights into, or knowings of, something other than themselves. What from the first point of view is the psychological transition from thought A to thought B, . . . is, from the thinker's point of view, a perception of an implication (if A, then B)'.[23]

In this passage, the weakest part is 'insights into, knowings of, something other than themselves'. For this he has used in the same paragraph to characterize 'acts of thinking': 'they are very special types of events',—yes, they are events, 'but they are a very special sort of events. They are "about" something other than themselves and can be true or false. Events in general are not "about" anything and cannot be true or false.'[24]

Indeed, he gives this as a ground why acts of inference have to be considered 'in two different lights'.[25] But his language suggests that acts of inference are always 'insights', 'knowings', and so they are not just a species of 'acts of thinking', as these 'can be true or false'. This raises the question that he does not raise, which is unavoidably raised in my mind, at any rate, by what he says, 'can acts of inference be false?' That is to say, can one infer what does not follow? Well, ordinary language certainly allows us to say so. 'The book is a farrago of false inferences,' you might read in some hostile review. Or one may make the observation, 'In committee meetings one is always hearing non-reasons for decisions being recommended'. Or again, commenting on a book, on an essay: 'He draws conclusions which simply do not follow from the premises he states'.

It looks as if Lewis might say, or might *have* to say, 'When you call an inference false, you are looking at it only as a "subjective" event, an item in someone's psychological history. It isn't an insight, a perception of an implication, it merely seems to the thinker to be that, if he isn't just pretending'. If this is right, then Lewis ought not to have said that 'from the thinker's point of view' an inference is a perception of an implication, intending to contrast it *as that* with what it is as a subjective event. If we allow that there *are* fallacious inferences, we *are* characterizing inference only as a 'subjective event', and it [is] as such that 'from the thinker's point of view it is a perception of an implication'. That is like saying, 'from the drunkard's point of view his experiences are perception of snakes swarming over him.'

Now Lewis didn't mean that. He merely meant, I think, that there aren't fallacious 'acts of inference'. What are called that, are not inferences at all. We may call them pseudo inferences. The thinker may have illusions of inference, but actual inference is the transition from a thought A to a thought B either in the form 'A, so B' or the form 'suppose A, then B', when this transition is correct, but only when it is correct.

My main reason for thinking this—that is, for thinking that this is what Lewis was getting at—is that he says: 'We cannot . . . reject the second point of view as a subjective illusion without discrediting all human knowledge.'[26] We certainly can in the particular case, where someone is engaged in 'fallacious inference'. Lewis is just not thinking of that case. Just as when he says, 'all possible knowledge . . . depends on the validity of reasoning. . . . Unless human reasoning is valid no science can be true.'[27] When he says that, he means to refer to reasoning rightly so called, as one might put it.

Again he says, earlier in the chapter, 'for that theory'—I think that he has in mind Naturalism, something like that—'would itself have been reached by thinking, and if thinking is not valid that theory would . . . be itself demolished.'[28] Now by thinking he here means 'argument', for he goes on to say, 'it would be an argument which proved that no argument was sound.'[29] I did because of one or two passages like that entertain the idea that perhaps Lewis was guilty of confusing truth and validity. I think on occasion he has done so, but I don't think after all he is doing so here. I think that he doesn't mean the thinking of thoughts which are true or false, but argumentation.

It's an interesting fact, by the way, that he can declare that thinking is valid where he would not and could not say 'arguing is valid' or 'arguments are valid'. For if anybody dared to say 'arguments are valid', anybody could reply at once 'but you mean some arguments are valid and some are not'. For whatever we say about thinking, reasoning and inference, we cannot say, 'there is no such thing as an invalid argument'.

Lewis was apparently unable to explain what he meant (at least as far as I can judge) by 'insights into, knowings of, something other than themselves' when he spoke of 'acts of inference'. One is puzzled by the expression 'something other than themselves'. I'm inclined to suppose that he is making a contrast with things like having a ringing in one's ears or an impression of a colour where what one has, Cartesianly considered, is a knowing of 'nothing but itself'. That act of consciousness, one might say, knows nothing of itself, unlike proper hearing and proper seeing.

The idea of 'something other than themselves' is clearly of importance to Lewis; he writes of it again at the end of the chapter (and I now stop considering the spread of pages 20 to 21, which in my mind is the strongest and most interesting part of the chapter).

In the chapter he speaks of attempts to fit our acts of inference into our picture of Nature. 'When we try to do this', he says, 'we fail. The item which we put into that picture and label "Reason" always turns out to be somehow different from the reason we are ourselves enjoying and exercising while we put it in. The description we have to give of thought as an evolutionary phenomenon always makes a tacit exception in favour of the thinking which we ourselves perform at that moment . . . our present act, claims and must claim, to be an act of insight, a knowledge sufficiently free from non-rational causation to be determined (positively) only by the truth it knows.'[30] This formulation 'knowledge determined only by the truth it knows' is extremely obscure.

How on earth is the truth that there is only one even prime number capable of determining and being the sole determinant of knowledge or can cause knowledge—because I suppose determinant means cause. If it doesn't, then I'm unclear what it means.

Well, it remains obscure to me. I take him, though, to mean, for example, that when considering a piece of knowledge or what claims to be knowledge, we consider the matter supposedly known and not only the condition of the supposed knower. Nor, to the extent that we do consider that, are we concerned with what may have caused some psychological state that he is in. I mean, we might consider about the condition of the supposed knower: 'Is the supposed knower somebody who was present on the occasion which he is purporting to report?', for example, which is something about the supposed knower. But we aren't concerned with what may have caused some psychological state that he is in, as we do consider causes of anxiety, losses of short term memory, fits of laughter—we look then into his psychological or indeed physiological state.

This is the nearest that I can get to an interpretation of this damnably obscure proposition, 'knowledge determined only by the truth it knows'. However, I hope to have shown that there is here in this chapter—Chapter III of the second edition of the book *Miracles*—material for serious discussion, material which is genuinely problematic. I don't mean problematic in the way in which what Lewis meant by 'knowledge determined only by the truth it knows' is problematic—problematic in the sense of the question 'what on earth did Lewis mean?' It's not obscure what he meant when he raises the question: what have the grounds to do with the actual occurrence of the belief that is a psychological event or, as I put it earlier, 'what is it for logical grounds not merely to exist for a conclusion but actually to have caused the conclusion?'

Notes

1. The following text is based on a very imperfect audiotape of Professor Anscombe's talk on 12 November 1985 to the Oxford C. S. Lewis Society, corrected in parts in the light of an incomplete draft manuscript of the talk.

2. G. E. M. Anscombe, *Metaphysics and the Philosophy of Mind: The Collected Philosophical Papers of G. E. M. Anscombe*, Volume II (Oxford: Basil Blackwell, 1981), 224–232.

3. J. B. S. Haldane, 'When I Am Dead', in *Possible Worlds: And Other Essays* (London: Chatto and Windus, 1927), 209; C. S. Lewis, *Miracles*, 1st ed. (London: Geoffrey Bles, 1947), 28–29; 2nd ed. (Fontana Books, 1960), 19.

4. *Miracles*, 2nd ed., 19.

5. *Miracles*, 2nd ed., 19.

6. *Miracles*, 2nd ed., 19.

7. *Miracles*, 2nd ed., 19.

8. *Miracles*, 2nd ed., 19.

9. *Miracles*, 2nd ed., 20.

10. *Miracles*, 2nd ed., 20.

11. *Miracles*, 2nd ed., 20.

12. *Miracles*, 2nd ed., 20.

13. *Miracles*, 2nd ed., 20.

14. *Miracles*, 2nd ed., 20.

15. *Miracles*, 2nd ed., 20.

16. *Miracles*, 2nd ed., 21.

17. *Miracles*, 2nd ed., 21.

18. *Miracles*, 2nd ed., 21.

19. *Miracles*, 2nd ed., 20.

20. *Miracles*, 2nd ed., 17–18.

21. *Miracles*, 2nd ed., 21.

22. *Miracles*, 2nd ed., 20.

23. *Miracles*, 2nd ed., 21.

24. *Miracles*, 2nd ed., 21.

25. *Miracles*, 2nd ed., 21.

26. *Miracles*, 2nd ed., 21.

27. *Miracles*, 2nd ed., 18.

28. *Miracles*, 2nd ed., 19.

29. *Miracles*, 2nd ed., 19.

30. *Miracles*, 2nd ed., 27–28.

3

C. S. Lewis and the Limits of Reason

Stephen Logan

ONE OF THE more beguiling errors of our times is that a highly developed intellect is an antidote for social and personal ills.[1] You can see how this error comes about: people ask themselves the question, 'what does a good life consist of?', or (more probably) 'how should I live?', and, almost as naturally as they'd consult certain people they know, they consult books. The more difficult books require a special effort to understand them, and people who make this effort have often developed the specialized mental abilities known as 'cleverness'; hence it's assumed that the cleverest people are the ones best placed to answer the question 'how should I live?'. Yet there are many indications that this is an error.

First, there is the evidence of experience. Universities are full of clever people, yet the public consensus is that, far from being well-qualified to discern and communicate the true nature of what might, for a particular person, constitute a good life, academics are very unreliable mentors in the arts of living. There's a special term in the vernacular to express this view: an 'educated idiot'. Then there's the evidence of what's been felt about professional mentors even in the spiritual realm. The Pharisees are presented in the gospels as clever, yet Christ is so consistently on guard against them[2] that the term Pharisee is a byword for people who show themselves ignorant by professing to be clever.[3] St Paul similarly is full of warnings about the dangers of getting caught up in foolish and idle speculations,[4] and there are clear parallels to this in the wisdom of the ancients of the Far and Middle East. And yet it took a clever man like St Paul to recognize the limitations of cleverness; and this is a way of saying that cleverness is very good for some purposes, bad for others, and that real intelligence, a different thing from cleverness, depends on recognizing both the strengths and limitations of intellectual agility.

In our own times we've seen the success of a book like Daniel Goldman's *Emotional Intelligence*, whose very title, as well as having now become a catchphrase in need of deconstruction, suggests a whole skein of difficulties we've got ourselves into as a result of misconceiving what intelligence might be.[5] F. R. Leavis, a literary critic not much honoured these days, began one of his later books with the assertion, 'L'intelligence is not the same as intelligence.'[6] This might be translated, 'intelligence is more than IQ'. The distinction doesn't seem very recondite, though I suspect Leavis resorts to French in order to surprise us back into a proper puzzlement. The whole issue needs, I think, careful unravelling, since the depth of our confusedness about the nature of reason goes beyond, in my opinion, the range of ordinary caution.

And it's here that Lewis can be crucially helpful. Lewis is widely regarded as a reasoner but outside academe, at any rate, he's best known, perhaps, for his non-discursive writings, pre-eminently the Chronicles of Narnia. Yet since these must derive their qualities from the character of his mind and since his mind is conspicuously characterized by, among other things, its dialectical power, it seems natural to suppose that even Lewis's fictional writings must benefit in some deep and subtle way from his reasoning powers. Yet it seems to me that his authority and appeal as a reasoner depend on his using reason in a special way, a way that doesn't isolate it from other modes and functions of our perceptual apparatus, such as those we call 'imagination'. And imagination—which I would define briefly in one of Coleridge's two senses as ordinary (and limitlessly extraordinary) perception—is a function of the whole being: the psyche, or soul.[7]

That imagination and reason are aspects of some more complex whole becomes evident if we try to classify Lewis's writings. If we call his space trilogy, his mythopoeic fiction, *Till We Have Faces*, and the Chronicles of Narnia, 'imaginative', we cannot help implying that the literary criticism and theological writings are unimaginative. A moment's thought may suggest that the distinction we habitually make between thinking and feeling is misleading. Imagine yourself walking into a glass door. What you feel is a sensation of pain, and it's natural to think of pain as a physical phenomenon—a matter of feeling; but if you imagine that at the moment of impact your brain was switched off, it's clear that you'd experience no pain. Sensation, in other words, is not exclusively an emotional or an intellectual phenomenon but somehow both, or, rather, a totality from which these two modes of experience are misleading abstractions. The structure of the English language, however, is such that we're impelled to assign experiences to the category of either thought or feeling. We have plenty of words that mean 'pertaining to thought': *rational, cerebral, intellectual, cognitive*, and so on. And we have plenty of words meaning 'pertaining to feeling': *emotional, sentimental, affective, touching*, and so on. What we don't have is a range of words relating to the complex whole experience from which thought and feeling are abstractions. So when we talk or write about experience, we are in certain ways impelled by the language to misrepresent it, or, in the case of English, to represent it within a scheme of conceptual categories which are misleadingly divisive. Hence the fact that books, particularly those written in an academic idiom, cognitively top-heavy, often seem foreign to the nature of experience; and hence the fact that philosophers like Wittgenstein or psychotherapists like D. W. Winnicott and Peter Lomas think ordinary usage a much more reliable index of the complexity of experience than any technical terminology could be.[8] I'm reminded here of Lewis's remark that learned language is easy but the vernacular is the real test if you have something difficult to express: 'Any fool can write *learned* language. The vernacular is the real test. If you can't turn your faith into it, then either you don't understand it or you don't believe it.'[9]

William Empson, similarly, said that if he wanted to find out whether something he had written was nonsense, he translated it into Basic English (a simplified version of the language developed for learners).[10]

Here perhaps is an indication of why poets writing in English often tend to give the Anglo Saxon parts of the language priority over the Graeco-Roman. Admittedly, the eighteenth century is a partial exception, since experiments there often tended the other way; yet the remark holds true for perhaps a majority of canonical poets. Milton—another apparent exception—uses Latin words with an awareness of their etymological implications that makes them, for him (as perhaps for Pope and Johnson), vividly sensuous. But other poets— Shakespeare, Wordsworth, Keats and Hopkins, for example—locate the sensuous primarily within the parts of the language which were established before the influx of Latin and Greek during the Renaissance. In the UK, the Graeco-Roman words in English are the prerogative of those people with a prolonged formal education. In my last two sentences, the words 'locate', 'sensuous', 'primarily', 'language', 'established', 'influx', 'Renaissance', 'Graeco-Roman', 'prerogative', 'prolonged', 'formal', and 'education' are all derived from Latin and Greek. Most of them do not figure much in common usage. Yet the words in the sentence I am writing now are all (except 'sentence' and 'except') taken from among the words that everyone knows. Because we've known many of these Anglo-Saxon words from our infancy, they have been enriched and modified by all the millions of contexts in which all the commonest words recur. These words ('sky', 'grass', 'mother', 'father', 'long', 'go', 'come', 'high', 'love', 'hot', etc.) pertain more directly to what we experience through our senses. Hence they are like buckets which we can drop down into the depth of our experience to haul out secret, elusive, forgotten, or unconscious meanings.

I put it to you that we value poetry, which I'm now going to discuss, because it has the power to heal such false distinctions as that between thinking and feeling and thereby put us in touch with the true heart and living tissue of our own being. It can help make us aware of the dimensions of our own capacity for living life richly and well. It serves in this sense a quasi-spiritual function since it's accessory to the grace by which we might hope to have life and have it more abundantly ('fully' in Anglo-Saxon). This, I believe, is close to the nub of the reason why Lewis valued poetry and why he was so disappointed when he argued himself into believing that he was not a distinguished poet. Even so, many of the qualities which made Lewis want to be a poet are fully manifested in his writings generally, including of course his poems, which, whatever their 'status', are perhaps like Matthew Arnold's, a unique and irreplaceable expression of the whole man.

But I must, to make sense of this argument, go back a bit and ask some questions which, like all the most staggering ones, are elementary. What are poems for? And where do they come from? Judging by the way that poets talk about the genesis of poems, they don't arise from the same regions, or activities, of the mind as discursive prose. ('Regions' is of course a metaphor; but given the specificity of the relations between particular abilities and particular parts of the brain, perhaps it is not, for all its crudeness, entirely unapt.) Here, for example, is C. H. Sisson, discussing how he actually writes a poem:

> All my poems are in a sense determined by the rhythm of the first line, which comes unasked and often when one is least expecting it. It is commonly followed by other lines, whether by one or two or by a whole poem. I am very relaxed about this. Nothing more may come than this fragmentary manifestation. It's important not to go on deliberately—wilfully making up, as it were, for the failure of the natural process. To know what one is going to say is a sign that one has nothing to say—nothing, that is, which needs a poem to convey it. If there is a poem there, it will present itself.[11]

Louis MacNiece makes a similar point, suggesting that poems justify themselves by expressing what we may not quite consciously be able to express. 'Poets', he says, '. . . do not know (exactly) what they are doing, for if they did there would be no need to do it.'[12] Seamus Heaney, talking ostensibly about T. S. Eliot's poem, 'Marina', but implicitly about how he himself writes a poem, says:

> . . . here we have 'de la musique avant toute chose'. The ear has incubated a cadence, a cadence which is to be found in the epigraph to the poem itself and which may well have constituted, in Valéry's terms, the poem's donné.[13]

The notion of incubating a cadence implies that a poet (Eliot, Heaney, Valery, Sisson, MacNiece, among innumerable others) will feel some trick of rhythm emerging in the mind and that by brooding on it, as a hen might sit on an egg, she or he will cause its meaning to hatch (or symbolize itself in words) and thereby turn into a complete poem. The poem results from incubating some vague but possibly strong urge towards meaning which comes more clearly before the conscious mind when words corresponding to it are found.

In a compilation of recordings of himself reading, Heaney makes some very interesting interlinking remarks about the poems. He says there that he was asked to write a poem on a public occasion and he had made many attempts at it but he couldn't produce anything which to him had a 'credible poetic life'. Again, there is an implication that the conscious effort to produce the poem somehow defeats this.

When Philip Larkin was asked how he felt when he'd written a poem, he said he felt 'as if I'd laid an egg'[14]; there you've got the metaphor of incubation coming back and something brought very surprisingly into an existence related to, but not easily imaginable from, the hen's first urge to lay or the poet's to write. Shelley was one of Lewis's favourite poets—very mysteriously, in some ways, because Shelley is obscure and indeterminate in all sorts of ways that Lewis in his prose tries not to be. Sometimes Shelley drafted a poem by literally writing in the shape of a stanza the words 'Ni, nal, ni, na, na, ni', for lines and lines and lines. In Shelley's manuscripts there are whole pages that are full of the notation, 'Na, na, na na ná, na' and so on.[15] What he's quite obviously doing there is incubating a cadence. He's caught a tune that somehow corresponds to the feel of the meaning that he's being impelled to express and he thinks that if he gets this tune down he'll be able to coax the poem out of him: to find, that is, an intelligible sequence of words which symbolizes more explicitly the significance latent in the tune.

Keats's early poem 'Sleep and Poetry' very strongly implies that the impulse to writing poems is to be found often in dreams. And Milton at three places in *Paradise Lost* tells us that his method of poem composition was to go to sleep, dream, wake up in the morning, remind himself of what his nightly slumbers had brought him, and then go and dictate the results of his dreams.

This is all quite close to implying that poetry comes from what we currently describe, and somehow attempt to conceive of, as the unconscious. Since Freud, it's become usual in many fields of discourse to distinguish between conscious and unconscious processes of the mind and to treat the unconscious ones with respect. We recognize, however, that the results of the unconscious processes can be difficult to catch. T. S. Eliot, in yet another metaphor of incubation, says that writing a poem is like trying to bring to birth 'a dark embryo of meaning': you didn't know what it was that was impelling you to write a poem (hence the origin and purpose of the impulse might be 'dark'); neither the poem nor your sense of purpose in writing it were fully formed (hence they were like an 'embryo').[16] The process of writing the poem, and of discovering whatever might become clear during it, was like bringing something to birth. It was an attempt to catch an impulse from the unconscious and to find a way of embodying its significance in a musical sequence of words. (The musicality of poetry is not an adjunct to its meaning, but the medium within which its meaning inheres.)

This attempt to release the unconscious into consciousness as a source of creativity parallels Wordsworth's attempts at recovering authenticity of expression (and so of experience). By sloughing off poetic jargon, and putting language back in touch with the current habits of thinking and feeling, it might be possible to experience the world freshly. Having been born into a poetic language gone stale, we might, by re-achieving freshness, be born again.[17] More prosaically, as he put it in prose, the endeavour was to evade what he called 'pre-established codes of decision',[18] to hop outside the tramlines of standardised feeling and get instead to something that was literally strange (because estranged) and true. Yet obviously there's a need to distinguish between avoiding the dullingly predictable and repudiating everything that might seem traditional or 'stock' within our responses.

Lewis professed himself in favour of preserving stock responses, though he did distinguish between good and bad ones. There is, I'll admit, a worrying kind of bluffness about this for me, swiftly succeeded by an equally worrying recognition that sometimes a simple distinction may be of more ethical value than a subtle one. Maybe the Modernist credo and associated technical innovations were overstrained; and there is the usual problem of Eliot's personal beliefs being treated as axiomatic; but we know for certain that Lewis as a younger man didn't like, or believed he didn't like, Modernism, and he disliked in particular its preoccupation with urban squalor. Like C. E. M. Joad and other influential spokesmen of his generation, he was troubled by the suspicion that all this talk about the authority of the unconscious was a pretext for self-indulgent and socially and culturally destructive barbarism. Thus, in quite a late poem of 1954, 'Confession', he writes, with an irony that makes self-denigration seem false, or faux-naïf:

> I am so coarse, the things the poets see
> are obstinately invisible to me.
> For twenty years I've stared my level best

> *To see if evening— any evening— would suggest*
> *A patient etherised upon a table;*
> *In vain. I simply wasn't able.*[19]

Lewis is here (and in some respects obtusely) parodying the opening of El-iot's poem, 'The Love Song of J. Alfred Prufrock', as though Eliot had been trying to write a loco-descriptive poem in the manner of John Masefield and the famous opening simile were a botched attempt at landscape. The only respect in which Lewis's poem truly simulates the manner of Eliot's is in the deliberate bathos of the rhyme, 'A patient etherised upon a table. In vain. I simply wasn't able.' From the standpoint which Lewis here seems to be as-suming—I'm remembering Barfield's point that Lewis could seem zeal-ously intent on subordinating himself to an image of the man he'd decided to become[20]—'Prufrock' might seem in the wilfulness of its own subver-sions an anti-poem. That, in some ways, is honourably its nature; but Lewis's poem soon settles (for the first six of ten lines in each of the first two stanzas) into a lucid, expository manner. This, aligning itself with satirical poems being written by George Orwell (among others), conducts a defence of stylis-tic traditions, and their associated forms of feeling, which the poetics of Modernism seemed to Lewis recklessly bent on displacing. A view congru-ent with Lewis's own has been more cautiously advanced by John Carey in his book *The Intellectuals and the Masses*, which argues that Modernism was a sort of hoax, by which Eliot, Pound, and Woolf diverted academic attention from the popular yet intelligent literary traditions represented by Arnold Bennett, H. G. Wells, and Jerome K. Jerome.[21]

Nonetheless, Lewis was as interested as the Modernists were and as the Romantics had been in evading uncreative rituals of experience. He, too, ar-dently wanted to liberate himself into a renovated style of living—though of course this entails risk, against which Lewis was heavily defended. Experi-encing the miraculous in the ordinary and writing about poetry so as to help others experience it might indeed help realize some the best potentialities of human nature; but the problem was to achieve this with minimal disruption to the conventions which gave a necessary assurance of stability, both per-sonal and cultural.

Lewis was a vivid dreamer and regularly confessed to being troubled by nightmares. Having found in the experience of watching a man go mad a pretext for scepticism about psychoanalysis, he didn't interpret his dreams with psychoanalytic seriousness; but he took the unsolicited promptings of what he called his imagination very seriously indeed, and the imagination it seems to me is, among other things, a name for the means by which we dissolve the distinction between unconscious and conscious; or, perhaps, for forms of perception in which the whole activity of the mind is more present. Lewis writes frequently about the genesis of his fictions, using words to the effect of, 'It all began with a picture', For example: 'In the Author's mind there bubbles up every now and then material for a story. For me it invariably begins with mental pictures.'[22] Lewis is insistent that he doesn't attach a moral to these pictures or try to make up pictures which illustrate a moral. He thinks you should let the pictures disclose their own moral inherencies. There's a relation, clearly, between this kind of process and the process of incubation which the poets I've quoted have said they were engaging in. The prompting to write, or the impulse behind, the poem comes to the poet unbidden (or bidden, but uncommanded); and it seems very important to most poets that they should not, in the initial stages, work on it too hard, but let the impulse manifest itself in its own way, given that they do possess appropriate kinds of technical know-how.

According to Tolkien, Lewis once described 'fairy-story making' as 'Breathing a lie through silver'.[23] That, for Tolkien, fairy stories were a type of myth is evident from his having replied to this remark in a poem which conflates the two.[24] More optimistically, Lewis later defined myth as 'a real though unfocused gleam of divine truth falling on human imagination'.[25] In saying that myth is 'a real though unfocused gleam of divine truth falling on human imagination', we have the same association found consistently in the Romantics and frequently in Eliot and his successors between an unsolicited and therefore (in our current post-Freudian terminology) 'unconscious' prompting and the deepest kind, in this case, a 'divine' kind of 'truth'. So the idea is that somehow what comes to you unbidden from the imagination contains within itself a truth which is potentially a divine truth; and this idea is taken very seriously by Lewis, much in the same way as the idea about the unborn poem as a dark embryo struggling to achieve intelligible form is taken seriously by Modernist poets.

But why should we want to gain access to the unconscious? In order to answer this question, we need to ask another staggering one. What is life? What are the deepest and most important moments of our experience? What does it mean to be fully and fruitfully alive?

The question 'What is life?', in various forms, is apt to produce a blankness in the mind from which we seek refuge, either in knowing mockery (such as often accompanies the related question, 'What's the meaning of life?'), or in scientific explanations which substitute a biological question for the philosophical one, or again in more innocent circumlocutions such as 'What is life for?', which leaves our conception of 'life' uninvestigated while we consider the purposes for which we might use it. In view of the difficulty, it seems reasonable—provided we are genuinely trying to focus on the philosophical issue—to reformulate the question slightly so as to provide some relief from the sensation of blankness, without merely providing escape. So we might ask, instead, what does it mean to be fully alive? Obviously this is more than a biological question, to which the answer is 'not dead, but capable of motion and thought'; and equally, though less obviously, it is a moral question, since the answer 'enjoying oneself at endless parties' seems both unsatisfactory (since endless parties wouldn't be fun) and slightly wrong (since the pursuit of fun seems too trivial a purpose to concern ourselves with exclusively). But the hedonistic answer serves to suggest that, in our attempts to be fully alive, to make use of our lives, we are governed, or at least prompted, by an idea, however vague and unexamined, about which elements of what we call reality are most worth cherishing, pursuing, or living for. 'Life', then, in the sense we are trying to bring a little more clearly into focus, is related to our sense of 'reality'. It is the purpose of many poems, such as Eliot's *Four Quartets*, I think, to subject conventional notions of 'reality' to searching, critical examination, so as to make possible a fuller, richer, and possibly better idea of 'life'.

But *Four Quartets* is a poem (or a suite of four poems); and whatever kinds of philosophical enquiry are going on in it, must be of a kind peculiar to poetry, or else they will render the formal characteristics of the poem superfluous. Eliot wrote an essay on 'Thinking in Verse'.[26] The title illustrates a difficulty which hinders most attempts to understand the relation between poetry and philosophy. It could mean 'Thinking, of the kind we usually assume the word to denote, done in the medium of verse'. Or it could mean 'Such thinking—not the usual kind—as can supremely be done in verse'. The first interpretation supposes thinking to be of a single unvarying kind, and verse to be modified by the introduction of thinking into it. The second interpretation supposes verse to condition the nature of whatever it includes, and the thinking that goes on in it, therefore, to be of a distinctive kind, characteristic of poetry. Lewis was, from the first—for example, his dialogue with E. M. W. Tillyard, *The Personal Heresy* (1939)—very interested not only in thinking, but in thinking about the nature of the thinking that poems make it possible to do. That he, throughout his life, continued to write poems (and occasionally expressed distaste for writing certain kinds of prose—for example, his volume in The Oxford History of English Literature, which he referred to as 'Oh Hell') reveals an abiding sense that poetry creates opportunities for certain kinds of thinking which the explicitness and even-pacedness of discursive prose will often preclude. And these kinds of thinking may be those which help us to encounter the miraculous as 'a simple produce of the common day'.[27]

In his book *Cultivating Intuition* and elsewhere (for instance, his forthcoming *Natural Psychotherapy*),[28] Peter Lomas argues that we need to take more notice of the ordinary, and people should try to rejoice in the ordinariness of their experience, not the special. He finds much resistance to this line of thinking in contemporary Anglo-American psychoanalysis, which is often caught up in professional orthodoxies and their corresponding technical idioms. He told me he had noticed when he was in Sweden that his ideas about the wondrous in the ordinary[29] were accepted very readily indeed. Possibly a reason for that is that the ethos of Swedish education is very different from that of Anglo American education, in that its emphasis is less exclusively put on developing the intellect. Especially since the Education Reform Bill of 1988 introduced testing at the ages of seven, eleven, and fourteen, children in Sweden, Lomas thought, go on very much further in their education before they take any kind of formal examination. Much of their learning is practical, out-of-doors, and non-discursive. It's usually found that when Swedish children start taking examinations they are behind other nations in Europe for about a year, but very quickly catch up. However accurate this account of Swedish education may be, Lomas believed that for his audiences in Sweden, the notion that we celebrate ordinariness wasn't at all bizarre. Debates about educational reform here in the UK seem inattentive to the possibility that education may not be, as currently conceived, altogether benign, even if it were delivered from the belief that one of its functions is to help students have money and have it more abundantly.

Language is an especially clear example of something that is ordinary and yet capable of being extraordinary, like a person. Lomas, like Wittgenstein and Lewis, believed that in the most ordinary forms of language there is potential for expressing the deepest, most complex parts of our experience—sometimes, for example, by pretence and ambiguities. William Empson explained how he was reading

> . . . a poem about strawberries in *Punch*, which I caught myself liking because of a subdued pun; here what was suggested was a powerful word, what was meant was a mere grammatical convenience:

> > *Queenlily June with a rose in her hair*
> > *Moves to her prime with a languorous air.*
> > *What in her kingdom's most comely? By far*
> > *Strawberries, strawberries, strawberries are.*

I was puzzled to know why the first line seemed beautiful till I found I was reading *Queenlily* as 'Queen Lily', which in a child's poetry-book style is charming; 'the lily with a rose in her hair', used of a ripening virgin and hence of early summer, in which the absolute banality of roses and lilies is employed as it were heraldically, as a symbol intended not to be visualised but at once interpreted, is a fine Gongorism, and the alternative adverb sets the whole thing in motion by its insistence on the verb. It is curious how if you think of the word only as an adverb all this playful dignity, indeed the whole rhythm of the line, ebbs away into complacence and monotony.[30]

It would have been easy—and conventional, within the terms of pre-1930s education—for Empson to discount his initial reading as a mistake; but when as an undergraduate working with his supervisor, I. A. Richards, on the essays that evolved into *Seven Types of Ambiguity*, he found himself able to think that perhaps the nexus of meanings he had glancingly picked up on was rising from the poet's unconscious into expression. The result was to transform into beauty—or to reveal the potentiality for beauty within—lines which otherwise seemed banal. This kind of hunch (much entertained by Freud) has been very influential in literary criticism since Empson's book was published in 1930. Alertness to ambiguity, or fugitive pluralities of meaning, can indeed transform our sense of how much of the extraordinary there can be in our experience of language, people, or anything else, that might purport to be ordinary.

Wordsworth ends his famous sonnet 'Mutability' with the line, 'We feel that we are greater than we know.' Again, there is an implication that the kinds of knowledge that you are conscious of possessing and can manipulate with your intellect may not always be the most important kinds.

Ted Hughes, in an interview, distinguishes between your real life and the representation of a life in a biography:

Once you've contracted to write only the truth about yourself—as in some respected kinds of modern verse, or as in Shakespeare's sonnets—then you can too easily limit yourself to what you imagine are the truths of the ego that claims your conscious biography. Your own equivalent of what Shakespeare got into his plays is simply forgone.[31]

This implies the view that Shakespeare was getting into his plays, however indirectly, the quality of his life: the quality of his mode of experience, with all the complexities that this entailed.

Matthew Arnold, too, is conscious of wanting to get at this less conscious, but more than conscious, life—this life beyond biography and the routines of ordinary living; beyond getting up when the alarm clock goes, putting on your clothes, and going to work. His poem 'The Buried Life' treats the rituals of routine existence as a burial, which stimulates a desperate longing for the knowledge that would revive and resurrect the soul:

> But often, in the world's most crowded streets,
> But often, in the din of strife,
> There rises an unspeakable desire
> After the knowledge of our buried life;
> A thirst to spend our fire and restless force
> In tracking out our true, original course;
> A longing to inquire
> Into the mystery of this heart which beats
> So wild, so deep in us—to know
> Whence our lives come and where they go.
> And many a man in his own breast then delves,
> But deep enough, alas! none ever mines. . . .[32]

This poem, written probably around 1850, comes at a point in intellectual history well before the publication of Freud in German, let alone English translation; further still before the popularisation of psychoanalysis and with that of the notion that you can gain and may benefit from gaining access to unconscious elements of your own experience: deepest currents of your own life. As Freud recognized, poets have for centuries been working with this enlarged conception of the mind's capabilities[33]; but the conscious awareness that a poem might investigate the psyche emerged fully in the Romantic period, having been adumbrated by (among many more ancient others) mediaeval dream-poets, by Shakespeare and by Milton. Even so, the difficulty of raising the unconscious into expression is suggested by Arnold's line 'There rises an unspeakable desire', where 'unspeakable' encompasses in its meaning 'disgraceful', 'unbearably intense', and 'not able to be spoken'. The depth of Arnold's preoccupation with the buried life is further suggested by a passage from Goethe's *The Ground Thought of Wilhelm Meister*, which Arnold translated in a notebook of 1847:

The first beginnings of 'Wilhelm Meister' arose out of an obscure presentiment of this great truth that a man may often endeavour after something, for which the necessary dispositions have been denied him by nature: that he may undertake and practise that in which he can never really get on: an inward feeling warms him to desist but he cannot get clear in himself about it and is driven on by a false path to a false end. . . . If a half light does rise upon him from time to time, then there arises a feeling bordering on despair, and yet on occasion he lets himself be carried onwards by the Wave, only half struggling against it.[34]

This passage might be quoted to illustrate the psychoanalytic theory of a defence: an unconscious strategy for deflecting thoughts assumed to be, or actually, traumatic. Where such a defence operates, it may be absolute, or allow fleeting intimations of its own provisional nature. And these intimations, if pursuable, may be sources of hope. Lewis, for instance, might have hoped to be a poet and defended himself against disappointment by becoming convinced that he wasn't one. But all these quotations suggest how widespread, in many different periods and contexts, are the forms of life that often we fail, or strive, to live. The failure can only imply the existence of obstacles: things that get in the way of success.

What are the obstacles? I'd like to touch on something I have touched on before. Perhaps in the sort of environment that members of universities inhabit, the single biggest obstacle is intellectualism, or the habit of attaching undue importance to conscious ratiocination and believing that that is the sole or principal means by which you gain access to truth. Most people outside universities would think that was quite a bizarre idea, I think. There's a problem about the very word 'intellectual' and when, for example, Milton uses the word from time to time in his poems he clearly does *not* mean 'pertaining to those powers of our minds by which we reason from propositions towards conclusions'. He means something much closer to what might be meant now by 'spiritual'. This change of idiom is one of the things which inclines us to equate intelligence with cleverness, or to equate philosophy (in the sense of a medium for communicating wisdom) with the mere cerebral sophistication of a modern academic discipline. You deal with this in practical life by developing a nose for falsity. Interviewing Richard Rorty in 1997, an interviewer said, 'He seemed distinctly reluctant to engage in small talk', and then a paragraph later noted, '. . . as soon as the conversation had turned to ideas however Rorty came alive'.[35] There seems to me something troubling about that. It's almost as if the only mode of being in which Rorty is able to be fully alive is a particular kind of intellectual discourse into which somehow the whole of experience has been transposed. And of course this is problematic for anybody who isn't an 'intellectual' because they are unlikely to understand the nature or function of any such practice. (The *psychological* nature and function of intellectualism may of course be disguised from its most accomplished exponents.)

Scholars aren't, in some respects wisely, allowed to make appeals to our noses—noses for falsity included. They need to be able to defend and vindicate an intuition by demonstrating that it isn't the same as a prejudice. T. S. Eliot in his essay 'Shakespeare and the Stoicism of Seneca' (1927) argues at quite some length that if thinking is what most philosophers do when they write, then poets don't think:

> The people who think that Shakespeare thought, are always people who are not engaged in writing poetry, but who are engaged in thinking. . . .[36]

Alternatively, one might say that what he means by that is poets don't think when writing poems in the way that critics think when writing critical essays. They are trying to find verbal equivalents for, and a way of making their readers participate in, what they do instead, which is be alive, experience the world as fully and sensitively and intelligently and vigorously as possible.

George Orwell's wonderful essay 'New Words' (1940) is about something much more important than its title may suggest.[37] It discusses the experiments of Modernism, for example Joyce's *Ulysses*, a book for which Lewis could hardly have shared Orwell's admiration. What this and other associated writings are trying to do, Orwell suggests, is to put into language the character of our usual (yet extraordinary) psychological processes. Most of the time when you're walking along you're not thinking in sentences; not, that is, in sequences of grammatically well-formed, complete, intelligible statements in words. Our thinking might comprehend stray words and phrases, quasi-visual images of varying degrees of inchoateness, fugitive sensations pertaining to all of our different senses, memories in variable depth of focus and distinctness, aspects of the immediate environment noticed and folded in when an infinitesimal break in concentration allows. And this whole jumble—or to use a favourite Lewis word, 'gallimaufry'—is what makes up most of our mental, or rather our psychic, lives. The moment that we try telling anybody what's going on in this psychic life of ours, we start using orderly sentences, disregarding the more elusive and evanescent elements of the experience, raising the rest to logicality and explicitness. It's inevitable that we should do this but, equally inevitably, it misrepresents our experience. When you ask somebody why they've made a decision, they're quite often impelled to answer you by saying, 'Well I did it mainly because of X and then because of Y', which suggests that making a decision is quite an orderly cerebral process; whereas I imagine that most of the decisions that we make have partly to do with working things out consciously, partly with waiting for stirrings in the unconscious mulch, and partly with learning to identify the direction of what we are careful to call with proper looseness our 'hunches'.

Sometimes Lewis himself expressed a fed-upness with, a recoil against, the effort to make sense of experience intellectually. He has a poem 'In Praise of Solid People'[38] which is really about people who are not intellectuals but who tend their gardens and sit quietly by the fire in the evening. He expresses, amid undertones of querulous distaste, a great yearning for what he perceives as this way of life because it doesn't, he thinks, involve those capable of it in endless ratiocination. Lewis, we might recall, had the chance to become a professional philosopher and was grateful to have been saved from it by the arrival of an academic job in English studies[39]—though that, too, would turn out to have its own tendencies to constrict and distort the fuller life of a rebaptised imagination.

If we are to oppose intellectualism, how are we to carry on reasoning? This is a problem raised by Lewis's own talk of the unconscious as an unregulated road system. Probably the best way round it is to distinguish between kinds of reasoning. Here I think Lewis is crucially helpful and clear. He's clear not only in replacing muddle with lucidity, but in helping us to respect various kinds of necessary muddle. He learnt how to be clear and properly unclear, I think, from the Romantics. Coleridge was in the habit of distinguishing between three terms, *sense, understanding, reason*: terms he had translated from corresponding ones in Kant (whom Coleridge was uniquely influential in promoting among anglophone readers). 'Under the term SENSE,' he wrote,

> I comprise whatever is passive in our being, without any reference to the questions of Materialism or Immaterialism; all that man is in common with animals, in *kind* at least—his sensations, and impressions, whether of his outward senses, or the inner sense of imagination. This, in the language of the Schools, was called the *via receptiva*, or recipient property of the soul, from the original constitution of which we perceive and imagine all things under the forms of space and time.

So he means sense impressions, what we make of those stimuli to creative perception which are conventionally represented as impinging on us from outside, but which are aptly suggested to be the results of our own imaginative activity by the Greek word 'phenomenon'—what shows itself (*phanein*) to us when we interact with *noumena*, or things as they might be in themselves.

We are unendingly involved in making up the world: what we see as 'the world' is a fiction, which we would only suppose therefore to be trivial and unrelated to truth if we had a depreciative idea of the truth-revealing power of fictiveness, of making things up, of creativity and poetry. Coleridge continues:

> By the UNDERSTANDING, I mean the faculty of thinking and form-
> ing *judgements* on the notices furnished by the sense, according to cer-
> tain rules existing in itself, which rules constitute its distinct nature.
> By the pure REASON, I mean the power by which we become pos-
> sessed of principle, (the eternal verities of Plato and Descartes) and of
> ideas (N.B. not images) as the ideas of a point, a line, a circle, in Math-
> ematics; and of Justice, Holiness, Free-Will, &c. in Morals. Hence in
> works of pure science the definitions of necessity precede the reason-
> ing, in other works they more aptly form the conclusion.[40]

Let me put the distinction in slightly different terms. If, on a day in high summer, you walked into a room and you found it freezing cold, you would compare your knowledge of the atmosphere outside with your sense impressions on entering the room and you'd think there must be an artificial source of this coldness. You would be applying your judgement to your immediate sensations and to your recollections of past experience in order to explain a puzzle: Why is the room colder than the temperature outside suggests it should be? Coleridge would call this type of reasoning 'understanding'; that is, ratiocination, or the act of deriving one proposition from another. If you were to decide that justice was a virtue, however, it's impossible that you should have arrived at that conclusion by ratiocination. You can *support* it by ratiocina-tion, but according to Coleridge seeing that something is good, or a virtue, is a pure intuition, comparable to the intuition that what lies at the centre of a circle is a point. We've never seen a geometrical point: the only way that you can represent a point is by a dot, a dot has 'extension' (it occupies space); but in geometry a point has no space. So a dot must itself have a centre. We can't imagine a point (or anything else) without supposing it to occupy space, be-cause (according to Kant) our minds are so constituted that we are obliged to interpret our experience in terms of space (and time). We can only think of the point at the centre of a dot by thinking of a smaller dot; but that smaller dot would have a centre too, and so on ad infinitum. Hence the idea of a mathe-matical point can't be derived from experience since we are not capable of any experience from which to derive it. And Coleridge, by what I can see as evi-dence and what Lewis saw as a problematic step, thought that you could move from this kind of mathematical intuition towards a moral intuition, towards, for example, a belief that it's good to be kind. These moral convictions—'the eternal verities of Plato and Descartes'—he thought were absolute intuitions.

What we call, or are in the habit of calling, the Romantic period, however, was not any more homogeneous than our own. It is characterized by tendencies which, though they may have a special dominance, exist in relation to other tendencies. All such 'tendencies' are abstractions from a complex whole which subsumes them. Still, because the Romantic period comes after the Enlightenment—a phase in European intellectual history characterized by intellectualism in all sorts of ways—there was a lot of worry lest Reason in this higher sense of intuition should get confused with ratiocination or self-consciously discursive thinking. In 1798, Wordsworth as a young man wrote an 'Essay on Morals' which he never published. It is a meditation on the supremacy of intuitive modes of reasoning and of the harm that may be done to them by over-reliance on ratiocination:

> I think publications in which we formally and systematically lay down the rules of the actions of men cannot be too long delayed. I shall scarcely express myself too strongly when I say that I consider such books as Mr Godwyn's and Mr Paley's and those of that whole tribe of authors as impotent to all their intended good purposes to which I wish I could add that they were equally impotent to all bad ones. Can it be imagined by any man who has deeply imagined his own heart that an old habit will be foregone, or a new one formed, by a series of propositions, which, presenting no image to the mind, can convey no feeling which has any connection with the supposed archetype or fountain or the proposition existing in human life. These moralists attempt to strip the mind of all its old clothing when their object ought to be to furnish it with new. All this is the consequence of an undue value set upon the faculty which we call reason.[41]

The books which Wordsworth deplores try, he felt, to argue you into what they regard as right ways of behaviour, and Wordsworth was suggesting that argument of this sort (ratiocination) has no power over the parts of our being which impel us to act: no power over our truer, deeper, less restrictively conscious life. Rowan Williams, for one, agrees:

> . . . we do need to remember that the number of people who come into a living personal faith as a result of argument is actually rather small.
> . . . St. Ambrose said that 'it did not suit God to save his people by arguments'.[42]

Wordsworth continues:

> You will at least have a glimpse of my meaning when I observe that our
> attention ought principally to be fixed upon that part of our conduct
> and actions which is the result of our habits. I mean here to exclude
> those accidental and indefinite actions which don't regularly and in
> common flow from this or that particular habit.

The argument here directs us towards features of our psychic experience
which, as Alasdair MacIntyre also notes, tend to be ignored in favour of what
it more prosilient.

And finally:

> I know of no book or system of moral philosophy written with suffi-
> cient power to melt into our affections, to incorporate itself with the
> blood and vital juices of our minds and thence to have any influence
> worth our notice in informing those habits of which I am speaking.

This clearly is a triumphant celebration of poetry, a form of writing which is
capable of incorporating itself with the blood and vital juices of our minds,
and it's also a justification for analogical exposition of the sort that Lewis
specialized in, presenting you with suggestively organic possibilities, rather
than with the bare bones of a logical argument.

The reason why there was so much feeling against mere ratiocination in
the Romantic period can be illustrated briefly by the most outrageous example of pure and unmisgiving ratiocination that I know. It's from a book that
Wordsworth referred to in the essay I've just quoted. William Godwin's *An
Enquiry Concerning Political Justice*, first published in 1793, was a massively
influential book, promising opportunities for moral improvement by the cul-
tivation of what Godwin calls 'reason'. It seduced many intellectually confi-
dent readers, including Wordsworth and Shelley. At one point Godwin asks
us to imagine there is a house on fire and that of two people trapped inside,
an archbishop and his valet, only one can be saved:

> In a loose and general view I and my neighbour are both of us men;
> and of consequence entitled to equal attention. But, in reality, it is prob-
> able that one of us is a being of more worth and importance than the
> other. A man is of more worth than a beast; because, being possessed
> of higher faculties, he is capable of a more refined and genuine happi-
> ness. In the same manner, the illustrious archbishop of Cambray was

of more worth than his valet, and there are few of us that would hesitate to pronounce, if his palace were in flames, and the life of only one of them could be preserved, which of the two ought to be preferred.[43]

Godwin, with an assurance the more astonishing, perhaps, in view of his having once worked as a non-conformist minister, argues that the Archbishop should be saved on the grounds that he's a more important person than the valet and could do more good to a greater number of people by virtue of his influence. Wordsworth, and eventually Shelley and Coleridge, thought this was a very pernicious kind of reasoning, partly because it goes so strongly against ordinary intuition but also because it falsifies the process by which you would decide how to act if you were standing outside a burning house. It assumes that the wise rescuer would engage in a process of deliberate calculation of which the result will arrive promptly because the relative values of the two people involved are self-evident. The effect of this type of reasoning was to suggest that ratiocination could be used as a means of finding out how to live.

Lewis in *The Discarded Image* draws on these Romantic distinctions between sense, understanding, and reasoning in explaining a number of mediaeval scholastic distinctions:

> Boethius, it will be remembered, distinguishes *intelligentia* from *ratio*; the former being enjoyed in its perfection by angels. *Intellectus* is that in man which approximates most nearly to angelic *intelligentia*; it is in fact *obumbrata intelligentia*, clouded intelligence, or a shadow of intelligence.

By this account, angels are supposed to have perfect intuition (*intelligentia*): they don't need to reason their way towards an understanding of what is the truth. They simply and without mediation see what is truly the case. Such is perfect intelligence. Human beings are intelligent in proportion as they share this ability to see what is truly the case. We have, as fallen or imperfect beings, traces of the angelic kind of intuition; but since human beings have never had this perfectly, the best that they can achieve is clouded intelligence (*obumbrata intelligentia*), which is also called *intellectus*. We support the inadequacies of our intuition by *ratio* or deduction:

> Its relation to reason is thus described by Aquinas: 'intellect (*intelligere*) is the simple (i.e. indivisible, uncompounded) grasp of an intelligible truth, whereas reasoning (*ratiocinari*) is the progression towards an intelligible truth by going from one understood (*intellecto*) point to

another. The difference between them is thus like the difference between rest and motion or between possession and acquisition' (Ia, LXXIX, art. 8). We are enjoying *intellectus* when we 'just see' a self-evident truth; we are exercising *ratio* when we proceed step by step to prove a truth which is not self-evident. A cognitive life in which all truth can be simply 'seen' would be the life of an *intelligentia*, an angel. A life of unmitigated *ratio* where nothing was simply 'seen' and all had to be proved, would presumably be impossible; for nothing can be proved if nothing is self-evident. Man's mental life is spent in laboriously connecting those frequent, but momentary, flashes of *intelligentia*, which constitute *intellectus*.[44]

'Man's mental life is spent in laboriously connecting those frequent but momentary flashes of intelligentia which constitute intellectus.' I suspect there is a relation between what Lewis is calling 'flashes of intelligentia' and what it is that poets are trying to get at when they write poems.

Perhaps the single most important account of reasoning in Lewis is that which occurs in his 1940 essay 'Why I Am Not a Pacifist'. It begins by explaining that by 'Reason'

> . . . I do not mean some separate faculty but the whole man judging, only judging this time not about good and evil, but about truth and falsehood. Now any concrete train of reason involves three elements.
>
> Firstly there is the reception of facts to reason about. These facts are received either from our own senses, or from the report of other minds; that is, either experience or authority supplies us with our material. But each man's experience is so limited that the second source is the more usual; Of every hundred facts upon which to reason, ninety-nine depend on authority.
>
> Secondly, there's the direct, simple act of the mind perceiving self-evident truth, as when we see that if A and B both equal C, then they equal each other. This act I call intuition.
>
> Thirdly, there is an art or skill of arranging the facts so as to yield a series of such intuitions which linked together produce a proof of the truth or falsehood of the proposition we are considering. . . .

This last activity is, I think, what Lewis specializes in, and it's probably one of the reasons that many people feel such affection and admiration for his

discursive writings. Yet in believing that the essential starting-point for ratiocination is a hunch or an intuition, Lewis aligns himself with Coleridge:

> . . . Thus in a geometrical proof each step is seen by intuition, and to
> fail to see it is to be not a bad geometrician but an idiot. The skill
> comes in arranging the material into a series of intuitable 'steps'. Fail-
> ure to do this doesn't mean idiocy, but only lack of ingenuity or inven-
> tion. Failure to follow it need not mean idiocy, but either inattention or
> defect of memory which forbids us to hold all the intuitions together.[45]

We see one of the difficulties into which over-intellectualized, academic discourse continually gets is that it may attempt to suggest that intuitions can be
simply produced by argument. If you counter that they operate under different conditions and are not produced by argument—that you can indeed work
towards intuitions through argument but they cannot in themselves be produced by argument—it might be objected that you are relying on something
which doesn't come from argument. Because this is indeed what happens
with prejudice—it's easily supposed that every conviction based on an intuition must be a prejudice. When this occurs, however, it's commonly the result
of failing to distinguish between different kinds of reason and of failing to
recognize that the power of purely discursive reasoning is limited.

Now the correction of errors in reasoning is really correction of the first or
third element. The second, the intuitional element, cannot be corrected if it
is wrong, nor supplied if it is lacking. You can give the man new facts. You
can invent a simpler proof, that is, a simple concatenation of intuitable truths.
But when you come to an absolute inability to see any one of the self-evident
steps out of which proof is built, then you can do nothing. No doubt this absolute inability is much rarer than we suppose. Every teacher knows that
people are constantly protesting that they 'can't see' some self-evident inference, but the supposed inability is usually a refusal to see, resulting either
from some passion which *wants* not to see the truth in question or else from
sloth which doesn't want to think at all.

Perhaps we can now understand a bit more clearly how it's possible to be,
as Lewis was, an intellectual and yet be at the same time an opponent of intellectualism. Admittedly it's a confusing state to be in, and emergence from
it is not a once-and-for-all simple process, not least because of what Freud
called 'the intellectual defence': using the intellect, that is, to deflect the reasonable questioning of its own authority. Lewis gradually changed his attitude towards the unconscious and thus towards the intellect. I think that he
had, first, a personal fight with the unconscious, then used the intellect as an

excuse for ignoring the unconscious and finally came to value the unconscious as the source of true intuitions.

T. S. Eliot in a private letter was dealing with this question of whether there is such a thing as truth perceived independently of ratiocination:

> I should say that it was at any rate essential for Religion that we should have the conception of an immutable object or Reality the knowledge of which shall be the final object of the will; and there can be no permanent reality if there is no permanent truth.
>
> This is the nub.
>
> I am of course quite ready to admit that human apprehension of truth varies, changes and perhaps develops, but that is a property of human imperfection rather than truth. You cannot conceive of truth at all, the word has no meaning, except by conceiving it as something permanent.[46]

So 'human apprehension of truth', Eliot is prepared to admit, 'changes and perhaps develops'. I want to suggest that such a development is also possible in the history of an individual. We have got used to books in which separate chapters are assigned to different aspects of Lewis's personality or writing as components of a fractured system: Lewis as a Literary Theorist, as a Poet, or as a Theologian, say.[47] Not all such essays imply that Lewis's work in each field excluded those aspects of his being which were operative in another. But the divisive implications of this way of thinking about Lewis corresponds to a similar divisiveness in his own way of thinking about himself. The split so many people see in Lewis is the result of his being drawn to imaginative embodiments of the qualities wilfully omitted from his conception of intellect and of himself at the earlier stages of his own development. These were subsequently to some extent reintegrated, and you can see effects of reintegration in the looser, less embattled tone of later writings such as *Letters to Malcolm Chiefly on Prayer* (1964) and *A Grief Observed* (1961); even in *Studies in Words* (1960) and *An Experiment in Criticism* (1961).

If in Lewis's poems we rarely see those striking peculiarities of expression which testify to emergence of a wholly new conception, we do find plainer statements of supra-rational—or imaginative—hunches. In 'Reason', for example, the intellect figures as a maid, the imagination as a mother:

> *Oh who will reconcile in me both maid and mother*
> *Who make in me a concord of the depth and height?*
> *Who make imagination's dim exploring touch*
> *Ever report the same as intellectual sight?*[48]

The poem despairs of achieving such integration, and may fail to do so as a result of trying too hard for a discursive resolution. It comes closest perhaps in recalling (unconsciously?) a passage from a letter in which Coleridge says

> . . . a great Poet must be, implicitè if not explicitè, a profound Metaphysician. He may not have it in logical coherence, in his Brain & Tongue; but he must have it by *Tact*/for all sounds, & all forms of human nature he must have the *ear* of a wild Arab listening in the silent Desert, the *eye* of a North American Indian tracing the footsteps of an Enemy upon the Leaves that strew the Forest—; the *Touch* of a Blind Man feeling the face of a darling Child.[49]

Another Lewis poem, called 'Poem for Psychoanalysts and/or Theologians', comes closer to bypassing mere intellect by conducting itself almost exclusively in symbolic figures and calculatedly alluring hints of cryptosexual analogy:

> *Naked apples, woolly-coated peaches*
> *Swelled on the garden's wall. Unbounded*
> *Odour of windless, spice-bearing trees*
> *Surrounded my lying in sacred turf,*
> *Made dense the guarded air*—[50]

This is presented as a joke, perhaps: a cluster of the sort of sexually suggestive images Lewis thinks a certain type of critic would rush to interpret. But the point of the poem is that these images are indeed made up: they do proceed from Lewis himself, the whole man, and make possible the expression of what his prose and more determinedly discursive poems refuse to admit. Along with its mockery, the poem will have unconscious revelations that Lewis cannot be in control of. (The line 'lying in sacred turf', for example, introduces, into what will strike many as a deliberately deceptive poem, an obvious pun on lying.) The poem's narrator remembers how he heard

> . . . *the golden gates behind me*
> *Fall to, shut fast. On the flinty road,*
> *Black-frosty, blown on with an eastern wind,*
> *I found my feet. Forth on journey,*
> *Gathering thin garments over aching bones,*
> *I went. I wander still. But the world is round.*

The significance of the ending here inheres in figurative embodiments of a sense of grim futility and exclusion from a more desirable state. And by its end, the poem has engaged firmly with one of Lewis's obsessive themes: the yearning for a world beyond the world, stimulated by elusive sensations of painful joy. That definite articles are so rare in the closing lines imparts an Anglo-Saxon severity to the tone, much at odds with the sensuous opening: a contrast from which much of the pathos of Lewis's experience derives. The fact that explaining the poem is harder suggests that the justification for its existence is stronger.

In *The Abolition of Man* (1943), Lewis puts forward the idea that feelings should be the servants, the supportive adjuncts, of thought; but the trouble with this claim is that it keeps intact that crude distinction between thinking and feeling which bedevils the verbal expression of experience in English. I believe that, ultimately, Lewis brought his discursive thinking on that subject closer to the level of subtlety he habitually achieved in his poems and narrative prose. Everyone can think of examples of the kind of reasoning in Lewis's critical, apologetic writings which make his critics dismiss him as a practitioner of chop-logic. Lewis was aware of this and referred sometimes to his 'bow-wow manner' or his 'police-court rhetoric'. Perhaps the most famous of the distinguished examples is Chapter 3 of the original edition of *Miracles*. There is, of course, a justification for the care with which Lewis followed up what he perceived as the humiliating and all-but-irrefragable criticism of G. E. M. Anscombe the philosopher, revising the chapter which, in a Socratic club discussion, she had assailed. It may be necessary, to have good philosophy in order to drive out bad, but it's also necessary to attempt good philosophy in order to identify the limits of even the best philosophical reasoning. I believe that as Lewis got older he became more mindful of the limitations of discursive reasoning as a means of discovering truth.

In cases of conscientious doubt, as well as in the making of many ordinary decisions, perplexity arises because there are reasonable arguments on several sides of a question. A question, moreover, may turn out to have unsuspected sides, or not to be quite the question you'd originally tried to answer. You may, indeed, suspect that imagining a question as having 'sides' at all is another of those misleading fictions which compromise the value of a discussion. (It seems to me that Lewis's deliberations on moral questions not infrequently have about them the air of scholastic irrelevance that Wordsworth condemns in Godwin.) Once confusion, or radical uncertainty, supervenes, you can either choose randomly, choose to suit your convenience, or postpone a decision by vacillation; but if you're trying to live well, none of these options may remain permanently open. One alternative is to appeal to authority, and it seems evident reading Lewis's letters that he would sometimes act in accordance with scripture where scripture seemed to him to give useful guidance on a point. Hence, in *Mere Christianity*, based on radio talks given in 1942, 1943, and 1944, he argues that for the Christian, sex outside marriage is a sin, so the only alternatives are marriage or sexual abstinence: a view which many Christians now might in various ways contest, not least for its being so decidedly a 'view'.

He gets into rather more difficulty with the argument from scriptural authority when it comes to the question of homosexuality. Replying in 1954 to a letter about this, he acknowledges that since, in his interpretation of scripture, the option of marriage is not available, chastity would seem to be the only option for the gay man on whose behalf he is being consulted. Yet he admits that this is a matter he is not certain about:

> All I have really said is that, like all other tribulations, it must be offered to God and His guidance how to use it must be sought.[51]

Again there is the problem some will find in 'tribulations', which Lewis seems to regard as an inevitable corollary of a sexual orientation which is now widely considered no more problematic than heterosexuality. Still, Lewis is responding to a letter about someone who is troubled; and there is a note of diffidence audible within his certitude. It seems to me that, in making this admission of uncertainty, Lewis is consulting a 'feeling' whose authority exceeds that of his intellect.

Lewis had at one time been dismissive about the authority of feelings. His own leaning towards intellectualism was, he realized, a consequence of the 'hostility to the emotions' which he refers to in *Surprised by Joy*[52] and which, it would seem, he regarded his relationship with Mrs Moore as somehow avenging for. It seems probable from the ways in which we talk about 'feelings', that we assume a complex hierarchy among them and use the term in a subtly shifting variety of senses. 'Is that what you *really* feel?' implies the existence of varying degrees of genuineness in the feelings a person is experiencing at any one time. 'I feel I shouldn't feel like that' implies that feeling is related to—indeed is sometimes synonymous with—moral intuition. In the case of his relationship to Joy Davidman, Lewis came up against a familiar conflict in a form he couldn't ignore or treat as he used to. Technically, Joy, as a Catholic by marriage, couldn't get divorced from her estranged husband, so any marriage between herself and Lewis was technically adulterous, as he says at one point. Lewis nonetheless married Joy. It seems difficult to resist the conclusion that in this case his intuition took priority over ratiocination.

In the view of the Romantics or of most modern psychotherapists, he wasn't on that account merely giving in to desire. Marrying Joy was an act of love, even if it did include compassion; intellectually, in terms of a broader understanding of the term *reason*, it was simply reasonable. It was consistent with Lewis's sense of the life that God wished him to lead. And to obey reason in that sense meant recognizing its limits in another.

Notes

1. This talk was given on 15 June 1999.

2. 'The Pharisees came and began to question Jesus. To test him, they asked him for a sign from heaven. He sighed deeply and said, "Why does this generation ask for a sign? Truly I tell you, no sign will be given to it"' (Mark 8:13). (NIV: all subsequent quotations from the Bible are given in this version.)

3. 'A person of the spirit or character commonly attributed to the Pharisees in the New Testament; a legalist or formalist; a self-righteous person, a hypocrite' (OED n. sense 2; first recorded in this sense in 1539).

4. 'Don't have anything to do with foolish and stupid arguments, because you know they produce quarrels' (2 Timothy 2:23).

5. Daniel Goleman, *Emotional Intelligence: Why It Can Matter More Than IQ* (London: Bloomsbury, 1996).

6. *Thought, Words and Creativity: Art and Thought in Lawrence* (London: Chatto and Windus, 1975), 15.

7. 'The primary IMAGINATION I hold to be the living Power and prime Agent of all human Perception, and as a repetition in the finite mind of the eternal act of creation in the infinite I AM.' In chapter 13 of the *Biographia Literaria* (1817), ed. James Engell and W. Jackson Bate, 2 vols. (London: Routledge and Kegan Paul, 1983), Vol. 1, 304.

8. E.g. 'Theory can never accommodate the subtleties and nuances of human intercourse. We require all the flexibility of ordinary language in order to make our interpretations as accurate as possible'. Peter Lomas, *Cultivating Intuition: An Introduction to Psychotherapy* (Harmondsworth: Penguin, 1994), 61.

9. C. S. Lewis, 'Version Vernacular', in *The Christian Century*, Vol. 75 (1958), 1515; reprinted in *Undeceptions: Essays on Theology and Ethics*, ed. Walter Hooper (London: Bles, 1971), 143.

10. 'I sometimes find myself turning a sentence into Basic from English in order to decide whether it is nonsense'. 'Teaching Literature' (1934); reprinted in *Argufying: Essays on Literature and Culture*, ed. John Haffenden (London: Chatto and Windus, 1987), 96.

11. 'The Best Words in the Best Order', in *The Poet's Voice and Craft*, ed. C. B. Mc-Cully (Manchester: Carcanet, 1994), 28.

12. 'Poetry Today' (1935); reprinted in *Selected Literary Criticism of Louis MacNeice*, ed. Alan Heuser (Oxford: Clarendon Press, 1987), 10.

13. 'The Fire i' the Flint: Reflections on the Poetry of Gerard Manley Hopkins' (1974); reprinted in *Preoccupations: Selected Prose 1968–1978* (London: Faber and Faber, 1980), 82.

14. *Required Writing: Miscellaneous Pieces 1955–1982* (London: Faber and Faber, 1983), 52.

15. See, e.g., *The Norton Anthology of English Literature*, ed. M. H. Abrams et al., 7th ed., 2 vols. (New York: Norton, 2000), Vol. 2, 2865, which reproduces MS drafts of 'O World, O Life, O Time'.

16. The phrase 'dark embryo of meaning' is Eliot's, from a note to the poems of Harold Munro, written in 1933 and quoted in C. K. Stead, *The New Poetic: Yeats to Eliot* (London: Hutchinson, 1964), 136.

17. The notion of being 'born into language' and acquiring in the process a system of concepts, implicit in the structure of the language, which organize perception derives from Lacan. In the New Testament, the process of repentance, closely linked with the idea of being born again, is often expressed by a Greek word μετάνοια ('metanoia'). This might roughly be translated as 'drastic change of outlook, spiritual orientation or style of perception'.

18. 'Advertisement' to *Lyrical Ballads* (1798); in *The Prose Works of William Wordsworth*, ed. W. J. B. Owen and Jane Worthington Smyser, 2 vols. (Oxford: Clarendon Press, 1974), Vol, 1, 116.

19. *The Collected Poems of C. S. Lewis*, ed. Walter Hooper (London: HarperCollins, 1994), 15.

20. '*Was* there something, at least in his impressive, indeed splendid, literary personality, which was somehow—and with no taint of insincerity—*voulu*? . . . some touch of a more than merely *ad hoc* pastiche?' *Light on C. S. Lewis*, ed. Jocelyn Gibb and Owen Barfield (London: Bles, 1965), xi.

21. Subtitled *Pride and Prejudice among the Literary Intelligentsia, 1880–1939* (London: Faber and Faber, 1992).

22. 'Sometimes Fairy-Stories May Say Best What's to Be Said' (1956); *Of This and Other Worlds*, ed. Walter Hooper (London: Collins, 1984), 71.

23. *On Fairy-Stories: Expanded Edition with Commentary and Notes*, ed. Verlyn Flieger and Douglas A. Anderson (London: HarperCollins, 2008), 65.

24. The surviving fragment of this poem was published directly after Lewis's reported comment.

25. *Miracles: A Preliminary Study* (1947, rev. 1960; Glasgow: Collins, 1974), 138n. In this note the belief that myth is 'priestly lying', akin to Lewis's own earlier view, is ascribed to 'the philosophers of the Enlightenment'.

26. See *The Varieties of Metaphysical Poetry*, ed. Ronald Schuchard (London: Faber, 1993), 153 n.

27. William Wordsworth, 'Prospectus to *The Recluse*', l. 55; *The Poems*, ed. John O Hayden, 2 vols. (Harmondsworth: Penguin, 1977), Vol. 2, 39.

28. Edited by myself and Paul Gordon [Stephen Logan's note].

29. A foretaste of Peter's work on this theme is afforded by his essay, 'Wonder and the Loss of Wonder'; in *Betweeen Psychotherapy and Philosophy*, ed. Paul Gordon and Rosalind Mayo (London: Whurr, 2004), 103–111.

30. *Seven Types of Ambiguity* (London: Chatto and Windus, 1930), 64–65.

31. Keith Sagar, *The Laughter of Foxes: A Study of Ted Hughes* (Liverpool: Liverpool University Press, 2000), xi. Quoted from a *Paris Review* interview of 1995.

32. *Poems*, ed. Miriam Allott (London: Longman, 2nd ed., 1979), 289.

33. '. . . creative writers are valuable allies and their evidence is to be prized highly, for they are apt to know a whole host of things between heaven and earth of which our philosophy has not yet let us dream. In their knowledge of the mind they are far in advance of us everyday people, for they draw upon sources which we have not yet opened up for science'. 'Delusions and Dreams in Jensen's *Gradiva*' (1907); rpt. in The Penguin Freud Library, Vol. 14: *Art and Literature*, ed. Albert Dickson (Harmondsworth: Penguin, 1985, rpt. 1990), 34.

34. Quoted in *Poems*, 288–289 n.

35. Sean Sayers, 'Is the Truth Out There?', *THES*, 6 June 1997.

36. *Selected Essays* (London: Faber and Faber, 3rd ed., 1951), 136.

37. *The Collected Essays, Journalism and Letters*, ed. Sonia Orwell and Ian Angus, 4 vols. (London: Secker and Warburg, 1968), Vol. 2, 3–12.

38. *Collected Poems*, 199–200.

39. See Roger Lancelyn Green and Walter Hooper, *C. S. Lewis: A Biography* (Glasgow: Collins, 1974), 83.

40. *The Friend*, ed. Barbara E. Rooke, 2 vols. (London: Routledge and Kegan Paul, 1969), Vol. 1, 177.

41. *The Prose Works of William Wordsworth*, ed. Owen and Smyser, 3 vols. (Oxford: Clarendon Press, 1974), Vol. 1, 103.

42. *Tokens of Trust: An Introduction to Christian Belief* (Norwich: Canterbury Press, 2007), 20.

43. William Godwin, *An Enquiry Concerning Political Justice* (1793; 3rd ed., 1798), Book II, Ch. 2 ('Of Justice').

44. C. S. Lewis, *The Discarded Image* (Cambridge: Cambridge University Press, 1964), 157.

45. 'Why I Am Not a Pacifist'; reprinted in *Essay Collection and Other Short Pieces*, ed. Lesley Walmsley (London: HarperCollins, 2000), 282–283.

46. Letter to Bonamy Dobrée, dated 12 November 1927; quoted in *Selected Prose of T. S. Eliot*, ed. Frank Kermode (London: Faber and Faber, 1975), 24–25 n.

47. As, for example, in *The Cambridge Companion to C. S. Lewis*, ed. Robert MacSwain and Michael Ward (Cambridge: Cambridge University Press, 2010).

48. *Collected Poems*, 95.

49. Letter to William Sotheby, 13 July 1802; in *The Collected Letters of Samuel Taylor Coleridge*, ed. E. L. Griggs, 6 vols. (Oxford: Clarendon Press, 1956–71), Vol. 2, 810.

50. *Collected Poems*, 127.

51. Letter to Sheldon Vanauken, 14 May 1954; in *Collected Letters*, ed. Walter Hooper, 3 vols. (London: HarperCollins, 2000–2006), Vol. 3, 472.

52. *Surprised by Joy: The Shape of My Early Life* (London: Bles, 1955), 188.

4

Sacramentalism in C. S. Lewis and Charles Williams

Kallistos Ware

THE OCCASION WHEN most often as an undergraduate in Magdalen I saw C. S. Lewis was not in fact in the lecture hall.[1] I used to meet him in the morning, about 7.30 or 7.45. He would go for a walk through the grounds of the college, along Addison's Walk and round by the Magdalen 'Water Walks', and I liked to do that too, and I used to meet him on those occasions, though our conversation was limited to saying, 'Good morning'.

Now I find it appropriate that I should most often have seen C. S. Lewis in a place of remarkable natural beauty, because Lewis was in fact very sensitive to the beauty of the world around us; and this sensitivity, so he tells us in his autobiography *Surprised by Joy*, went right back to his early childhood. He speaks about the view which he remembers from his nursery windows, from the Lewis house in Belfast. They could see, he tells us, 'what we called "the Green Hills"; that is, the low line of the Castlereagh Hills. . . . They were not very far off but they were, to children, quite unattainable. They taught me longing—*Sehnsucht*.'[2]

But while Lewis was sensitive to the beauty of the natural world, what mattered to him was not merely the external aesthetic appearance of nature around us. What mattered to him was that the world of nature has sacramental value. Through the world of nature we are brought into communion with God. We might say that for Lewis the world of nature was both solid and transparent. It was solid: he valued the 'is-ness' of material things, and he conveyed this distinctive character very effectively in his writing. But while he valued the material world around us in and for itself, he valued it still more because of its transparency, because of the way in which the material world brings us to an apprehension of God. Significantly, Lewis in his anthology from the writings of George MacDonald quotes the words of his Scottish master about what MacDonald terms 'the deeper meanings of nature and her mediation between us and God.'³ Such exactly is Lewis's view: nature mediates between us and God, the world is a sacrament of the divine presence.

So tonight in my talk about the world, the sacrament, creation, and theology in C. S. Lewis and Charles Williams, I would like to explore with you this particular approach towards the created world.

Now C. S. Lewis is an original thinker, at times bold and unexpected, but he is also a traditionalist, rooted in the past. If he's original, it is above all because he goes back to the *origines*, the sources or origins, and this is as true of his creation theology as of other things. The idea of the world as sacrament is first of all characteristic of much Anglican theology, particularly seventeenth-century Anglican theology. Let us recall, for example, the words of Thomas Traherne in his *Centuries of Meditations*: 'Heaven and Earth did sing my Creator's praises. . . . Eternity was manifest in the Light of the Day, and something infinite behind everything appeared.'⁴ Or take again the words of George Herbert in his poem 'The Elixir', well known, I'm sure, to many of you as a hymn: 'Teach me, my God and King, In all things Thee to see, And what I do in anything, To do it as for Thee. . . . A man that looks on glass, On it may stay his eye; Or if he pleaseth, through it pass, And then the heav'n espy. All may of Thee partake.' So Herbert continues, 'Teach me, my God and King, In *all* things Thee to see', in each blade of grass, in each rock and stone, in each animal, in each living person. This is not pantheism but panentheism. Pantheism says, 'The world is God and God is the world', but the panentheist says, 'God is in the world and the world is in God'.

This, then, is what Traherne and Herbert say from the classic tradition of Anglicanism, and this is what Lewis also believes, but this idea of the sacred, sacramental character of nature is far more ancient than the seventeenth century. It has its roots in Judaism, in the Old Testament. As we are told at the end of the creation story in Genesis I, 'God saw everything that he had made, and behold, it was very good.' And the Psalms say, 'The heavens declare the glory of God.'⁵

This sacramental approach to the universe is evident equally in ancient Christianity. One saying that is attributed to our Lord—not actually recorded in the Gospels, but circulated among the early Christians—is this: 'Lift the stone and you will find me; cut the wood in two and there am I.'⁶

The early monks of the fourth century may have renounced earthly possessions, but they didn't thereby reject the material world. There is a story told of the father of Christian monasticism, Anthony of Egypt. One day some philosophers came to see him and they said to him, 'How can you endure to live in this horrid wilderness, deprived of any consolation from books?' and Anthony replied, 'My book, o philosophers, is the world around me, and whenever I wish I can read in it the wonderful works of God.' The world, nature, is God's book.

Indeed, in the spirituality of the Orthodox Church it is customary to distinguish three main stages or levels upon the spiritual way. The first level, known in Greek as *praktiki* or *praxis*, is the active life—the life of moral effort, of serving God through a sense of ought, uprooting the vices and acquiring the virtues. The third and final stage is *theoria*, contemplation of God. But in between, there is a second stage, which is known as *physis* or *physiki*, natural contemplation or the contemplation of nature, apprehending God, not this time through a sense of *ought*, but through a sense of *is*. We do not pass straight from active moral effort to contemplation of God, but first learn to open our eyes to the wonder and mystery of the visible world around us. First we apprehend God in each thing, then we transcend each thing, pass beyond it, and apprehend Him in His transcendent being.

The tradition of natural contemplation, apprehending the divine in the world around us, treating the world as sacrament, remains very much alive in the Orthodox Church today. I can remember when as a deacon I was living in the Monastery of St. John the Theologian on the island of Patmos in Greece. The spiritual father at that time, Father Antiochanus, used to say, 'He who does not love trees does not love God', and when the farmers came to see him for confession, for a penance he would tell them to go and plant a tree. And then he would go round the island every now and then on a pastoral expedition, to see how the penances were getting on: Were they being properly watered and protected from the goats?

'Do you know', Father Antiochanus used to say, 'that there is one more commandment not written in the Bible, and it is the commandment, "Love the trees"?' He was an ecologist long before ecology had become fashionable. The Russian Orthodox theologian Father Alexander Schmemann says, 'The Christian is the one who, wherever he or she looks, sees everywhere Christ and rejoices in him.'[7] So one means of being a Christian is to see all things in God and God in all things. That is the essence of natural contemplation.

Now, I would like to ask how important this sacramental view of creation is to C. S. Lewis, and, at the end, to make comparison more briefly with Lewis's friend Charles Williams. At many, many points in C. S. Lewis's writings, there is evident a keen sense of the wonder and mystery of the created world. Lewis was far-ranging in his imaginative power, masterly in his command of words, and he used both imagination and language to full effect when describing the realm of nature. Take, for example, the first story in his space trilogy, *Out of the Silent Planet*. This to me conveys very well a sense of the is-ness of physical things. Lewis writes with great force about Ransom's experiences in the old world Malacandra, his sense of light, colour, touch, taste. Here, for example, is the description of Ransom's journey through space to the planet of Malacandra, what he sees when he looks out in that night into the firmament:

> There were planets of unbelievable majesty, and constellations un-dreamed of: there were celestial sapphires, rubies, emeralds and pin-pricks of burning gold; far out on the left of the picture hung a comet, tiny and remote. . . . The lights trembled: they seemed to grow brighter as he looked. . . . Almost he felt, wholly he imagined, 'sweet influence' pouring or even stabbing into his surrendered body.[8]

Ransom, travelling through space, realizes that in fact space is not empty, dead or black, but is full of living and transfiguring light.

How well Lewis conveys images of the scenery of Malacandra: the beauty of the Handramit, the deep valley; the strange journey through the high ground of the Harandra. This same sense of the value of material things, of their wonder, comes out, I think, even more powerfully in his second novel, *Perelandra* or *Voyage to Venus*. Once more we've got here a vivid expression of the *haecceitas* of each created thing: the floating islands, the powers of the thunderstorm, the taste of fruit on Perelandra, the sound of the singing beasts. A very strong sense of nature.

Again, for a sense of what creation meant to Lewis, let us recall his mar-vellous retelling of the creation story in *The Magician's Nephew*, when Aslan, the lion, sings the world into existence. 'Narnia, Narnia, Narnia, awake. Love. Think. Speak. Be walking trees. Be talking beasts. Be divine waters.'[9]

Along with this sense of the beauties of the material world, Lewis empha-sizes its thinness. There's a story told by the Anglican theologian and spiri-tual guide Evelyn Underhill. One time she was going to go to the island of Iona in Scotland. The friend with whom she was staying had a Scottish gar-dener, and when he heard she was going to Iona, the gardener said to her, 'Iona's a very thin place.' 'What do you mean?' asked Evelyn Underhill, and he replied, 'There's not much between Iona and the Lord.'[10] Now for Lewis, the world was a very thin place. He's conscious not just of its is-ness but of its transparency. He's conscious of the interpenetration between the natural world and the supernatural world. This world opens out onto other worlds of which we are usually unaware, but these other worlds are much closer to us than we think. Here I would recall the very telling symbol that he uses in his first Narnia book, the symbol of the wardrobe. Just by going through a ward-robe, out you come into another world. That was what Lewis felt the nature of the world around us to be. He valued it for itself—he loved walking in the country—but he also felt it pointed beyond.

But if this world is a place of beauty and wonder, it's also a place of danger and terror, marred by sin and evil.

Much of Lewis's most effective writing concerns precisely the presence of evil. In such books as *The Problem of Pain* or *The Screwtape Letters*, in a novel such as *That Hideous Strength*, in the Narnia septet, a master theme is the battle between good and evil. In *Mere Christianity* he underlines the paradox of the world round us. He is speaking of the sense of Somebody above us, with a capital S. We have two bits of evidence about the Somebody. One is the universe He has made. Now, if we use that as our only clue, then I think we should have to conclude that He was a great artist (for the universe is a very beautiful place), but also that He is quite merciless and no friend to man, for the universe is a very dangerous place.

Of course Lewis goes on to point out that if the world is a dangerous place, that is not because of the way that God has made it but because of the way in which it has been distorted by the Devil.

Lewis's view of the Devil is well summed up by William Luther White in his book *The Image of Man in C. S. Lewis*, written almost half a century ago, but still one of the best books about Lewis: 'Though the Devil could make nothing . . . he has infected everything.' Lewis wrote in a letter, quoted by Luther White, 'I have always gone as near Dualism as Christianity allows— and the New Testament allows one to go very near.'[11] Yet Lewis is only a moral dualist, not an ontological dualist—indeed he rejects ontological dualism as logically flawed. 'If good and evil are two co-equal powers', he says in *Mere Christianity*, 'then there must exist beyond them a third reality; otherwise by what standard can we call the one power good and the other bad?'[12] Yet however forceful evil may be, the universe in itself is God's creation and therefore good. As Lewis puts it, 'Evil is a parasite, not an original thing.'[13] It's an adjective, not a noun. It has no substantive existence. It's simply the distortion of what in its basic essence remains fundamentally good.

If the creation as a whole is good, then more particularly, Lewis insists that the world of matter is good, and more specifically still, the human body is good. As he says in *Mere Christianity*, 'There is no good trying to be more spiritual than God. God never meant man to be a purely spiritual creature. That is why He uses material things like bread and wine to put the new life into us. We may think this rather crude and unspiritual. God does not. He invented eating. He likes matter. He invented it.'[14]

Again he writes, 'I know some muddle-headed Christians have talked as if Christianity thought that sex, or the body, or pleasure, were bad in themselves.

But they were wrong. Christianity is almost the only one of the great religions which thoroughly approves of the body—which believes that matter is good, that God Himself once took on a human body, that some kind of body is going to be given to us even in Heaven and is going to be an essential part of our happiness, our beauty, and our energy."[15]

Equally, in his anthology from George MacDonald, he quotes his Scottish mentor on the value of the body. As MacDonald says,

> It is by the body that we come into contact with Nature, with our fellow-men, with all their revelations to us. It is through the body that we receive all the lessons of passion, of suffering, of love, of beauty, of science. It is through the body that we are both trained outwards from ourselves, and driven inwards into our deepest selves to find God. There is glory and might in this vital evanescence, this slow glacier-like flow of clothing and revealing matter, this ever uptossed rainbow of tangible humanity. It is no less of God's making than the spirit that is clothed therein.[16]

So in this way Lewis insists on the unity of the human person. We are to see ourselves in holistic terms, as an undivided unity of soul and body.

I remember a story told about a professor of philosophy in London University some years ago, Professor Hywel Lewis (who was, I think, no relative of C. S. Lewis). Professor Hywel Lewis was much inclined to emphasize the difference between the soul and the body in a rather Platonist way. His students used to say, 'Professor Lewis does not go for a walk, he takes his body for a walk.'

Regarding the complications of the body/soul relationship, I also recall a story about a nineteenth-century Anglican Archbishop of Dublin, Archbishop Trench. Archbishop Trench was travelling back from England to Ireland across the North Sea in a storm, and he fell and broke his leg on the boat. Thereafter, though the breakage was healed, he was obsessed with fear that he would lose the use of this leg. On one occasion, at a dinner party, he cried aloud, 'I knew it would happen. I knew it. I have lost all power of sensation in my leg.' Whereupon the lady sitting next to him turned to him and said, somewhat coldly, 'It may comfort you to know, your Grace, that during the last twenty minutes it is my leg you have been pinching.'

We are a unity of body and soul, and that is why Lewis saw spiritual value in sexual love. However, the point he emphasizes when he deals with this in the chapter on *eros* in his book *The Four Loves* is not the sexual, physical aspect in itself, but the all-embracing personal relationship. He thinks that if you isolate sex, you deprive it of its true value. So he says about the state of being in love:

> A man in this state really hasn't leisure to think of sex. He is too busy thinking of a person. The fact that she is a woman is far less important than the fact that she is herself. He is full of desire, but the desire may not be sexually toned. If you asked him what he wanted, the true reply would often be, 'To go on thinking of her.' He is love's contemplative. And when at a later stage the explicitly sexual element awakes, he will not feel . . . that this had all along been the root of the whole matter.[17]

Yes, for Lewis sexuality is a gift from God, to be used for his glory within marriage; but once sexual union is isolated from the *total* union of the persons, it becomes a distortion and a snare. That is precisely why sex outside marriage is wrong.

Lewis's positive attitude towards God's material creation is evident also in his vision of the age to come. Heaven is not an abstraction. It is palpable. It is solid. This is apparent in his sermon 'The Weight of Glory,' preached in the University Church here in Oxford. The glory of the age to come which Lewis envisages is, among other things, a physical glory, a glory of physical things transfigured. The solidity, the transfigured physicality of heaven, is memorably conveyed in his work *The Great Divorce*. Here is his experience as he goes into heaven and tries to pick a daisy:

> It was the light, the grass, the trees that were different; made of some different substance, so much solider than things in our country that men were ghosts by comparison. Moved by a sudden thought, I bent down and tried to pluck a daisy which was growing at my feet. The stalk wouldn't break. I tried to twist it, but it wouldn't twist. I tugged till the sweat stood out on my forehead and I had lost most of the skin off my hands. The little flower was hard, not like wood or even like iron, but like diamond. There was a leaf—a young tender beech-leaf, lying in the grass beside it. I tried to pick the leaf up: my heart almost cracked with the effort, and I believe I did just raise it. But I had to let it go at once; it was heavier than a sack of coal.[18]

Most of the ghosts who come to visit the heavenly realms cannot endure this solidity of heaven. The grass tortures their feet, they experience it as horrible spikes, and the people in heaven are also solid. In every way, including the physical, heaven is real.

So in this dream parable *The Great Divorce*, George MacDonald says to Lewis, 'Hell is a state of mind. . . . Heaven is not a state of mind. Heaven is reality itself.'[19] And later Lewis, speaking again through MacDonald, says of the age to come, 'Every natural love will rise again and live forever in this country: but none will rise again until it has been buried.'[20] Thus there is indeed continuity between this present world—the world of physical nature, the physical pleasures, and natural love—and the realm of heaven. This world is a true foreshadowing of the next, but there also has to be a death and resurrection.

In the last chapters of the final Narnia book, *The Last Battle*, heaven and eternal life are clearly spelt out in physical terms. There will be animals and trees in the age to come. Everything good will be preserved in heaven. Peter, looking down from heaven, exclaims: 'Why!', as he sees the distant region, 'It's England. And that's the house itself—Professor Kirk's old home in the country where all our adventures began!' 'I thought that house had been destroyed', said Edmund. 'So it was', said the Faun, 'But you are now looking at the England within England, the real England just as this is the real Narnia. And in that inner England no good thing is destroyed.'[21] All that is good will be preserved in the age to come.

This applies to our own self above all else. C. S. Lewis gave full value to the Christian belief in the resurrection of the body. The separation of body and soul at death are no more than temporary: at the end of time, they will be reunited. The integrity of our total personhood will be restored. We shall have a body once more—a transfigured, spiritual body, but a body continuous in some real sense with that which we have at present. Speaking of the resurrection body, Lewis, in his book *Miracles*, uses the telling and helpful analogy of a waterfall.[22] He points out that if you look at the waterfall, the drops of water are constantly changing, but the arc of water, the shape of the waterfall, remains the same; and in that sense, though the material constituents are all the time altering, yet it is the same waterfall. And he suggests that this might help us to understand the relationship between our present body and our body in the age to come. Perhaps it will not have the same physical constituents, but it will be the same body, because it will have the same form. Our body expresses our soul, and just as our body in this life expresses our personality, it will do so in the age to come. In the sense in which we are the same person, it will be the same body.

When we say that the body expresses the soul, this leads me to recall the saying, 'In the case of all of us who are more than 40 years old, we are responsible for the appearance of our faces.' A somewhat daunting thought. You show what kind of a person you are.

Through all of this, it becomes clear how high is the value that C. S. Lewis attaches to this world as God's creation, and within this world to our physical, material bodies. For him, the world is indeed a sacrament of divine presence and divine glory. 'Teach me, my God and King, in all things Thee to see.'[23] Lewis did precisely that.

Now, how far does Charles Williams share his standpoint? The two are, as we might expect, often in striking agreement, but there are differences of emphasis. I think Charles Williams was less sensitive to the beauty of this world than C. S. Lewis was. Charles Williams, after all, was a city dweller in a way in which Lewis was not. Charles Williams did not usually go for long walks in the hills on his holidays. He didn't have many holidays.

In the novel *The Place of the Lion* (which I think is in many ways the most successful of Williams's novels, the one in which the plot holds together best), what I particularly love is the chapter called 'The Coming Of The Butterflies': Mr Tighe's vision of butterflies. '"O glory, glory", Mr. Tighe says, "O glory everlasting! . . . O that I should see it!" he said again, "O glory be to it!"'[24] If space permitted, I would reproduce the whole of that section, but it goes on for several pages. There, I think, Williams expresses, as Lewis does, a strong sense of the beauty and wonder of the world, and therefore its sacred character.

You will remember that a key theme in Charles Williams is the contrast between the way of affirmation and the way of negation. There are two different forms of theology, as you know: Either you can try to describe the divine by saying what it is, or you can try and describe it by saying what it is not. You can use both methods, and indeed you have to. To sum up the difference between the affirmative or cataphatic way and the negative or apophatic way, I recall a publication I read some years ago called *Signs of the Times*, published by the *Times* newspaper. They had run a competition inviting people to send in photographs of strange notices that they had observed, and a collection of them appears in the book. Someone from Uganda sent in a road sign saying, 'Elephants have right of way'. Someone in Wales sent in a sign from a car park saying, 'Parking is limited to 60 minutes in each hour'. And I leave those of you who are Welsh in my readership to work out what that means. Anyway, I am thinking of two notices from this book, one of which illustrates the way of affirmation and one the way of negation. The first shows a level crossing over a railway line. Near the railway line, there is a box attached to a post, inside the box a bell, and above the box a notice. The notice says, 'Danger: stop, look and listen. If the bell is ringing, do not cross the line. If the bell is not ringing, stop, look and listen anyway, in case the bell is not working'. So there you see the affirmative approach: Every possibility is allowed for. But then there was another notice, from Australia: a signpost which said, 'This road does not lead either to Sydney nor to Canberra'. We are not told where it does lead. That's the way of negation.

Now Charles Williams believed in both of these ways, but he stressed especially the way of affirmation, and this surely signifies the affirmation of this world as sacrament. His key principle, 'this also is thou, neither is this thou',[25] corresponds exactly to the role of natural contemplation in Patristic spirituality. God is in everything, but God is above and beyond everything. Charles Williams, in common with Lewis (indeed far more emphatically than Lewis), was conscious of the thinness of the world, the interpenetration of the natural and the supernatural, the way in which this world reflects and interacts with the world beyond. As the actor Martin Browne said of Williams, 'I have never met any human being in whom the divisions between body and spirit, natural and supernatural, temporal and eternal, were so non-existent, nor any writer who so consistently took their non-existence for granted.'[26] Typically, Williams observes in his *Outlines of Romantic Theology*: 'There are minds for whom the mere kerb of the pavement falls away into incredible abysses.'[27] And he had exactly that kind of mind.

For Williams, created things are to be valued in and for themselves. They are solid, not just shadows, and yet they always point beyond themselves. Again Williams, along with Lewis, is profoundly conscious of the power and dynamic force of evil, and this comes out in his novels. I would agree, indeed, with Anne Ridler, who says of Williams: 'The evil is too much described.' Yet if, like Lewis, Williams was a moral dualist, like Lewis he was never an ontological dualist. He believed, again in Anne Ridler's words, 'in a universe ruled by love', and he always emphasized the danger of what he calls 'unofficial Manichaeism', which he passionately rejected. Williams was acutely aware that evil has more particularly infected matter. We may think here of his chilling descriptions of the materiality of magic. Yet he never waivers in his conviction that matter is good, and is endowed with sacramental value. 'It is quite clear', he says in one of his letters, 'what matter ought to be. It ought to be the *significant* presence of God.'[28] Williams rejects fiercely the notion that the body has, as he puts it, 'fallen a good deal farther than the soul.'[29] He values our physical sexuality, quoting Julian of Norwich, 'The worshipful City that our Lord Jesus sitteth in is our sensualite.'[30] 'We experience', he says, 'physically, in its proper mode, the kingdom of God.'[31] Valuing the body, Williams, much more definitely than Lewis, emphasizes that romantic love involves the whole person, body and soul together. So there are differences of emphasis, but a shared underlying vision of the world as sacrament.

To sum up, let me read one more sentence from Lewis, emphasizing the wonder and variety of nature: 'Never did He make two things the same; Never did He utter one word twice.'[32]

Notes

1. This talk was given on 20 October 1998.
2. C. S. Lewis, *Surprised by Joy* (London: Geoffrey Bles, 1955), 14.
3. C. S. Lewis, *George MacDonald: An Anthology* (London: Geoffrey Bles, 1946), entry '150. Nature', 69.
4. Thomas Traherne, *Centuries of Meditations*, ed. Bertram Dobell (London: P. J. & A. E. Dobell, 1948), 152–153.
5. Psalm 19:1.
6. Gospel of Thomas (Saying 77).
7. Paraphrasing Alexander Schmemann, *For the Life of the World* ([Crestwood, NY]: St. Vladimir's Seminary Press, 1982), 113.
8. C. S. Lewis, *Out of the Silent Planet* (London: Pan Books, 1971), 34.
9. C. S. Lewis, *The Magician's Nephew* (New York: Macmillan, 1961), 103.
10. *Collected Papers of Evelyn Underhill*, ed. Lucy Menzies (London: Longmans, 1946), 196.
11. William Luther White, *The Image of Man in C. S. Lewis* (Nashville: Abingdon Press, 1969), 93–94.
12. Paraphrasing C. S. Lewis, *Mere Christianity* (London: Geoffrey Bles, 1952), 34.
13. Lewis, *Mere Christianity*, 35.
14. Lewis, *Mere Christianity*, 50.
15. Lewis, *Mere Christianity*, 77.
16. Lewis, *George MacDonald*, entry '52. The Body', 40.
17. C. S. Lewis, *The Four Loves* (London: Geoffrey Bles, 1960), 108.
18. C. S. Lewis, *The Great Divorce* (London: Geoffrey Bles, 1945), 27.
19. Lewis, *The Great Divorce*, 63.
20. Lewis, *The Great Divorce*, 88–89.
21. C. S. Lewis, *The Last Battle* (New York: Macmillan, 1956), 171–172.
22. C. S. Lewis, *Miracles: A Preliminary Study* (London: Geoffrey Bles, 1947), 180.
23. George Herbert, 'The Elixir' from *The Temple* (1633).
24. Charles Williams, *The Place of the Lion* (Grand Rapids, MI: William B. Eerdmans, 1978), 43.
25. Charles Williams, *He Came Down From Heaven* (London: Faber and Faber, 1950), 25.
26. E. Martin Browne and Henzie Browne, *Two in One* (Cambridge [England]: Cambridge University Press, 1981), 101.

27. Charles Williams, *Outlines of Romantic Theology*, ed. Alice Mary Hadfield (Grand Rapids, MI: William B. Eerdmans), 72.

28. Alice Mary Hadfield, *Charles Williams: An Exploration of His Life and Work* (New York: Oxford University Press, 1983), 107.

29. Charles Williams, *The Image of the City and Other Essays*, selected by Anne Ridler (London: Oxford University Press, 1958), 68.

30. Williams, *Image of the City*, 68.

31. Williams, *Image of the City*, 87.

32. C. S. Lewis, *Perelandra* (London: Bodley Head, 1943), 246.

5

Charles Williams and the Problem of Evil

Paul S. Fiddes

THE NAME OF Charles Williams is often linked with that of C. S. Lewis, not only because they were friends, fellow 'Inklings', and mutual critics of each other's work, but because they both wrote novels that would now be classified as 'fantasy'.[1] They themselves believed they were alerting the reader to the spiritual dimension within the world of the everyday, and this perhaps was in the mind of the publisher who attached a blurb to the dust jackets of Williams's seven novels[2] advertising them as 'supernatural thrillers'. But a comparison between Williams and Lewis flounders at several points, and not least in Williams's treatment of the nature of evil; the reader of both sets of novels will find something rather more daring, more ambiguous—and thus more disturbing—about Williams as he portrays radical evil within human life.

Williams is perhaps best known for such ideas as 'the theology of romantic love', 'the way of exchange', 'the affirmation of images', and 'the image of the city'. These themes are woven throughout the fabric of his astonishing range of writing—novels, plays, poetry, literary criticism, popular theology, history, and biography. But basic to these main themes is, I believe, his understanding of evil and human fallenness. His various genres of writing all show an unusual working out of the Augustinian concept of evil as *privatio boni*, a negation and absence of the good, and here I want to suggest he has both made an original contribution to Christian thought *and* stumbled into some theological problems. This accounts, I believe, for the ambiguous portrayal of evil that readers feel even when they do not analyse it. But while his presentation undermines itself, this does not destroy the effect of his writings; rather, I want to suggest that the inconsistencies and ambiguities prevent us as readers from bringing our understanding of evil to any final closure, and prompt us to question the way that the 'classical' theological tradition has presented the image of God as the Supreme Good.

For a portrayal of Augustine's dictum that evil is strictly 'nothing', we may begin with Williams's novel *Many Dimensions*. The story concerns the Stone of King Solomon, which has the remarkable properties of being able to be divided and so replicated without being diminished, and of being able to transport its bearer through space and time. Sir Giles Tumulty is one of the characters who tries to exploit this spiritual power for his own advantage, and is finally drawn into the Stone itself. As he is carried towards the centre of the many dimensions of the Stone, he is confronted by the eternal light at its heart and is destroyed.

> He was conscious of a myriad other Giles Tumultys, of childhood and boyhood and youth and age, all that he had ever been, and all of them were screaming as that relentless and dividing light plunged into them and held them. He was doing, it seemed, innumerable things at once, all the things that he had ever done, and yet the whole time he was not doing, he was slipping, slipping down, and under and over him the Glory shone, and sometimes it withdrew a little and then pierced him again with new agony. And now he was whirling round and round, having no hold above or footing below, but being lost in an infinite depth. Above him the light was full of eyes, curious and pitiless, watching him as he had often watched others. . . .[3]

As Williams describes it, everything that Giles had done was a 'not doing', simply a turning away from the light, a slipping away from the good. This is a graphic picture of Augustine's definition of evil as absence of good, *privatio boni*. Evil has no positive ontological standing, no reality of its own; it is strictly nothing or non-being, a turning away from being. It is always parasitic upon the good.[4] Drawing upon an already existing tradition of thought in Neo-Platonism,[5] Augustine was thus able to answer his critics who asked him whether God had created evil; this was a nonsense question, he replied, as evil was not a created thing at all, but simply a slipping away from the created good through the free will of the creature.

I. Evil as Privatio Boni

In the first section of this essay I want now to trace Williams's handling of this idea through three stages of human life: fall, the predicament of existence, and salvation. Corresponding to Williams's own treatment of these three phases, we can call them the act of *alteration of consciousness*, the state of *divided consciousness*, and the gift of *transformation of consciousness*. Acknowledging

Williams's contribution here will set the scene for some problems in his thought that we shall have to face later.

1. The Alteration of Consciousness: Seeking to Know Good by Means of Evil

Augustine's portrayal of the human fall from fellowship with God seems straightforward enough at first sight. The world was created perfect, and Adam and Eve were created enjoying a state of bliss. However, they chose freely to turn away from the Good; in pride they were pleased with themselves and refused to have God to rule over them. Augustine perceives that they *could* do this because as finite beings they had been made from nothing (*ex nihilo*); they only had to let go of the Good to slip back towards nothing.[6] The slipping away was evil, a loss of the Something which was the good. It is *privatio boni*. We, for our part, inherit this depravity; we have slipped far down the scale of being, and cannot pull ourselves back up again. That needs the grace of God and a new act of creation.

But there is a problem with this kind of theological sketch, and it has been readily pounced upon by Friedrich Daniel Ernst Schleiermacher in the last century and by John Hick in this.[7] If Adam and Eve were created perfect, 'wrapped around with grace', and in the bliss of communion with God, why should they *want* to turn away from the good? Granted, they would not be unable to sin, but they would be able not to sin.[8] They *could* turn away, but why would they *want* to? Would not their experience of the good overwhelm and satisfy them? Augustine himself admitted he was baffled by this, both with regard to the fall of the angels and human beings, and the fact that he could come to no explanation simply confirmed for him that evil was in fact strictly nothing.[9] There was a kind of self-creation of evil *ex nihilo*.

Now, in his theological work *He Came Down from Heaven* (1938), Williams does attempt to offer an answer to this objection, while he does not explicitly raise the question. He takes up the part of the Adam myth in Genesis 3, where the snake tempts Adam to eat the fruit of the 'knowledge of good and evil'. Williams suggests this means that Adam wanted to know the good, but he wanted to know it in a new way, through its opposite, evil.[10] This is an ingenious answer as to why someone living in the illumination of Paradise would *want* to do evil; as a denizen of bliss, Adam naturally wants to know the good, but he seeks to know it through its contradiction, to see what it is like from God's point of view. ('You shall be like God, knowing good and evil'; Genesis 3:5.)

Here Williams deliberately combines Augustine and Aquinas. Augustine had said that, since evil is strictly nothing, it could only be known by way of the good.[11] Aquinas had said that God could know the good through its opposite, evil, as a purely intellectual matter.[12] Williams adds that, unlike God, Adam could only know evil through *experience,* and so wanting to know good through its contradiction brought on the disaster of actually experiencing evil. There was an 'alteration of knowledge' or alteration of consciousness, whence from henceforth good would be known *as* evil.

This is a fascinating use of the tradition of evil as *privatio boni,* in order to answer a problem that must be vexing to all Augustinians. The very existence of the problem leads most modern theologians, of course, away from the idea of a single-point historic fall in which a perfect creation suddenly falls into disaster through one act. It leads theologians such as Paul Tillich to prefer an account in which creation and fall always coincided, though as a matter of fact rather than as a logical necessity.[13] Nor does Williams himself actually attempt in his fiction to depict the Adamic act of seeking the good through evil. While he constantly describes the present human predicament of only knowing good *as* evil, for example being tempted to misuse what is good for evil ends, he does not portray anyone really wanting to know and serve the good through its opposite. Perhaps this in itself indicates that he also regards the Adam story as a timeless myth, a way of talking about the actual predicament in which human beings find themselves now. If so, then Williams provides a complementary insight to the solution offered by Hick, that human beings are created at an 'epistemic distance' from the divine glory in order to allow room for genuine response.[14]

Williams does rewrite the story of Adam in his poetry, and so makes it live in the imagination. In his Arthurian cycle of poems, *Taliessen through Logres,* the ideal Empire is pictured in the form of a body, its four provinces being the head, the breasts, the hands, and the buttocks—the prophetic intellect, the milk of doctrine, the acts of creation and the foundation of the senses.[15] The Adam within the body is tempted to know good through evil as God does:

> The Adam in the hollow of Jerusalem respired:
> softly their thought twined to its end,
> crying. . . .
> *Does not God vision the principles at war?*
> *Let us grow to the height of God and the Emperor:*
> *Let us gaze, son of man, on the Acts in contention.*[16]

The result is horrifying:

> Phosphorescent on the stagnant level
> a headless figure walks in a crimson cope,
> volcanic dust blown under the moon.

The body of Christendom is perverted:

> A brainless form, as of the Emperor,
> walks, indecent hands hidden under the cope,
> dishallowing in that crimson the flush on the mounds of Caucasia.

It is perhaps no accident that Williams's conversation partner C. S. Lewis comes to exactly the same conclusion as Williams about the nature of the human fall, and in his novel *Perelandra* he *does* attempt what Williams declines: to depict in *narrative* form the temptation to know good by means of evil. The Lady is tempted to disobey God's command not to remain on the 'fixed land'—echoing a constant theme of Lewis, that it is the heart of sin to want to hold on to the same experience. The tempter urges that the Lady can only truly know what the will of God is when she disobeys it: 'a real disobeying, a real branching out, this is what he secretly longs for. . . .'[17] The whole novel is an attempt to describe how someone who desires and loves the good could still be seduced into evil. But then, it is also in the form of a myth.

2. The Divided Consciousness: Knowing Good as Evil

Williams's own interest is less in any moment of past fall than in the continuing human predicament. Because evil is strictly nothing, only the good can actually be known. So it is the human agony 'to know good *as* evil'.[18] That is, evil is always the good corrupted and so the human consciousness is divided; we know the good only in a distorted form. This was the perception of St Paul, who saw the Old Testament law as a good thing spoilt, and who describes in Romans 7:19 the pain of knowing that 'the good I want to do, I do not'. In this century the theologian Karl Barth summed up sin as 'the impossible possibility'.[19]

Williams works out this division of consciousness not only in characters in his novels, but in his literary criticism. In *The English Poetic Mind* he finds the key to Shakespeare's vision of reality in the play *Troilus and Cressida*. Faced by the evidence that his beloved Cressida has been sleeping with the enemy, Troilus cries out:

> *This she? No; this is Diomed's Cressida.*
> *If beauty have a soul, this is not she. . . .*
> *. . . This is, and is not, Cressid!*
> *Within my soul there doth conduce a fight*
> *Of this strange nature, that a thing inseparate*
> *Divides more wider than the sky and earth. . . . (5.2.137–149)*

Troilus finds himself living in two worlds, one in which Cressida is his faithful love and one in which she is the faithless lover of Diomed. What connection can there be between these two worlds, divided wider than earth and heaven?

> Nothing at all, unless that this were she. (5.2.135)

In Troilus's experience, he knows the good only as soiled and perverted: 'this is and is not Cressid'. As Williams puts it, reviewing several major tragedies of Shakespeare in one magnificent sweep:

> The crisis which Troilus endured is one common to all men; it is in a sense the only interior crisis worth talking about. It is that in which every nerve of the body, every consciousness of the mind, shrieks that something cannot be. Only it is.
>
> Cressid *cannot* be playing with Diomed. But she is. The Queen *cannot* have married Claudius. But she has. Desdemona *cannot* love Cassio. But she does. Daughters *cannot* hate their father and benefactor. But they do.[20]

Williams goes on to suggest that each tragic hero has a preconceived idea about life and the way people will behave—Romeo has a vision of death, Macbeth of kingship, Anthony of love; in a conflict of perception with the world around, they have to lose the idea, and to suffer intensely while losing it. It cannot be, and yet it is. 'This is and is not Cressid'. And all stems from the nature of evil as *privatio boni*, so that we have to say 'this is a good, and yet it is not'. Only Milton's Satan deliberately embraces this divided consciousness, vowing 'evil, be thou my good'.

This is all highly illuminating as a study of Shakespeare, though the idea of evil as a perverted good is not in itself original to Williams. What does appear as highly original, however, is the ambiguous meaning of the phrase, 'this is and is not. . . .' 'This also is Thou; neither is this Thou.'[21] In the first place it means, as we have seen, that every earthly good slips towards nothingness. 'This is, and is *not*, Cressid'. But conversely, it means that every earthly good, mixed as it is with non-good, can be the way to the Supreme Good, the *Summum Bonum*.[22] This is, and is not, Beatrice. Here we touch Williams's theology of Romantic love: we are disturbed from our self-absorption and self-sufficiency by the shock of love, as Dante was led towards the vision of divine love through Beatrice.[23] As Glen Cavaliero aptly expresses it, 'the Beatrician moment is itself a moment of judgement.'[24]

3. The Transformation of Consciousness: Knowing Evil as the Occasion for Good

The solution to the human predicament, according to Williams, is not merely to try to sort out good from evil. In his view the Old Testament prophets attempted this without any real success. Since evil is *privatio boni*, the authentic way of salvation is 'to know the evil of the past itself as good', which means knowing evil as the opportunity for the good, or as 'an occasion for love'.[25] This is the way of transformation of consciousness. In the fall, Adam tried to know good *by means of* evil; the consequence is that we know good *as* evil; the solution is to know evil *as occasion for* good. It was in this latter way that Christ knew evil, affirming all things as a place for good, seeing all things by the pattern of heaven. But we cannot by ourselves simply know evil in the way that Christ did, as occasion for love; we must be enabled to do so, and the way of enabling is the way of exchange. In the cross, affirms Williams, Christ took on our experience of the loss of the good, so that we might share his knowledge of evil. This is the pattern of coinherence, and it is one into which we can enter with others now in the fellowship of the cross, bearing each others' burdens.[26]

So Williams binds together a traditional thought—the cross as a substitution—not with any concept of penal satisfaction, but with a redeeming of human life from evil. This is a remarkable remaking of images, all based upon the idea of evil as *privatio boni*. In none of the novels is it worked out more thoroughly than in *Descent into Hell*.

In this novel a young woman, Pauline, has since childhood been haunted by a Doppelgänger, a duplicate figure of herself whom she often sees on the road in the distance, and whom she has an extreme fear of meeting face to face. She is released from her crippling anxiety by the offer of Peter Stanhope to carry her burden of fear for her, described in a chapter called 'The Doctrine of Substituted Love':

> It was necessary first to receive intensely all her spirit's conflict. He sat on, imagining to himself the long walk with its sinister possibility, the ogreish world lying around, the air with its treachery to all sane appearance. His own eyes began to seek and strain and shrink, his own feet, quiet though they actually were, began to weaken with the necessity of advance upon the road down which the girl was passing. The body of his flesh received her alien terror, his mind carried the burden of her world. The burden was inevitably lighter for him than for her, for the rage of a personal resentment was lacking. He endured her

sensitiveness, but not her sin; the substitution there, if indeed there is
a substitution, is hidden in the central mystery of Christendom which
Christendom itself has never understood, nor can.[27]

Pauline has an ancestor who was burned at the stake as a Protestant
martyr, and who is described in the history books as going to his death in an
ecstasy of joy, shouting in the midst of the fire, 'I have seen the salvation of
my God'. She wonders how he could have made such a great evil an occasion
for good, and she discovers *how* when at the climax of the book she is trans-
ported back through time to the martyr's condemned cell. She finds him in
trembling of the coming fire. She sees a counterpart of herself, full of joy,
appearing to the condemned man, offering to carry his fear for him: she
hears her own voice saying, 'Give it to me, give it to me, John Struther.' He
does so in thanksgiving, and at that moment Pauline understands why she
has been so afraid of her counterpart; in fact, the fear she was carrying was
not of the Doppelgänger at all, but John's fear of the fire.

> She had lived without joy so that he might die in joy, but when she lived
> she had not known and when she offered she had not guessed that the
> sacrificial victim had died before the sacrificial gift was accomplished.[28]

So she is reconciled with her real self: 'she whirled on the thing she had so
long avoided, and the glorious creature looked past her at the shouting martyr
beyond.' The reconciliation with her own true being is possible because 'she
had all her life carried a fear which was not hers but another's, until it had
become for her in turn not hers but another's.' She carries John's burden and
Peter Stanhope carries hers. This is the way of exchange that makes it possible to embrace even the fire, so that the flames of evil become an occasion for
good and warm the heart. 'He that hath much, to him shall more be given',
cries John as he goes to his death. Battle Hill on which this takes place merges
with another hill, that of Gologotha, on which 'far off beyond vision in the
depths of all worlds, a god, unamenable to death, awhile endured and died.'[29]

In all Williams's novels, the characters take the way of exchange to find that
the nothingness of evil is the path to the good. If it is symbolized by fire in *Descent into Hell*, it is symbolized by water in *All Hallows' Eve*. Another dead soul,
Lester, gazes upon the dirty waters of the Thames, full of sewage and rubbish:

> The evacuations of the City had their place in the City; how else could
> the City be the City? Corruption (so to call it) was tolerable, even

adequate and proper, even glorious. . . . A sodden mass of cardboard and paper drifted by, but the soddenness was itself a joy, for this was what happened, and all that happened, in this great material world, was good.[30]

This vision of evil as strictly nothing, as *privatio boni*, does, however, produce a theological problem which takes shape in various ways in Williams's work, and which gives rise to that feeling of discomfort I mentioned at the beginning of this paper. It is the danger of justifying the presence of evil in the world.

II. The Theological Problem: Justifying Evil
1. The Will of God

The problem arises in the first place from the affirming of evil as the opportunity for good. ('Corruption was . . . even glorious. . . .'). This might lead us to a theodicy in which the presence of evil and suffering in the world was justified on the grounds that they were necessary as a means of personal growth and moral development. This is usually called by philosophers of religion an 'instrumental' or 'educational' theory of evil, and it might be viewed as educating either the sufferer or those who witness the suffering. If applied to the existence of *moral* evil, that is, the evil that results from human moral choices, it would of course have the effect of making the fall itself a necessary part of human growth towards maturity. While there are theologians who argue this, it would nullify Williams's own view that the attempt to know God through evil was a catastrophe. There is a danger, then, that Williams's universal and generous recognition of evil as an occasion for the good ('corruption was glorious') might actually lead to an affirming of evil as a necessary means of knowing the good.

Even more perilously near is a theodicy applied to *natural* evil, that is, the suffering which flows from disruptions in nature such as earthquakes, floods, viruses, and genetic disorders. It might seem an easy step to move towards a view in which the Creator intends such evils in order to provide an opportunity for love. This is the theory argued by C. S. Lewis in his early book *The Problem of Pain*: 'What is good in any painful experience is, for the sufferer, his submission to the will of God, and, for the spectators, the compassion aroused and the acts of mercy to which it leads.'[31] It is the latter good, the virtue created in those who have to cope with the suffering of others, that a more recent philosopher, Richard Swinburne, emphasizes in his own theodicy.[32] Williams did in fact reject this whole approach, as becomes clear in a review he wrote of Lewis's book:

> All my own emotions rebel against the pattern of this book. I do not want to be shown that pain is, or may be, a good; that (given our present state) its inevitability is a good.[33]

Lewis himself, in the agony of the slow death of his wife from cancer, came to feel that he did not want to be shown this either. In his later book *A Grief Observed*, he writes:

> Someone said, I believe, 'God always geometrizes'. Supposing the truth were 'God always vivisects'?[34]

Lewis now finds abhorrent the idea that God designs the world and its suffering with the skill of a master mathematician. Williams had always reacted against this, though we may note in passing that Lewis has apparently recalled the phrase 'God always geometrizes' from Williams's own book *He Came Down from Heaven*, used in another context and correctly ascribed to Plato.[35]

Against all Williams's intentions, however, there is a danger that the celebrating of evil as a pathway to the good may result in a view of the necessity of evil, suffering and fallenness such as found—for example—in Georg W. F. Hegel. Williams's use of the concept of evil as *privatio boni* has this ironic possibility within it: 'The evacuations of the City had their place in the City. . . corruption was . . . even glorious, . . . all that happened was good.' Williams partly, but *only* partly, succeeds in resisting this tendency through three strategies.

First, he exults in the protests of Job, as he himself protested against Lewis's argument. The story of Job keeps alive the need for a 'stark rage' against all evil and suffering, whether natural or moral evil, and whether the anger is directed against the banal comments of friends, the universe, or God himself. 'Humility has never consisted in not asking questions', says Williams. 'It does not make men less themselves or less intelligent, but more intelligent and more themselves.'[36]

In the second place, Williams understands the cross of Jesus as a kind of accepting of responsibility by God for the sufferings of the world. This is consistent with a belief that God has *allowed* human beings free-will to make perverse choices, but not that God has *intended* them as a necessary stage of growth. The educationalist does not regret his means of education, but God does feel that amends must be made:

> Our justice condemned the innocent, but the innocent it condemned was one who was fundamentally responsible for the existence of all injustice—its existence in the mere, but necessary, sense of time, which His will created and prolonged.[37]

This leads us to the third and major strategy of Williams: a mysterious relation between God's eternal will and the temporal will of human beings. In his revision of Augustine's thought in *The Descent of the Dove*, Williams suggests that what the great predestinarian was aiming at all the time was not just a remorseless divine will, but a mingling of wills: 'The City of God leaps upon its citizens. . . . But its choice is (beyond human thought) inextricably mingled with each man's own choice.'[38] This theory, over-charitably ascribed to Augustine, is fleshed out in all the novels.

In *War in Heaven*, for example, Gregory Persimmons tries to manipulate the Holy Grail, as Sir Giles Tumulty tries to exploit the stone of King Solomon in *Many Dimensions* (in fact, Sir Giles makes his first appearance in this earlier story). The Archdeacon refuses to bargain for the Grail, and apparently lets it go into Gregory's hands without concern. In this he is proved right. At the climax of the book Gregory tries to use the Grail as an interface between the worlds of the living and the dead, placing it—filled with blood—upon the bare chest of the bound Archdeacon; Gregory is attempting a ghastly marriage between the soul of the living priest and the soul of a dead man whom he killed. When the magic charm seems to have worked, the centre of the Grail awakes and takes over: 'suddenly from it broke a terrific and golden light; blast upon blast of trumpets shook the air.'[39] The light does not destroy Gregory as it does Sir Giles in *Many Dimensions*; it propels him into the arms of the London police force. Earlier in the novel, the Archdeacon had reflected:

> 'When the time comes, He [God] shall dispose as He will, or rather He shall be as He will, as He is.'
> 'Does he will Gregory Persimmons?' Kenneth said wryly.
> 'Certainly He wills him', the Archdeacon said, 'since He wills that Persimmons shall be whatever he seems to choose. That is not technically correct, perhaps, but it is that which I believe and feel and know.'
> 'He wills evil, then?' Kenneth said.
> 'Shall there be evil in the City and I the Lord have not done it?' the Archbishop quoted.[40]

Williams, through the Archdeacon, is not merely claiming that God *permits* evil while not *intending* it, so that God can use evil as occasion for good while not actually designing it this way. That claim is what the narrator of the story calls 'the simpler idea'[41] on which the Archdeacon's friends fall back. That the Archdeacon intends a more direct will of God in the matter is clear by his evasive use of the phrase 'he wills that Persimmons shall be whatever he [Persimmons] *seems* to choose', not just 'whatever he chooses'. Williams wants to maintain the mystery of an interlocking of divine will and human will, rather than having a God who merely plans evil and suffering, but he is prevented from what he calls the 'simpler idea' that 'agony and evil were displeasing to God, but that He permitted them'. In this Williams shows himself an acute theologian, *given his presuppositions*: the distinction between causing and permitting is indeed a very fine one, *if* we keep a classical theistic picture of a God who is outside all movement of time and who acts coercively in a way that cannot be resisted. This is the received image of what God as Supreme Good must be like, in contrast to all relative earthly goods.

Williams does have such a picture of God, as is clear from his discussion of time in the novel *Many Dimensions*. Like Boethius, he understands God to exist eternally in the sense of experiencing our every moment—past, present, and future—simultaneously.[42] Elsewhere he cites Boethius, claiming that the events for which we implore the fulfilment of God's will on earth 'are already perfectly concluded by it in heaven . . . they already exist as events in heaven.'[43] Those theologians (such as Wolfhart Pannenberg)[44] are right who argue that it is impossible with such a concept to give any real force to human free will, as a matter of open choice and open future. As Sir Giles is dragged towards the annihilating light at the heart of the stone of King Solomon, he remembers a vision he once had of this end. Using the Stone to travel in time, he had once tried to enter the future, but apparently could not because 'the future had as yet lain only in the Mind to which it equally with the past was present'; instead, the Stone had *revealed* the future to him, a vision that he had mercifully forgotten until now. However, we are bound to ask how the future in that case could have been any different, whatever choices Sir Giles had made. He seems to have had an illusory freedom based only in his lapse of memory. In theory he could have travelled into it without making any difference to his destiny. We are caught in as many tangles of thought here as the unfortunate Sir Giles is to be trapped in the Stone.

Williams obviously hopes that his idea of a mysterious mingling of wills will be sufficient to allow for evil as a genuine enemy of God's will, and so prevent the absolute necessity of evil and suffering. However, he seems to be hampered by his Boethian concept of God's omniscience and his Augustinian concept of God's *irresistibile* grace. Despite his strategies, Williams's novels demonstrate the problem with following through the view of evil as *privatio boni* to its logical conclusion, that evil will not only be *de facto* an occasion for good, but *must* happen in order to be so. We shall always be in danger of justifying evil. To avoid this danger we might refuse to make too tight a system of thought about evil as *privatio boni*, and stress instead the fragmentary and incomplete nature of any understanding of evil as 'nothing'. But a complementary approach is to allow the impasse we have reached to prompt us to revise our notions of God. That is, we may maintain that God is redeeming a situation God does not in any way design or intend, and work out the consequences of this 'simpler idea' for the nature of God.

This would mean, I suggest, a God who has limited God's self for the sake of the freedom of creatures. If we think of a divine self-emptying (*kenosis*) in which God freely chooses not to operate in a unilateral way, but desires instead only to work with the consent and response of creation, then it is possible to think of a God who can be frustrated and thwarted in God's own plans, and who does not know every detail of the future.[45] There is, in fact, just a hint of this idea in *He Came Down from Heaven*, when Williams comments on the continual lack of response to God from the people of Israel in the Old Testament, which leads to the recurrent phrase 'the Lord repented him'. God, as it were, changes his design (though not his ultimate purpose)— or as Williams puts it, 'The Will of the Omnipotence is to be turned aside and to submit itself.'[46]

Such a picture of a self-limiting God, involved in time, change, and suffering, might indeed enable us to speak of evil as an occasion for good. That is, the God who limits God's self in allowing created beings to make their wrong choices can still make the evil and death God does not want into servants.

2. The Dark Side of the Good

In Williams's plays, the same theological problem appears in a different way, with the appearance of a Satan-like figure. Ambiguities are bound to occur when knowing God as evil is catastrophic, and knowing evil as occasion for good is salvation. Williams obviously felt that some kind of image or symbol would help in the understanding of the ambiguity, some character standing outside the main plot who would act as a kind of stimulant to make us aware of the ambiguous nature of the good.

In his plays, therefore, there appears such a figure. The precursor is Satan in *The Rite of the Passion*,[47] who points out that the effects of works of love can be evil as well as good (a successor to the series of accusers in Oscar Wilde's parable, *The Doer of Good*). In *Seed of Adam* the figure is the Third King, who stands for the state of 'everlasting perishing'. His two brother kings have tried to lose him on the journey to Bethlehem, but he turns up after all, explaining that 'earth is always leaving clues for hell, / and hell has only to follow that news of earth.'[48] He introduces himself as the core of the fruit that Adam and Eve ate, and with the aid of his alter-ego, a threatening figure with a scimitar, he attacks Mary: 'the worm / of that fruit. . . has a great need to feed / on living form.' But the result of the conflict between the Third King ('King of the core') and Mary, stylized in a dance, is that Mary falls into labour: 'Parturition is upon me; blessed be He!' Under the sword-blade of death, love has been born:

> . . . *my son took flesh under its flash.*

The Third King warns Adam, present in the person of Augustine, of the ambiguities of his desire:

> *Do not speak too soon; you desired the boon of salvation—*
> *have it! You desired twice—me and not me,*
> *the turn and the Return; the Return is here,*
> *take care that you do not prefer me.*[49]

The turn away from the good (*privatio boni*) has been redeemed in the 'Return' to God in Christ and, mysteriously, the Third King has been the occasion for both events, as 'me' and 'not me'. Aptly he joins in praising God as 'the only Necessity', whose 'necessity [is] in himself alone' (an idea we must come to in a moment). The Third King's persona as Accuser, the prosecuting Counsel who insists the truth be told, is taken up in the figure *called* the Accuser in *Judgement at Chelmsford*. He introduces himself as the one who stands

> *at the right hand of all men in their hour of death;*
> *but also they may see me at any hour. Their breath*
> *catches, their blood is cold, they remember their sins.*[50]

He reviews the history of the Church in Essex throughout the ages, and shows convincingly that all its so-called virtues have actually produced few acts of love. The See of Chelmsford is thus shaken from any claims on her own virtue, and driven back simply to rely on the love of God. With that, the Accuser declares himself to be 'God's true knowledge of all things made', is greeted by Chelmsford as 'dearest of all lovers', and takes her down from the cross saying:

> Most sweet lady,
> I have waited an hour, and yet an hour for this;
> now I will lift you where we have willed; on,
> on to the City, the Love between all lovers.[51]

Accusation and transfiguration are thus fused together. In *The House of the Octopus* there appears similarly the figure of the Flame, though it is perhaps in the earlier play *Thomas Cranmer of Canterbury* that the figure makes the most impression as 'The Skeleton'. This character describes itself as the way to salvation *and* the way of death:

> I am the way,
> I the division, the derision, where
> the bones dance in the darkening air,
> I at the cross-ways the voice of the one way,
> crying from the tomb of the earth where I died
> the word of the only right Suicide,
> the only word no words can quell,
> the way to heaven and the way to hell.[52]

The Skeleton ('I am the back of Christ') constantly shows how the very best intentions can produce the worst results. He puts Cranmer to the test, continually interrupting his writing of fluid prose of the Book of Common Prayer with cynical comments:

CRANMER [writing]. It is very meet, right, and our bounden duty, that we should at all times and in all places, give thanks . . .

THE SKELETON. Ah, how the sweet words ring their beauty.
it is meet, right, and our bounden duty.
But will you sing it with unchanged faces
when God shall change the time and the places?[53]

This figure with its various names—Satan, Third King, Accuser, Flame, and Skeleton—is of course modelled on the Satan of the Book of Job. When this figure finally makes its appearance towards the end of the Old Testament, it is not the utterly evil character—the Prince of Demons—of the

Gospels, Milton, and the later Christian imagination. He is originally God's prosecuting counsel with a legitimate place in the courts of heaven among the Sons of God. He is the Adversary who accuses sinners before the bar of divine justice, as we see in the stories of the testing of Job and the prosecution of the high priest Joshua.[54] Truly, he is somewhat over-zealous in defending the honour of the Law. The account of his provoking of David into a presumptuous sin[55] show him sliding from the role of prosecutor to *agent provocateur*.[56] In order to secure a conviction, he is ready to incite the committing of a crime. So it is easy to see how the name 'Satan' or 'Adversary' came to be applied to the one who was later pictured as the Great Enemy of God and humankind. The Satan of later Rabbinic thinking and of the New Testament is a mixture of the earlier 'Accuser' with a newer personification of all that is evil, the sum total of rebellion against God's purpose for human life. It appears to have become necessary to symbolize the collection of all individual human darkness, and it was given the name Satan.[57]

There are, then, two Satans in the Scriptures: the accuser who works for God and the accuser who works against God. In the popular religious imagination, the one evolves into the other, and though they are often mixed together we should remain aware of two distinct roles at play. Using this biblical key to interpretation, we may perceive that in Williams's plays the two identities become fused and even confused. The Accuser who has a legitimate function of testing the good is always slipping into the persona of the opponent to true life, death incarnate. We cannot but feel the cold breath and the shadow that comes from the Third King and the Skeleton in particular.

This becomes problematic when, as often, there appears to be no awareness of a shift between roles. Then the symbol of the Accuser in the plays reflects the same ambiguity about the status of evil we find portrayed in the novels. There is always the danger of evil as a contingent occasion for good becoming a *necessary* occasion for good. The symbol of the Skeleton vividly makes clear the peril of a movement towards monism. The proper anxiety to avoid dualism and to make good the only final reality, the only Thing that exists, has led to the danger that evil may be presented as the dark side of the good. We might trace the sources for this in Williams's thought within Gnosticism, Neo-Platonism, or the hermetic mysteries of the Order of the Golden Dawn.[58] However, its direct source is much simpler, and much more within traditional Christian theism. It comes from an imaginative working out of the principle of evil as *privatio boni*, against the background of the assumptions of classical theism—a timeless, immutable, impassible, and irresistible God.

Williams did not consider the possibility that God might permit a strange reality to appear within creation, a distortion unintended by the Creator, but emerging from a free-will 'turn' of created beings from God towards nothing. To conceive this does, of course, require that God in humility is willing to suffer injury and change from beyond God's self in covenant with the world, that—as Karl Barth put it—'God has the prerogative to be free without being limited by His freedom from external conditioning' so that 'God must not only be unconditioned but, in the absoluteness in which He sets up this fellowship, He can and will also be conditioned.'[59]

3. Necessity and Fatalism

A third way we may identify the problem of evil in Williams's work is in the concept of *necessity*, which appears continually in the novels, plays, poems, and theological writing. 'Necessity' is not intended to represent sheer fate or compulsion, as this would undermine the human free will that Williams wants to affirm:

> In the Crucifixion of Messias necessity and freedom had mutually crucified each other, and both (as if in an exchanged life) had risen again. Freedom existed then because it must; necessity because it could.[60]

W. H. Auden was impressed by the last phrase, and it appears in his poem 'New Year Letter'.[61] What Williams seems to intend is a consent to God that 'we do . . . of necessity and yet voluntarily' so that 'we have chosen necessity' (this at least is his interpretation of Calvin),[62] a notion that comes extraordinarily close to the theologian Karl Barth's talk of the divine decision 'whereby it is decided who I am in my own [really free] decision.'[63] For Williams, the vision of love in Beatrice points us towards 'the great union of necessity and . . . free-will'.[64] But in both Barth and Williams there is always the danger of necessity's slipping into a mere force of fate or destiny, into what Williams identifies as Virgil's 'great invocation of Necessity' in Dante's *Inferno*: 'Thus it is willed . . . ask thou no more.'[65]

At its highest, to affirm 'the Necessity' means accepting everything as an occasion for love and joy, including evil. Again Williams quotes from Dante: 'love is indeed necessity . . . we are in-willed to will, in-loved to love'.[66] This fusing of love, necessity and free-will is exemplified in Williams's exegesis of Shakespeare's play *Antony and Cleopatra*. I have already remarked that in this couple's love Williams finds a divided consciousness, which reflects the basic tragedy of human life: 'this is, and is not, thou'. In the death of Cleopatra, however, this begins to be healed as Cleopatra vows:

> *My desolation does begin to make*
> *A better life. . . . (5.2.1–2)*

Cleopatra dies apparently defeated, having been unable to hold the two worlds of her dream of love and political reality together. As Williams reminds the reader inclined to be sentimental, she does in fact die, so 'she cannot be said to triumph over death'.[67] But in expressing her love in the moment of death she does begin to hold 'the two *fatalities* of love and death' in a union of 'intense opposites'. The stroke of death is as a 'lover's pinch that hurts and is desired'. She recognizes the necessity of her desolation for what it is, and using what has befallen her, she can say that Caesar, the consummate politician, is 'Ass unpolicied', and claim in her defeat that:

> *I am again for Cydnus,*
> *To meet Mark Anthony.* (5.2.228–229)

In his final plays, as Williams finds it, Shakespeare invites us to look on things just as they are. 'With all kinds and classes of men, with the great globe itself and all which it inherits, poetry has done what it can. The elemental simplicities of the last plays, the facts of being uttering their essential nature, alone remain.'[68] So Beatrice, in Williams's interpretation of Dante, is the one who constantly asks us to 'look, only look well':

> Open your eyes; see what I am. You have seen things by which you are
> able to endure my smile.[69]

In this context that we begin to understand why the Skeleton can be associated with necessity,[70] as these various Satan-figures certainly help us to 'look' ('We see our servant Thomas; we see how pure his desire . . .').[71] As with evil as a 'glorious' opportunity for good and the figure of the Accuser, we are presented again with the problem of whether greeting all things as 'necessity' may not make evil also a necessary part of the process.

In handling this concept of the Necessity, Williams does, however, present two ideas which work against the location of sin and evil in any process of mere fate. In the first place, he takes up the classical idea that only God is necessary being—that is, only God has causes of existence entirely in the self: 'that which is beyond all categories and has only within itself its necessity of being'.[72] So sin is making *ourselves* necessary, just as Adam in pride behaved 'as if he had a necessity of being in himself'.[73] This is a self-centredness which distracts us from the whole pattern of things, the dance of coinherence which is God's purpose in creation. In *Descent into Hell*, the historian Wentworth makes his final plunge into the abyss when he refuses to recognize truth and puts himself in its place. Meeting his hated rival at a historians' dinner,

> the shock almost restored him. If he had ever hated Sir Aston because of a passion for austere truth he might even then have laid hold of the thing that was abroad in the world and been saved. [But] He looked at Sir Aston and thought, not 'he was wrong in his facts' but 'I've been cheated'. It was his last consecutive thought.[74]

So, in the *Taliessen* cycle of poems, Arthur makes the fatal mistake of preferring his own kingship to the whole pattern of the Empire.[75] In other words, 'our only true necessity is in love' and not in ourselves; sin only becomes a necessity when we make ourselves necessary, and then 'the universe is always unfair'.[76] Evil, then, cannot be a 'necessary' part of development as long as that growth is ruled by love.

A second insight that undercuts any logical necessity of evil is Williams's placing of the incarnation at the heart of the Necessity. That is, the making flesh of the eternal word in space and time was not dependent upon the fall and human sin.[77] Like Duns Scotus and Gerard Manley Hopkins,[78] Williams here insists that it was the eternal decision and purpose of God for the Logos to become a human being, 'coinherent' with all flesh, regardless of the fall. Given the state of the human predicament, this incarnation took on the particular form of suffering and death, so that 'intolerable charity . . . killed him',[79] but it would have had some form anyway. The incarnation supremely is the necessity of love, quite apart from any need to deal with evil.

III. Conclusion: The Ambiguities of Evil

The force of necessity, the role of the 'Accuser', and the absolute decree of God all give evil an ambiguous status in Williams's art. Arising from Williams's original use of the tradition of *privatio boni*, these themes tend to justify evil as a necessary part of God's good creation, while at the same time any logical necessity is being continually undermined by the 'necessity of love'. The novel *The Greater Trumps* offers the image of a cosmic dance for the Necessity of the universe, symbolized by a set of golden dancing images, and this does seem to be understood by one of the characters, Henry, as a dance of mere fate:

> [The dance] is always perfect because it can't be anything else. It knows nothing of joy or grief. . . . If you cry, it's because the measure will have it so; if you laugh, it's because some gayer step *demands* it.[80]

It is because he understands necessity in this totally predetermined way that Henry thinks he can control the world around him; if only he can read the movements of the dance, he can exploit them to his own advantage. Thus he uses the matching images of the dancers on Tarot cards to beat up a storm in which he aims to kill the father of the girl he loves, and who is standing in the way of their happiness.

The portrayal of Henry as being in serious and tragic error might lead us to suppose, however, that Williams is critical of this view of an inflexible dance of destiny. C. S. Lewis, using the same image of the dance, for which he appears to be indebted to Williams,[81] clearly presents a more dynamic picture. The angelic hosts who celebrate the Great Dance at the end of *Perelandra* cry aloud, 'Never did he make two things the same. Never did he utter one word twice.'[82] It is an evil to repeat the same steps when the measure has moved on. The temptation that the Lady in *Perelandra* experiences is to stay on the fixed land, but, in the memorable phrase of C. S. Lewis, 'the same wave never comes twice.'[83] There is a hint of the same idea in Williams's account of the Beatrician vision. At the very point when the beloved becomes a way of contemplating Almighty Love itself, the temptation is to turn aside and 'to linger in the moment, to live only for the recurrence of the moment.'[84] Truly for Dante the sight of the Lady at the window recalls the love that had been lost at the death of Beatrice,[85] but if this happens we are not to dwell upon it. We are not to seek repetition. It is consistent with this that one character in *The Greater Trumps* exclaims of the divine Fool, supposedly immobile at the heart of the dance of golden figures: 'but I saw him move'.[86]

Thus the very image of necessity as a dance, into which we are invited to enter with its patterns of coinherence and exchange, may help to dissipate the idea of the necessity of evil and to resist justifying its presence in the world. It may help to subvert Williams's own concept of a God formed in the mould of classical theism, which—I have argued—exacerbates problems with the tradition of *privatio boni*. We may be led to think that if we are really to participate in the dance, there has to be partnership and mutuality between God and the world.

But we should also not ignore the real gains of the ambiguities of evil as Williams presents them, as in the vivid image of the Skeleton. They prompt us to deconstruct the absolute binary oppositions with which we interpret the world, and especially to seek for some integration within the human self which appears to have a 'shadow' side, named by William Blake as the Spectre, which cannot be dealt with by merely excluding it.[87] We must not attempt to unify good and evil, but as Mary Grey puts it in her plea for 'connected knowing', we should acknowledge the messy 'interweaving of good and evil'.[88] We can, for example, recognize the way that an overconfidence about identifying the polarity between good and evil can lead to the scapegoating and demonizing of others. These loose ends in experience can point us to a remaking of the concept of God in which we cannot see all the problems of evil resolved, but in which we can see how they might be.

Notes

1. This is an expanded and revised version of a talk given on 25 February 1992. An unrevised version has previously been published in *Baptist Reflections on Christianity and the Arts. Reflections on Beauty. A Tribute to William L. Hendricks*, edited by David M. Rayburn, Daven M. Kari and Darrell D. Gwaltney (Lewiston: Edwin Mellen Press, 1997), and is here used and revised by kind permission of the publishers.

2. The publisher was Faber and Faber, which republished all the novels in a uniform edition.

3. Williams, *Many Dimensions* (London: Gollancz, 1931/London: Faber and Faber, 1947), 246.

4. Augustine, *The City of God*, 11.9; *Enchiridion*, 4.13.

5. See Plotinus, *Enneads*, 1.8.3–5.

6. Augustine, *On Free Will*, 3.1, 2, 18.

7. Friedrich Schleiermacher, *The Christian Faith*, translated by H. R. Mackintosh and J. S. Stewart (Edinburgh: T. & T. Clark, 1928), 295. John Hick, *Evil and the God of Love* (London: Fontana, Collins, 1968), 75.

8. Augustine, *On Rebuke and Grace*, 32–33.

9. Augustine, *The City of God*, 12.7; 14.13.

10. Williams, *He Came Down from Heaven* (London: Heinemann, 1938), 16–18.

11. Augustine, *Confessions*, 3.7.

12. Aquinas, *Summa Theologiae*, 1a.14.10: 'God would not know good things perfectly if he did not also know evils'.

13. Paul Tillich, *Systematic Theology*, Combined Volume (Welwyn: Nisbet, 1968), vol. 2, 45–50.

14. Hick, *Evil and the God of Love*, 317.

15. See Sørina Higgins on 'Anatomical Geography as Metaphysics', in 'Double Affirmation: Medievalism as Christian Apologetic in the Arthurian Poetry of Charles Williams', *Journal of Inklings Studies* 3/2 (2013), 73–79.

16. 'The Vision of the Empire', in *Taliessen Through Logres* (London: Oxford University Press, 1938; 1969), 10. In her exegesis, Anne Ridler explicitly links this part of the poem to the 'alteration in knowledge' of the Fall; see *Notes on The Taliessen Poems of Charles Williams* by Various Hands (Oxford: The Charles Williams Society, 1991), 16.

17. C. S. Lewis, *Perelandra* (London: Bodley Head, 1943; 1967), 132.

18. Williams, *He Came Down from Heaven*, 77. My emphasis.

19. Karl Barth, *Church Dogmatics*, English translation edited by G. W. Bromiley and T. F. Torrance (Edinburgh: T. & T. Clark, 1936–1977) IV/2, 410–424.

20. Williams, *The English Poetic Mind* (Oxford: Clarendon Press, 1932), 59.

21. See Williams, *He Came Down from Heaven*, 25.

22. The phrase thus holds together the two ways of the affirmation of images and the rejection of images: see Charles Williams and C. S. Lewis, *Arthurian Torso* (Oxford: Oxford University Press, 1969), 151; cf. 'The Departure of Dindrane', in Williams, *The Region of the Summer Stars* (London: Oxford University Press, 1969), 32.

23. Charles Williams, *The Figure of Beatrice: A Study in Dante* (London: Faber and Faber, 1943), 47–51, 207–210.

24. Glen Cavaliero, *Charles Williams: Poet of Theology* (Basingstoke: Macmillan, 1983), 155.

25. Williams, *He Came Down from Heaven*, 77.

26. Williams, *He Came Down from Heaven*, 124–129; Charles Williams, 'The Way of Exchange', in Williams, *The Image of the City and Other Essays*, ed. Anne Ridler (London: Oxford University Press, 1958), 147–154.

27. Williams, *Descent into Hell* (London: Faber and Faber, 1937; London: Faber and Faber, 1949), 101.

28. Williams, *Descent into Hell*, 171–172.

29. Williams, *Descent into Hell*, 125.

30. Charles Williams, *All Hallows' Eve* (London: Faber and Faber, 1945), 197.

31. C. S. Lewis, *The Problem of Pain* (London: The Centenary Press, 1940), 98–99.

32. Richard Swinburne, *The Existence of God* (Oxford: Clarendon Press, 1979), 214–215.

33. Charles Williams, book review of *The Problem of Pain* by C. S. Lewis, *Theology*, 42.247 (January 1941), 63.

34. C. S. Lewis, *A Grief Observed* (London: Faber and Faber, 1961, published as written by 'N. W. Clerk;' 1964), 26.

35. Williams, *He Came Down from Heaven*, 40.

36. Williams, *He Came Down from Heaven*, 36.

37. Williams, 'The Cross', in *Image of the City*, 133–134.

38. Charles Williams, *The Descent of the Dove: A Short History of the Holy Spirit in the Church* (London: Longman, 1939), 71.

39. Williams, *War in Heaven* (Gollancz, London, 1930; repr. Faber, London, 1947), 244.
40. Williams, *War in Heaven*, 180.
41. Williams, *War in Heaven*, 181.
42. Boethius, *The Consolation of Philosophy*, 5.6.
43. Williams, *He Came Down from Heaven*, 4.
44. Wolfhart Pannenberg, 'Speaking about God in the Face of Atheist Criticism,' *Basic Questions in Theology*, vol. 3, trans. R. A. Wilson (London: SCM Press, 1973), 107–108.
45. For a working out of this concept, see Paul S. Fiddes, *The Creative Suffering of God* (Oxford: Clarendon Press, 1988), 63–76, 91–109.
46. Williams, *He Came Down from Heaven*, 38.
47. Printed in Williams, *Three Plays* (London: Oxford University Press, 1931).
48. *Seed of Adam*, reprinted in *Collected Plays by Charles Williams*, with introduction by John Heath-Stubbs (London: Oxford University Press, 1963), 164.
49. *Seed of Adam*, 169.
50. *Judgement of Chelmsford*, in *Collected Plays*, 72.
51. *Judgement of Chelmsford*, 147.
52. *Thomas Cranmer of Canterbury*, in *Collected Plays*, 12.
53. *Thomas Cranmer*, 32.
54. Job 1:6–12; Zechariah 3:1–5.
55. 1 Chronicles 21:1.
56. So G. B. Caird, *Principalities and Powers: A Sudy in Pauline Theology* (Oxford: Clarendon Press, 1956), 36–9.
57. See Walter Wink, *Unmasking the Powers: The Invisible Forces That Determine Human Existence* (Philadelphia: Fortress, 1986), 22–30.
58. See Roma Alvah King, *The Pattern in the Web: The Mythical Poetry of Charles Williams* (Kent: Kent State University, 1990), 11–17.
59. Karl Barth, *Church Dogmatics*, trans. and ed. G. W. Bromiley and T. F. Torrance (Edinburgh: T. & T. Clark, 1936–77), II/1, 303.
60. Williams, *Descent of the Dove*, 174–175.
61. W. H. Auden, *Collected Poems*, ed. Edward Mendelson (London: Faber and Faber, 2007), 238; see also 'The Quest', in Auden, *Collected Poems*, 285.
62. Williams, *Descent of the Dove*, 174.
63. Karl Barth, *Church Dogmatics*, I/1, 161–162.
64. Williams, *Figure of Beatrice*, 165.
65. Williams, *Figure of Beatrice*, 115.
66. Williams, *Figure of Beatrice*, 196.
67. Williams, *English Poetic Mind*, 93–95.
68. Williams, *English Poetic Mind*, 108.
69. Williams, *Figure of Beatrice*, 215.

88 C. S. LEWIS AND HIS CIRCLE

70. Cf. Williams, *Thomas Cranmer*, 55–56: 'love necessity; I am he'. 'I am necessary Love where necessity is not'.

71. Williams, *Thomas Cranmer*, 6.

72. Williams, *Descent of the Dove*, 62.

73. Williams, *Descent of the Dove*, 67. Williams accuses the church of the same sin, imposing necessity on others: 150–152, 154.

74. Williams, *Descent into Hell*, 218–219.

75. Charles Williams, 'The Crowning of Arthur', in *Taliessin*, 21.

76. Williams, *Figure of Beatrice*, 147–148.

77. Williams, *The Forgiveness of Sins* (London: Bles, Centenary Press, 1942), 29–32.

78. Gerard Manley Hopkins, *Sermons and Devotional Writings*, ed. Christopher Devlin (London: Oxford University Press, 1959), 170; cf. Scotus, *Parisensia*, 3.7.4.

79. Williams, *Forgiveness of Sins*, 31.

80. Williams, *The Greater Trumps* (London: Gollancz, 1932; London: Faber and Faber, 1954), 95, my emphasis. Compare the dance of the Skeleton in Williams, *Thomas Cranmer*, 13.

81. See Paul S. Fiddes, '"For the Dance All Things Were Made": The Great Dance in C. S. Lewis's *Perelandra*', in *C. S. Lewis's* Perelandra: *Reshaping the Image of the Cosmos*, ed. Judith Wolfe and Brendan Wolfe (Kent: Kent State University, 2013), 40–44.

82. Lewis, *Perelandra*, 246.

83. Lewis, *Perelandra*, 164, cf. 77–79. Sanford Schwartz proposes the influence of Henri Bergson on Lewis's thought here: see Schwartz, *C. S. Lewis on the Final Frontier: Science and the Supernatural in the Space Trilogy* (New York: Oxford University Press, 2009), 55–73.

84. Williams, *Figure of Beatrice*, 123.

85. Williams, *Figure of Beatrice*, 123; cf. 41–43, 54–56.

86. Williams, *Greater Trumps*, 139.

87. For the reclaiming of the Spectre within the self, see William Blake, *The Four Zoas* 8:339–360 in *Blake: Complete Writings with Variant Readings*, ed. Geoffrey Keynes (London: Oxford University Press, 1957, 1966), 328–329. But as Williams comments, to *prefer* the Spectre is indeed to be lost; see *Forgiveness of Sins*, 95.

88. Mary Grey, *The Wisdom of Fools: Seeking Revelation for Today* (London: SPCK, 1993), 107–110.

Literature

6

That Hideous Strength:
A Reassessment

Rowan Williams

I DECIDED WHEN asked to speak to the society simply to talk about one of the books that I find most interesting and most challenging, though in some ways also most deeply flawed, of Lewis's major works, and that's *That Hideous Strength*.[1]

It's a novel that has been often under-rated. In my own judgment it's second only to *Till We Have Faces*, which I think is without a doubt Lewis's finest fictional work. I think *That Hideous Strength* is inferior to *Till We Have Faces* in sheer psychological penetration. And I think it's also inferior theologically to *Till We Have Faces,* offering a less fully 'converted' model than the later book. I'll elaborate a bit later on what I mean by those comments.

But, assuming that not absolutely everybody has the plot at their finger-tips, I'll very briefly summarize quite a complicated story. The setting of *That Hideous Strength* is a small university town, Edgestow, which of course, says Lewis in the Foreword, bears no relation to any university town in any place he's ever been. But he says it's just a little bit like Durham; and of course may seem a little bit more like Oxford in certain respects. In Edgestow, one of the colleges, Bracton, owns a historic piece of woodland which various people are unaccountably eager to get their hands on. A new group, the National Institute for Coordinated Experiments, the N.I.C.E., are about to set up their institute near Edgestow and they wish to acquire the college's land. One of the young fellows at Bracton, Mark Studdock, is a major figure in the novel. He is lured to assist the institute in their work, which is of a very nebulous character indeed, at first. But meanwhile, his (rather estranged) wife, Jane, becomes involved with another group of people who clearly represent values utterly at odds with those of the N.I.C.E. and their headquarters at Belbury, which apparently owes not a little to Harwell and the atomic power station in Lewis's own imagination at the time.

The novel is about the conflict between the group in which Jane becomes involved at St Anne's-on-the-Hill, centred around the mysterious figure of Ransom, and the group around the N.I.C.E. at Belbury. The interest of the story turns on Mark Studdock, the young academic sociologist. In one sense, it's a novel about the saving of Mark's soul, but this is dressed up with a great deal of detail, a kind of preternatural thriller element, with which Charles Williams is normally more associated than is Lewis. At the climax of the book—a very dramatic and remarkable climax—interplanetary (we are to suppose) angelic powers are drawn into battle to bring about the destruction of the N.I.C.E. and Belbury, indeed of much of Edgestow too, as a result of the mediation of the strange figure of Merlin, who has been kept in cold storage for many centuries under Bragdon Wood. (This is why it's such an important place.) His suspended animation is ended; he returns to full life and becomes the agent or 'channel' of the heavenly powers which bring about the destruction of the evil forces at Belbury. That's a very inadequate summary, and I shall be reading bits and pieces of the book as I go through; but this is just to remind you of the overall structure of the plot.

What I want to do is to follow a good literary critical pattern, a pattern of rhetorical 'chiasmus', to start out by talking about superficial virtues, then superficial vices in the book, then deeper weaknesses in the book, and then deeper strengths. So it's an A-B-B-A structure, if you are interested in that sort of thing.

I. Superficial Virtues

First then, the superficial virtues and excellences of the book. The first thing to say quite simply is that Lewis is a magnificent narrative stylist. The book has enormous pace, and Lewis has extraordinary skill with realistic dialogue. Here, more than in almost anything else he wrote, he taps a kind of deep well of natural English comedy. It's a very, very funny book in places. The observation of, and the creation of, comic character I think excels anything he did in any of his other writings. If I were looking for comparisons, I'd say that this is a book in which more nearly than any other Lewis sounds rather like Trollope as a narrative stylist—the same relaxed fluency and the same gentle irony towards many of the characters; the same ability to get inside the skin of characters in an ironic yet charitable way so characteristic of Trollope's best narration.

Of the humour, let me give you two of my favourite examples. (I'm afraid quite a lot of this address will be my favourite bits. But I make no apology for that.)

There is a very fine scene early on in the book where some of the academics are discussing the future of their institution and how it's going to be related to the National Institute for Coordinated Experiments. The main characters here are Curry, the sub-warden of the college; Feverstone, the man from the great world outside, a very sinister and important figure in the book as a whole; and Busby, the bursar. Part of the comedy of this scene turns on the fact that nobody can remember what academic subject Curry is supposed to practise.

'That's the worst of the whole system,' said Curry. 'In a place like this you've either got to be content to see everything go to pieces or else to sacrifice your own career as a scholar to all these infernal college politics. One of these days I *shall* chuck that side of it and get down to my book.'

'I see', said Feverstone. 'In order to keep the place going as a learned society, all the best brains in it have to give up doing anything about learning.'

'Exactly!' said Curry. 'That's just—' and then stopped, uncertain whether he was being taken quite seriously.

'All that's very well in theory', said Busby, 'but I think Curry's quite right. Supposing he resigned his office as sub-warden and retired into his cave. He might give us a thundering good book on economics—'

'Economics?' said Feverstone, lifting his eyebrows.

'I happen to be a military historian, James,' said Curry.[2]

And another indication of this indigenous comic root that Lewis so effectively taps into is a scene in a pub near Edgestow.

The bar was at first empty. During the next half-hour men dropped in one by one till about four were present. For some time they did not talk at all. Then a very little man with a face like an old potato observed to no one in particular, 'I seen old Rumbold the other night.' No one replied for five minutes, and then a very young man in leggings said, 'I reckon he's sorry he ever tried it.'[3]

It's all we ever learn about Rumbold.

Curry, the sub-warden of the college, is a brilliant comic creation—an eternal survivor, a character who manages to come through even the appalling holocaust at the end. We meet him for the last time beginning to plan how to start all over again.

> The well-informed man, who was Curry, got out. Such a man always knows all officials, and in a few minutes he was standing by the fire in the ticket collector's office . . .
>
> 'Well, we don't exactly know yet, Mr. Curry', said the man. 'There's been nothing coming through for about an hour. It's very bad, you know. They're putting the best face on it they can. There's never been an earthquake like it in England from what I can hear. And there's the floods too. No, Sir, I'm afraid you'll find nothing of Bracton College. All that part of the town went almost at once. I don't know what the casualties'll be. I'm glad I got my old Dad out last week.'
>
> Curry always in later years regarded this as one of the turning-points of his life. He had not up till then been a religious man. But the word that now instantly came into his mind was 'Providential' . . . He'd been within an ace of taking the earlier train: and if he had . . . The whole College wiped out! It would have to be rebuilt. There'd be a complete (or almost complete) new set of Fellows, a new Warden. It was Providential again that some responsible person should have been spared to deal with such a tremendous crisis' . . . The more he thought of it, the more fully Curry realised that the whole shaping of the future college rested with the sole survivor. It was almost like being a second founder. Providential—providential.[4]

More seriously, the characterization of some of the main figures is no less brilliant. Mark Studdock himself, the 'hero' of the book, is beautifully realized: as Lewis says of him early on, he is 'young and shy and vain and timid'.[5] He is a very typical young academic, in fact. And the way in which the National Institute appeals to the basic instincts of the younger academic (which some of us I'm sure will recognize) is very well brought out. He is a man with no tradition of the interior life, no inner ethical structure, and so a man peculiarly vulnerable to the blandishments of the technocratic promise of the National Institute. Because of this vulnerability, because of his eagerness to be on the controlling organizing side of things, he can put up with an amazing amount of nonsense in other people. Wither, the deputy director of the National Institute, another remarkable creation, is trying to explain (or rather trying not to explain) to Mark what his work will be in the institute.

> 'We do not really think, among ourselves, in terms of strictly demarcated functions, of course . . . Everyone in the Institute feels that his own work is not so much a departmental contribution as a moment or grade in the progressive self-definition of an organic whole.'

> And Mark said—for he was young and shy and vain and timid—'I do think that is so important.'[6]

We'll hear more of Mark later on.

To me, the best of all is the characterization of Merlin, rather surprisingly: Merlin, the Dark Age magician, restored to the twentieth century and beautifully realized, a quiet, solid, and also earthy and violent character all at once.

Merlin in some ways stands in the book for precisely that contact with the organic which the National Institute attacks and undermines at every point. And Merlin's almost animal shrewdness, the pre-moral character of his insight and judgment (and yet the reality of his wisdom), and the enormous scope of his power in the book, all these are fused together in a very plausible portrait indeed. He's a humorous man. It takes some time to persuade him that the twentieth century is serious, and indeed one's not quite sure whether he is persuaded. He's also a Christian of a very peculiar kind because he's a magician, too. He is, as many people remark in the book, somewhere on the edge of Christianity and a deeper paganism. And it's precisely that marginality that gives him his centrality and power in the book.

I've heard it said that some aspects of the portrait of Merlin are based on Lewis's own memory of W. B. Yeats. I think in terms of character that's unlikely. But the physiognomy, the massive prophetic presence, tall, fat, Celtic, and overpowering, does certainly sound remarkably like Yeats in his later years.

So the narrative energy is enormous, the characterization is often superb. It reads easily. There is a great deal of narrative cross-cutting where you are left in situations of suspense in one bit of the plot and whisked off elsewhere. It is, quite simply, a well-told story that holds the attention. Its humour is very great and very subtle. Stella Gibbons wrote that it has the best account of a college meeting outside C. P. Snow. Those of us not wholly persuaded of the literary merits of C. P. Snow might prefer to say it has one of the best accounts of an academic meeting outside Malcolm Bradbury (readers of *The History Man* will recall that it contains a particularly scarifying account of a departmental meeting).

These then are some of the superficial virtues—the vigour, the energy, and attractiveness of the book. I want next to turn to what I regard as superficial vices, leading to some rather deeper vices of the book.

II. Superficial Vices

I find some of the superficial difficulty most evident in St Anne's-on-the-Hill, the centre of the 'good' party in the book. There is here an uncertainty of tone. How do good people talk to each other?—a question that very few writers of fiction really manage to resolve. There's an uneasy blend, I think, of the pious and the jocular and the pre-Raphaelite (that is, a rather elaborate idiom with a sort of William Morris mediaevalism). Some of what these people say sounds remarkably like a sort of boy's school retelling of the Arthurian legend. And when Ransom gets talking to Merlin, curiously enough Merlin sounds plausible and Ransom doesn't. The Dark Age character sounds plausible and the twentieth-century one doesn't sound like the twentieth century—even the twentieth century trying to sound like the Dark Ages, if that isn't too complicated.

Ransom himself, I have to say, doesn't work for me. Dorothy Sayers said of him (remember he is a figure who appears of course in the two earlier works of the science fiction trilogy) that she found him much less appealing now that he had become pale and interesting and had taken to lying around on sofas like the Heir of Radclyffe (the hero of a Victorian novel by C. M. Yonge). And there is some truth in that charge. Ransom has become a kind of ageless, not exactly sexless, but slightly super-human figure, lying in his chair holding the household at St Anne's together in the force of his personality with his flowing golden beard and his piercing eyes. I don't think it comes off; it seems theatrical. And I think (and I'll say more about this later) that the dehumanizing of Ransom is a very deep failing in the imagining of this book.

This is of course (as I've hinted) to say that Lewis suffers from the typical difficulties of the novelist in portraying virtue, let alone holiness. It was Lewis himself who wrote that in order to imagine an evil character you simply have to project a few lines out of your own temperament a little bit further, and in order to imagine a virtuous character you have to imagine grace which you don't actually have and can't project from yourself. That's very insightful. If you asked yourself (and you may find this a very interesting question to reflect on) who are the successful virtuous characters in modern fiction, the list is rather short.

(Just to put in a footnote, I think Tallis Browne in Iris Murdoch's *A Fairly Honourable Defeat* is a successful virtuous character—just, and *only* just.)

The other characters at St Anne's are uneven. The Ulster philosopher-gardener, MacPhee, is superbly done, but that's largely because he's drawn from life. He is, of course, Lewis's own tutor, Kirkpatrick, with some of his idioms and some of his peculiarities—and that distinctive kind of rationalist decency which Lewis recognized as being something quite different from the agnostic emptiness of Mark Studdock. It's an atheistic piety, if you like, an atheism still profoundly informed by just that inner life that Mark Studdock lacks. And it's this combination and the many personal quirks that make MacPhee such a persuasive and attractive character.

The rest of them I'm not happy with. As regards Dr and Mrs Dimble, the aging middle-aged, childless couple, the name Dimble says rather more than perhaps Lewis intended it to. They are a bit dull. Now in part their dullness is important in the book, and I'll come back to that later, too; but in part it is *just* dullness—and characteristically again Lewis is disposed to see Mrs Dimble with her energetic domesticity, her instinctive reduction of questions to personalities, as the ideal of a good woman. Lewis on women is certainly something we'll need to talk about a bit later.

The Dennistons, Arthur and Camilla, are meant to be younger representatives of the party of virtue, but for most of the book they are cardboard figures. We hear that Arthur Denniston resigned his fellowship; and early in the book we hear that he has tested his vocation as a monk—or at least there is a story to that effect. No sign of anything like that inner struggle remains in the Arthur of the book. He and Camilla are, I suppose, the kind of romantically committed couple who represent the saving of active erotic love, just as the Dimbles represent the saving of a kind of matured married love. But they need more flesh if they are to do their job, and I'm not sure they've got it.

Grace Ironwood, the spinster in the household, and Mrs Maggs, the cleaning lady, are, I'm afraid, characters out of the Agatha Christie property basket. They are compounds of clichés. They're lively and cleverly done, but they have no life apart from the plot's requirements.

More important, Lewis runs a very deep risk in setting up two conflicting groups, two conflicting *companies of interest*, Belbury and the N.I.C.E. and St Anne's-on-the-Hill—because it's very difficult to portray the seductions of the inner ring, the inner circle (a very important theme in the book) when goodness is itself represented by *another* kind of inner ring, another kind of closed circle. Let me give you an example. Camilla is trying to persuade Jane, Mark Studdock's wife, to assist the party of virtue of St Anne's-on-the-Hill:

'It's all so strange and—*beastly!*' said Jane . . . Her habitual inner prompter was whispering, 'Take care. Don't get drawn in. Don't commit yourself to anything.'[7]

And she mentions another prophetic dream she has. She's of interest to both parties because she has a gift of clairvoyance.

> 'I saw the murder—Mr. Hingest's murder.'

> 'There you are', said Camilla. 'Oh, Mrs. Studdock, you *must* come in. You must, you must.'[8]

Now 'you must come in' is dangerously like the sort of thing that the other side is also saying to Mark, and I'm not sure how well Lewis handles this. The stuff about the inner ring, of course, looks back to a justly celebrated paper, which is reprinted in *They Asked for a Paper*, on 'The Inner Ring'. It's a paper which shows Lewis at his moralist best, talking about the enormous seduction of the sense of belonging, being on the inside.

> At the word 'we' you try not to blush for mere pleasure—something 'we always do'. And you will be drawn in, if you are drawn in, not by desire for gain or ease, but simply because at that moment, when the cup was so near your lips, you cannot bear to be thrust back again into the cold outer world. It would be so terrible to see the other man's face—that genial, confidential, delightfully sophisticated face—turn suddenly cold and contemptuous, to know that you had been tried for the Inner Ring and rejected.[9]

In his paper and in many passages of *That Hideous Strength*, Lewis describes the way in which we can spend our whole lives trying to get to the inside of mysterious groups where the power and the sophistication seem to be. He qualifies it a bit towards the end of this paper.

> If in your spare time you consort simply with the people you like, you will again find that you have come unawares to a real inside: that you are indeed snug and safe at the centre of something which, seen from without, would look exactly like an Inner Ring. But the difference is that its secrecy is accidental, and its exclusiveness a by-product, and no one was led thither by the lure of the esoteric: for it is only four or five people who like one another meeting to do things that they like. [That's the Inklings in fact.] This is friendship. Aristotle placed it among the virtues.[10]

That's well said, but I'm just not sure whether in *That Hideous Strength* the virtuous of St Anne's-on-the-Hill manage to be a group of friends or whether there isn't also the lure of the esoteric there. And Camilla's 'You must come in' haunts me as I read the book as an ambiguity in this area.

Ransom is told to 'collect', I quote from the same passage, 'a company to watch for this danger, and strike when it came.'[11]

Again there is an ambivalence here. St Anne's-on-the-Hill is dangerously near to being defined as a mirror image of Belbury, a company which strikes, which takes action, which gains control. But how does that curious hothouse at St Anne's-on-the-Hill relate to the Church Catholic, to put it bluntly? If this is meant to be a Christian novel, where's the church? There's part of an answer to that which I'll come to later on, but I don't think it's St Anne's-on-the-Hill.

Perhaps some of this can be illuminated by reflecting that this is the novel in which the influence of Charles Williams is most apparent in Lewis's work. These concepts of a company with a kind of shared power in an intensely interior community gathered around a charismatic personality has a lot to do with Charles Williams, and, for my money, Ransom, in this book, is Charles Williams in many important respects—in his doctrine of love and in his curious relations of dominance to people around him, especially the women. It's in the St Anne's episodes that the influence of Williams is most clear; and maybe that accounts for why they are to me the least satisfactory. Williams could do it, really rather well. Lewis 'doing Williams' is another matter, and I think that's part of the problem.

And then, leading on to what I think are the serious weaknesses, there is of course the notorious business of the great dénouement at Belbury, the massacre (as in effect it is) of the evil characters. 'Over the top', I think, is the only expression one can use for this. I think it's when the elephant breaks loose and comes into the dining room and begins trampling people to death that I feel something has snapped in the authorial psyche.

Lewis obviously had an uncertain conscience about this himself, but characteristically, he gives the uncertain conscience to Mrs Dimble in the book.

'I wanted to ask about Edgestow . . .' said Mother Dimble. 'Aren't Merlin and the *eldila* a trifle . . . well, *wholesale*. . . .'

'Who are you lamenting?' said MacPhee. 'The jobbing town council that'd have sold their own wives and daughters to bring the N.I.C.E. to Edgestow?'

'Well, I don't know much about them', said she. 'But in the University. Even Bracton itself. We all knew it was a horrible College, of course. But did they really mean any great harm with all their fussy little intrigues? Wasn't it more *silly* than anything else?'[12]

And then after a bit more . . .

> 'You are all forgetting', said Grace, 'that nearly everyone except the very good (who were ripe for fair dismissal) and the very bad, had already left Edgestow.'[13]

I think that is a very dangerous doctrine. It reminds me of the story of a papal legate during the Albigensian Crusade urging on the warriors of Simon de Montfort to kill everybody in sight because 'the Lord will know his own'. And I think Lewis gives way a little bit to that towards the end. It is that kind of *totality* of judgment on evil in the massacre at Belbury, and remarks like that from the conversation afterwards, that threaten to push *That Hideous Strength* over the borders of what any novel can or should do. Novels are about moral growth and moral ambiguity, and the resolutions they offer are resolutions within a human narrative. The importation of angelic powers to wreak wholesale destruction seems to me not to belong in a novel. That's a very dogmatic statement, but I'm trying to articulate some of my uneasiness about what's actually going on there—which leads me into my reflections on what I think are maybe deeper weaknesses.

III. Deeper Weaknesses

Should fiction deal in heaven and hell? Lewis says in the preface that 'This is a "tall story" about devilry'.[14] Fair enough. But the tone shifts uneasily between an almost allegorical, that is a very fixed, set of oppositions, and a realistic novel with all the great virtues which Lewis could bring to realistic fiction. Novels can't easily have saints and demons in them, because if novels are about the ambiguities of personality, people with the moral fixity of angels and demons are not characters you can introduce, or at least not without taking great risks.

Or if you *are* going to do that sort of thing—if you *are* going to have a demon in your novel—it's important not to try *at all* to get 'inside', important to let them be a kind of cipher. And unfortunately we are taken from time to time inside, or a little bit inside, the minds of the villains, especially Wither. The episode of Wither's death, later on in the novel, is, I think, a mistake—all the worse a mistake because Wither himself is so superbly done in the novel as a whole. There is an element of what one could call the 'Ronald Merrick' syndrome. Those of you who know Paul Scott's novels will know what I mean: in *The Raj Quartet*, Merrick begins as a partly comic, partly pathetic figure;

and by the end of the quartet he has become a genuinely diabolical figure, a very frightening character indeed.

Wither, likewise, begins as a rambling old chump and we slowly see the terrifying vacuity that exists behind. Wither becomes profoundly sinister, perhaps one of the most menacing of the evil characters in the book as the narrative proceeds. But there are two points where we are, just a little bit, taken 'inside' his mind.

> The Deputy Director hardly ever slept. When it became absolutely necessary for him to do so, he took a drug, but the necessity was rare, for the mode of consciousness he experienced at most hours of day or night had long ceased to be exactly like what other men call waking. . . . The manner and outward attitude to men which he had adopted half a century ago were now an organization which functioned almost independently, like a gramophone . . . his inmost self was free to pursue its own life. That detachment of the spirit, not only from the senses but even from the reason, which has been the goal of some mystics, was now his.[15]

I think that's a mistake, because it sets out to explain what ought be left as sinister and unresolved, Wither's own emptiness. Likewise, the episode of his death later on—he's realizing that his spirit guides, the evil powers that have been using him, have failed.

> It is incredible how little this knowledge moved him. It could not, because he had long ceased to believe in knowledge itself. . . . He had passed from Hegel into Hume, thence through Pragmatism, and thence though Logical Positivism, and out at last into the complete void.[16]

Lewis the author here turns aside to spit at his colleagues at High Table in a rather unhelpful way. Again we're taken inside Wither but not in any sense that explains anything. That string of philosophical names is negative name-dropping, if you like. It explains nothing.

So the question arises, are the evil characters in this book actually persons? Are they demons or are they characters? And they hover somewhere in between.

I think Feverstone *is* a character, very much so. He escapes early from the dining room where the frightful carnage is taking place and watches it through the serving hatch; that I think is brilliant and horrible. It is the right note of plausible horror to strike, and it makes him paradoxically more of a person, a very evil one, but a person. But if they *are* persons, then the absolute judgment at the end is questionable. They're not demons. And if they're *not* persons, then you ought to leave their interiority alone; you ought to leave them as menacing ciphers, as Wither is in much of the book.

It's this irresolution that seems to me to betoken a deeper uncertainty with how to deal with evil characters. In other words, Lewis is not doing either the very good or the very bad very well. And that gives one pause. It is an *interesting* weakness. A pertinent comparison might be Graham Greene's *Brighton Rock*, where you have an attempt to create a damned character, in the figure of Pinky. It's very important that we are never really allowed into Pinky's mind at all. He comes from and goes into a particular kind of darkness, a particular kind of void. The energy, the force, and the plausibility of the book depend on us not seeing how he works, or hardly at all.

(One other comment on the characters. Jules, the nominal head of the Institute, is, it seems, a remarkably malicious portrait of H. G. Wells—or rather H. G. Wells with all his least attractive characteristics accentuated. I think he has a rather raw deal both as the character in the book Jules and as a picture of H. G. Wells. But, that's by the way.)

Then again, partly connected with the question, 'are these evil characters persons or not?', several of them are characterized by some sort of a barren or suspect sexuality. The appalling and terrifying head of the secret police, Fairy Hardcastle, is quite clearly a lesbian (we are told that in almost so many words) and a sadist, who enjoys torturing women. She again, oddly, has more character than some of the other evil figures. But when we look at Wither once again and at Filostrato, the Italian scientist, who is a very important figure at Belbury, what exactly is going on? Are we to see them as persons with a personal sexuality or not? There is a small hint at one point that Wither is homosexual. Filostrato is described as a 'eunuch' and clearly is a kind of sexless figure, or at least an unsexed figure. His huge bulk and his treble voice tell us as much. Does this again suggest some uncertainty about how to characterize evil? I don't know. You can see where Lewis is coming from: all the features of evil that crop up and are discussed and portrayed in this book have something to do with a rejection or suppression of the 'natural'. Technocracy, diabolism, and perversion are all parts of the Belbury complex. And the rejection of the natural, the rejection of the *body,* is an important part of how evil is defined in this book. The Belbury people can't understand why the rejection of the organic or the material is such a terrible thing. But it is hard to miss an uncertainty of register and focus in this, and what is for many readers an uncomfortable resort to stereotypes of sexual eccentricity. And perhaps the most worrying thing from the point of view of the sexual profile of the book is the sadism of the massacre scene. Lewis admitted in some of his private correspondence his own temptations to sadistic fantasy; and I think he is exorcising it rather too thoroughly in this scene at the end—which I do not propose to quote.

One other weakness I've already touched on. What exactly is the relation of St Anne's-on-the-Hill to the Christian faith and the Church Catholic? The language of St Anne's tends to be a language of *power and mystery*, not of grace. In some ways it's the most problematic aspect of Charles Williams, a confusion of the supernatural with the *preternatural*, as if revelation and church and sacraments are not enough. You need an injection of something 'extra', some preternatural element, some preternatural link between persons, some charismatic influence from a personality—Ransom, Charles Williams—plus the notion of super-terrestrial powers. So St Anne's weathers the conflict at the end of the day through Merlin, possessed by the angelic powers of the spheres—just as Belbury itself is possessed by evil forces. It's a rather sharply focused instance of how St Anne's comes dangerously close to being defined by its opposite.

What interests me is that what seems to be the narrative heart of the book is the battle for Mark Studdock's soul. This is where the subtlety and a great deal of the moral excitement of the book is located. And in the case of Mark, his discovery of Christianity has nothing to do with what people seem to be talking about at St Anne's, nothing to do with power and mystery, with the preternatural. It has everything to do with the Gospel; and in the finest passage on this, in the second half of chapter fifteen, we have Mark being invited to spit on a crucifix as part of his training in objective thinking. He has got to cure himself of his prejudices if he is to be a proper servant of the N.I.C.E., and this entails abusing a crucifix. Mark suddenly feels resistance. He's aware of rising danger.

> If he disobeyed, his last chance of getting out of Belbury alive might be gone. Even of getting out of this room. . . . He was himself, he felt, as helpless as the wooden Christ. As he thought this, he found himself looking at the crucifix in a new way—neither as a piece of wood nor a monument of superstition but as a bit of history. Christianity was nonsense, but one did not doubt that the man had lived and had been executed thus by the Belbury of those days. And that, as he suddenly saw, explained why this image, though not itself an image of the Straight or Normal, was yet in opposition to crooked Belbury. It was a picture of what happened when the Crooked met the Straight—what it would do to him if he remained straight. It was, in a more emphatic sense than he had understood, a *cross*.[17]

. . .

He was thinking, and thinking hard. . . . Christianity was a fable. It would be ridiculous to die for a religion one did not believe. This Man himself, on that very cross, had discovered it to be a fable, and had died complaining that the God in whom he trusted had forsaken him—had, in fact, found the universe a cheat. But this raised a question that Mark had never thought of before. Was *that* the moment at which to turn against the Man? If the universe was a cheat, was that a good reason for joining its side? Supposing the Straight was utterly powerless, always and everywhere certain to be mocked, tortured, and finally killed by the Crooked, what then? Why not go down with the ship? He began to be frightened by the very fact that his fears seemed to have vanished. They had been his safeguard . . . they had prevented him, all his life, from making mad decisions like that which he was now making as he turned to Frost and said, 'It's all bloody nonsense, and I'm damned if I do any such thing.'[18]

Now that is the Gospel in a nutshell, and it is interestingly echoed by a marvellous passage in Hilda Prescott's book, *The Man on a Donkey*, where Robert Aske, hanged in chains at York Castle, looks despairingly into an empty heaven and feels betrayed by God; and yet his heart turns to the God who, though betrayed, helpless, and useless, is yet the last refuge of a dying man. It's precisely this dimension which is so unforgettably developed in *Till We Have Faces*, and of course in *A Grief Observed*; but that's another story.

So that's one of the paradoxes of the book. The Christianity that we meet at St Anne's-on-the-Hill is a bit too Technicolor. Mark is saved by the cross; England is saved by the intervention of angelic powers through Merlin. I'm not quite sure what's going on there. But you may see what I mean by claiming that *Till We Have Faces* has a greater *convertedness* about it.

And finally in these weaknesses, let me turn to the controversial bit about relations between the sexes. Ransom interrogates Mark's wife Jane about why her marriage is such a disaster and suggests it is because she hasn't learned obedience. Obedience, he says, is an 'erotic necessity'. Charles Williams is again very much in the background here. Jane may, says Ransom, escape the male, but she can't escape the cosmic *masculine*, so to speak. 'In relation to God we are all feminine'—a sentiment Lewis uses elsewhere as well. It's very much the view of Milton in *Paradise Lost*, and Lewis accordingly mentions it in that masterpiece, *Preface to Paradise Lost*. 'He for God only, she for God in him.'[19] Women have got to experience the masculine. They've got to be, if not literally, then metaphorically and spiritually, broken into by the masculine, the irruptive, the violent.

> 'Yes,' said the Director, [Ransom] 'there is no escape. If it were a virginal rejection of the male, he would allow it. Such souls can by-pass the male and go on to meet something far more masculine, higher up, to which they must make a yet deeper surrender. But your trouble has been what old poets called *Daungier*. We call it Pride. You are offended by the masculine itself: the loud, irruptive, possessive thing—the gold lion, the bearded bull—which breaks through the hedges and scatters the little kingdom of your primness. . . . The male you could have escaped, for it exists only on the biological level. But the masculine none of us can escape.'[20]

What has Lewis said here? Is this a problem *women* have particularly? How do men encounter the 'masculine'? Why is the masculine defined in these really rather startling terms, the *irruptive* and *possessive*? I note 'possessive' there. Isn't there actually a rather dangerously trivial account of masculinity being wheeled on here, not quite thought-through enough?

Jane is represented as being resentful about 'the loud careless masculine laughter on the lips of bachelor uncles' in her childhood, and when Ransom laughs at her, he has just that kind of bachelor laughter which had often infuriated her on other lips. What has *that* kind of masculinity, that assertive, possessive, irruptive thing to do with what I imagine Lewis wants to say about the ultimate otherness of God? Aren't we having particular (and rather dubious) cultural models of masculinity blended with something quite important being said about the divine, in a way which in fact *does* confuse the male and the masculine in a deeply unhelpful way? Shouldn't erotic necessity be a *mutual* obedience and cannot the man discover, in Lewis's rather curious sense, the masculine, the other, the transcendent in the woman? But I don't like those bachelor uncles—and I note with interest their bachelorhood.

The erotic necessity of obedience is in fact just as ambiguous as Jane feels it to be. Twice in the book she is represented as feeling a very seductive twinge of something or other when Ransom starts talking about obedience, and Ransom has to stop her. But of course I don't blame Jane. This is very ambiguous language. When a very powerful and charismatic man is sitting there talking to you about erotic obedience, it is, I imagine, rather difficult not to feel something other than pure intellectual interest at work.

I've spent quite a bit of time on what I think are major weaknesses and I think they *are* major; but I want to end with talking about major strengths.

IV. Major Strengths

They are major enough for me to think it *is* a good book, one of my favourites in spite of everything. And there are two things I want to underline especially. One is of course what Lewis was absolutely brilliant at in all his works, and that is what you might call the phenomenology of evil, or the phenomenology of temptation. What's it like to want to be bad? In *The Screwtape Letters* of course we have one of the classic expositions among modern moralists of this theme. And here he identifies it beautifully, and of course identifies it in Mark—not in the evil characters of Belbury so much, as in Mark himself: the urge to be on the inside, the urge to be in the know, the urge to be in control. This is finely done. And what's more, this urge is identified by Lewis with a whole repertoire (as I've already mentioned) of anti-natural, anti-organic, anti-material elements. It's a book in which the goodness of the earth, the goodness of the created order, is very firmly underlined, and you can see just how firmly when you see what the opposite is. Mark is taken to Filostrato.

> Filostrato turned sharply from him and . . . flung back the window curtains . . . the full Moon—Mark had never seen her so bright—stared down upon them . . .
>
> 'There is a world for you, no?' said Filostrato. 'There is cleanness, purity. Thousands of square miles of polished rock with not one blade of grass, not one fibre of lichen, not one grain of dust. Not even air.' . . .
>
> 'Yes. A dead world,' said Mark, gazing at the Moon.
>
> 'No!' said Filostrato . . . 'No. There is life there.'
>
> 'Do we *know* that?' asked Mark.
>
> 'Oh *si*. Intelligent life. Under the surface. A great race, further advanced than we. A *pure* race. They have cleaned their world, broken free (almost) from the organic.'[21]

Filostrato goes on:

> 'They do not need to be born and breed and die. . . . The Masters live on. They retain their intelligence.'[22]

Evil as bodilessness is a brilliant stroke.

Another feature of the portrayal of Belbury, again part of the phenomenology of evil, has to do with *political* evil. Lewis was a conservative. He made no secret of that and yet in this book he rightly sees that political evil is in a sense something beyond left and right. Fairy Hardcastle is quite right, though chilling, when she points out to Mark that the real political power is neither left nor right in the ordinary sense.

> 'I don't see how one's going to start a newspaper stunt [asks Mark] . . . without being political. Is it Left or Right papers that are going to print all this rot . . . '

> 'Both, Honey, both,' said Miss Hardcastle. 'Don't you understand *any-thing*? Isn't it absolutely essential to keep a fierce Left and a fierce Right both on their toes and each terrified of the other? That's how we get things done . . . *Of course* we're non-political. The real power always is.'[23]

Political evil is the urge to control, the urge to suppress, the urge to amputate the organic. Call it left or right, it doesn't matter; and Lewis is right to see that the N.I.C.E. has a blend of fascism and a certain kind of progressivist drivel that was perhaps rather more common in left-wing circles in the 40s and early 50s than it is now. (We have different kinds of drivel today.)

So he manages to portray a political evil, a political threat, that evades normal political labels. The symbol of the N.I.C.E., a naked male holding a thunderbolt, is a brilliant type of fascist iconography. And fascism is often what's behind much of this. But the point is that Lewis refuses to see totalitarianism in ordinary political terms. In fact he's rather like Hannah Arendt in her brilliant essay on the origins of totalitarianism. Totalitarianism is something which can't simply be pinned down to left or right by prospective opponents. It's a deeper problem—and of course a *spiritual* problem.

Evil as absolute control by a bodiless mind is part of how Lewis identifies it. And it's a fine portrayal of a typical corruption of the enlightenment ideal, a sort of rake's progress that runs from the enlightenment and the sense of the independent mind down to the ideal of the disembodied controlling ego.

And then too, as in *Screwtape*, one of the things about evil is that it's incapable of recognizing good. That it is to say, it doesn't know how good works. Belbury fails not just because of eldils and Merlin and all the rest of it, but also because it doesn't know where the real threat is coming from. It doesn't understand about St Anne's. More important, it doesn't understand about the Cross. This comes over neatly, without being pointed up at all, when some of the senior villains at Belbury are trying to work out where the threat's coming from.

'Only three possible people left the College after him [Mark]'[24] says Fairy Hardcastle, trying to identify who the dangerous people are.

'—Lancaster, Lyly, and Dimble. I put them in that order of probability. Lancaster is a Christian, and a very influential man. He's in the Lower House of Convocation. He had a lot to do with the Repton Conference. . . . He has a real stake in their side. Lyly is rather the same type, but less of an organiser. . . . Both these are dangerous men. Dimble is quite a different type. Except that he's a Christian, there isn't much against him. He's purely academic. . . . Impractical . . . he'd be too full of scruples to be much use to them.'[25]

Dimble of course is the only one who *is* a significant agent in the book, and the idea that Christian power doesn't necessarily lie in General Synod, as it were, may be worth taking to heart. Needless to say, we never hear anything else about Lancaster or Lyly. The evil characters can only think in terms of people defending a 'stake' in goodness, supporting a party or interest group. But, alas, that again is why St Anne's-on-the-Hill can seem so unsatisfactory, since it so constantly drifts towards sounding like another in-group.

So that's one thing, one deep virtue: the portrayal of a phenomenology of evil, especially of political evil. And the second point which I think is enormously positive (and I've already hinted at) is that at best Merlin and the other preternatural elements in the book represent an alliance of good with *matter* and *createdness* over against a false spiritualism. At the end, where Mark and Jane are reunited and Mr Bultitude the bear at last finds his mate, and so forth, there is a healthy eroticism—all the healthier for at least breaking through some of the self-consciousness of St Anne's-on-the-Hill—but it doesn't fit with Ransom at all. Ransom remains too disembodied. He's ceased to be very recognizably human and that's part of the difficulty. So we have an enormously positive, enormously imaginative alliance of the good and the created and the material over against the attempt to escape from creation as a fundamental form of evil—but not quite carried through imaginatively. We can acknowledge the real and major strength all the same.

V. Conclusion

So the overall balance on the sheet is still pretty favourable for the book; the great flaws are more than compensated for by the depth of insight. I read it and re-read it quite regularly, feeling not that I have to accept all the ideas in it, but that, as with much of Lewis's work (to use a phrase of his own) it's a 'mouthwash for the imagination'[26] at its best. It restores a sense of what evil is and what good might be. It may be less mature than *Till We Have Faces*; but it's more ambitious and more profound than the earlier science fiction books. Its weakness has something to do with Lewis trying to be Charles Williams, but it is still readable as morality. As theology it is not perhaps so uniformly good as some other things that Lewis did, but it's a remarkable book and I'm very glad to have had the opportunity of talking about it.

Notes

1. This talk was given on 10 May 1988.
2. C. S. Lewis, *That Hideous Strength* (London: HarperCollins, 2005), 35.
3. Lewis, *That Hideous Strength*, 292.
4. Lewis, *That Hideous Strength*, 521–522.
5. Lewis, *That Hideous Strength*, 62.
6. Lewis, *That Hideous Strength*, 62.
7. Lewis, *That Hideous Strength*, 148.
8. Lewis, *That Hideous Strength*, 148.
9. C. S. Lewis, *They Asked for a Paper* (London: Geoffrey Bles, 1962), 146–147.
10. Lewis, *They Asked for a Paper*, 149.
11. Lewis, *That Hideous Strength*, 147.
12. Lewis, *That Hideous Strength*, 518–519.
13. Lewis, *That Hideous Strength*, 518–519.
14. Lewis, *That Hideous Strength*, Preface.
15. Lewis, *That Hideous Strength*, 342–343.
16. Lewis, *That Hideous Strength*, 490–491.
17. Lewis, *That Hideous Strength*, 466–467.
18. Lewis, *That Hideous Strength*, 468.
19. John Milton, *Paradise Lost*, Book IV, line 299.
20. Lewis, *That Hideous Strength*, 437.
21. Lewis, *That Hideous Strength*, 235–236.
22. Lewis, *That Hideous Strength*, 236–237.
23. Lewis, *That Hideous Strength*, 125–126.
24. Lewis, *That Hideous Strength*, 324.
25. Lewis, *That Hideous Strength*, 324.
26. See letter to Jane Gaskell, 2 September 1957, in *C. S. Lewis, Collected Letters: Volume III: Narnia, Cambridge and Joy*, ed. Walter Hooper (London: HarperCollins, 2006), 881.

7

Yearning for a Far-Off Country

Malcolm Guite

I'M CONSCIOUS THAT many of you will be people who perhaps have had not only, as I have, a lifelong love of Lewis but some personal connections with him, having received correspondence from him, or personally met him.[1] I was born too late for that, but I can say that from the time I first read Lewis (like so many others, as a child, reading the Narnia books), I felt him as a kind of companion. He was one of those authors I really longed to meet and when, later on, as a schoolboy and then as a University student, I began to read his literary criticism and his theology and got involved in the philosophical, the theological, and above all, the argumentative Lewis, I wanted to have known him even more. He was one of those people with whom I found myself either profoundly agreeing or very profoundly disagreeing, so much so that the imaginary conversation continued long after I had closed the book. Often it was this working through the disagreements in my own mind and coming back again to Lewis as an interlocutor that led to real growth and development.

So, I've always read and enjoyed Lewis, and I've found myself at different stages in life coming back to him for different reasons. At first it was to 'travel in the realms of gold', then it was to seek him as a companion and guide across the literary landscape, now I seek him out as a conversation partner in the contemporary discussion about the role and meaning of imagination and its multifold relations to truth, especially theological truth. So I'm finding him still at this stage, and I expect still to be finding him when I'm 80, as a welcome and at the same time endearingly infuriating interlocutor. I can never quite let him go, and perhaps many of you have similar feelings.

But I've called tonight's talk 'Yearning for a Far-Off Country', and what I want to focus on is that theme that runs so deeply through so much of Lewis of yearning and longing, a theology of desire. I've called the talk 'Yearning for a Far-Off Country'—I suppose I could equally have called it 'The Inconsolable Secret' or even 'Committing an Act of Indecency', all of which are phrases from that wonderful sermon 'The Weight of Glory'.

I'd like to start with a passage from 'The Weight of Glory' which is typical of Lewis, both in its eloquence and in the way Lewis puts his finger both where it hurts and where the key to things is, the way he dares to reach out and touch you and say, 'What is this doing to you as a person?' And it's not only in sermons like this that he makes such an appeal. In his literary criticism, too, he expects you to engage from the quick of your soul with the very quick of what a writer is saying, and he expects you to deploy your knowledge and your literary-critical abilities to enable that engagement rather than to prevent it. This approach, which we will see in the extract from 'The Weight of Glory', is the exact opposite of the kind of writing which has dominated academia in the last thirty years and with which most of us were brought up. I am thinking of that apparatus of critical theories cobbled out of Derrida and the whole kind of structuralist, post-structuralist, hyper-theory and meta-criticism. The kind of theory, which, far from bringing you to the quick of your own soul or the author's, seems to keep you at an infinite distance, interposing layer upon layer of social or linguistic theory between you and the text. So that modern literary criticism, instead of being something that enables you to be touched to the quick and changed by what you read, is really almost like the sort of lead-lined gloves that people in nuclear stations have to wear to protect them from any reaction with what they're handling. But in this passage Lewis reaches out through all the layers of defence and distance and irony with which academics wrap themselves, and touches his listeners almost in spite of themselves. No wonder he is afraid they will think he is committing an indecency. Here's what he says:

> In speaking of this desire for our own far-off country, which we find in ourselves even now, I feel a certain shyness, I am almost committing an indecency. I am trying to rip open the inconsolable secret in each one of you—the secret which hurts so much that you take your revenge on it by calling it names like Nostalgia and Romanticism and Adolescence; the secret also which pierces with such sweetness that when, in very intimate conversation, the mention of it becomes imminent, we grow awkward and affect to laugh at ourselves; the secret we cannot hide and cannot tell, though we desire to do both.

I pause to note this acute psychological insight from Lewis, his alertness to how ambivalent our deepest feelings are: 'cannot hide and cannot tell, though we desire to do both.'

> We cannot tell it because it is a desire for something that has never actually appeared in our experience. We cannot hide it because our

experience is constantly suggesting it, and we betray ourselves like lovers at the mention of a name. Our commonest expedient is to call it beauty and behave as if that had settled the matter. Wordsworth's expedient was to identify it with certain moments in his own past. But all this is a cheat. If Wordsworth had gone back to those moments in the past, he would not have found the thing itself, but only the reminder of it; what he remembered would turn out to be itself a remembering. The books or the music in which we thought the beauty was located will betray us if we trust to them; it was not in them. . . .

Then comes a very key distinction here for Lewis, the distinction between *in* and *through*:

> . . . it was not *in* them, it only came *through* them, and what came through was longing. These things—the beauty, the memory of our own past—are good images of what we really desire; but if they are mistaken for the thing itself they turn into dumb idols, breaking the hearts of their worshippers. For they are not the thing itself; they are only the scent of a flower we have not found, the echo of a tune we have not heard, news from a country we have never yet visited.[2]

It's extraordinary how the prose rises to the condition of poetry in that beautiful peroration: 'the scent of a flower we have not found, the echo of a tune we have not heard, news from a country we have never yet visited.' There is a double admission here both of what's found and what's not found; the combination of yearning and the incompleteness is tremendously honest.

It seems to me that passages and even phrases like this give the lie to the facile caricature of Lewis as a sort of tweed-coated, hide-bound, blustering, donnish person full of prejudice and bombast. This is not the language of a boorish and blustering person who's trying to browbeat you with his conservative dogmatism. For people of my generation, coming freshly to this sermon, preached here in 1941, it feels more like the open-ended music that stirred us in a song like U2's *I Still Haven't Found What I'm Looking For* than like the Lewis that dismissive modern English dons or liberal theologians had told us to expect.

So that's a starting point, and obviously this theme of a yearning for something that's there but not quite, something that's eternally receding, is not unique to Lewis. But he picks it up and expounds it in his works from its three great sources in scripture, classical philosophy, and classical literature. In scripture, there is a pervasive sense of being 'strangers before thee, and sojourners, as were all our fathers: our days on earth are as a shadow and there is none abiding' (1 Chronicles 29:15 AV). We yearn for that which is to come, a theme picked up in Hebrews and elsewhere, and there is a sense of moving through the images and trying to find what's really there behind them. Clearly there's that same sense in Plato, which Lewis picks up so beautifully at the end of Narnia in the notion of the Shadowlands; and finally, it's there again in Virgil in his sense of that receding shore—of a journey on which you hope each stopping-place might be the destined shore, only to discover that the shore is further on. Indeed, Lewis dedicated a whole poem, 'The Landing,' to that Virgilian metaphor, whose last verse runs:

> *Hope died—rose again—quivered, and increased in us*
> *The strenuous longing. We re-embarked to find*
> *That genuine and utter West. Far astern and east of us*
> *The first hope sank behind.*[3]

Returning to 'The Weight of Glory', one of the things that interests me is the way in which Lewis, having given that very passionate, quite 'subjective' account of what it feels like from the inside to have that yearning, doesn't capitulate to what I think is really a kind of cultural apartheid of his time and ours. I mean the terrible split, since the Enlightenment, between so-called 'objective' truth and so-called 'subjective' truth—that 'apartheid' whereby we divide the world between objective and subjective, and then have all 'the facts' on the objective side and all the 'values' on the merely subjective side.

It's as though we have all agreed to 'cleanse' the so-called objective and real world, the world of actual, factual truth, of all value or meaning at all, so that it becomes the realm of quantity, not quality. But then it turns out we can't live without the values and meanings, so we kind of transport them all across the dividing line to the 'subjective' realm and say, 'You can have your beliefs and values as much as you like, providing it's your private universe, your private beliefs, and you don't pretend to think that it's "out there", or true for anyone other than yourself.'

Now Lewis could have capitulated to that, as many of his contemporaries did. He could have become a great psychological writer, a master of the inner realm, a mover of images within, conceding that his images were just internal symbols recombined to make a series of beautiful but essentially private patterns. But there's the honesty in Lewis that says, 'However beautiful the pattern is and however pleasantly arranged by my art, it's still not complete, nor is it only or essentially self-referential, there's still something beyond.' And the beyondness of this something beyond is not a *subjective* beyondness, it's not a beauty that I just haven't got around to imagining yet, it's an *objective* beyondness as well. He's actually saying in this sermon that what we are yearning for is, in a profound sense which we can scarcely grasp, 'really there'. And our yearning for it is part of the evidence that it's really there. So I see in Lewis, in all his writing, an attempt to bridge or heal that historic 'Enlightenment' split; I think he does it with his imagination, in his fiction and in his sermons, and I think he and Owen Barfield between them begin to do it philosophically. I think Barfield maybe does it more than Lewis.

Perhaps we can just flesh out that address to the reader or listener about having such longing with a little passage that I'm sure many of you are familiar with from *Surprised by Joy*, where Lewis talks about his own experience of longing. He does it with a beautiful kind of double regress, a memory which itself triggers a memory:

As I stood beside a flowering currant bush on a summer day there suddenly arose in me without warning, as if from a depth not of years but of centuries, the memory of that earlier morning at the Old House when my brother had brought his toy garden into the nursery. It is difficult to find words strong enough for the sensation which came over me; Milton's 'enormous bliss' of Eden (giving the full, ancient meaning to 'enormous') comes somewhere near it. It was a sensation, of course, of desire; but of desire for what? not, certainly, for a biscuit-tin filled with moss, nor even (though that came into it) from my own past. . . . and before I knew what I desired, the desire itself was gone, the whole glimpse withdrawn, the world turned commonplace again, or only stirred by a longing for the longing that had just ceased. It had taken only a moment of time; and in a certain sense everything else that had ever happened to me was insignificant in comparison.[4]

It's wonderful, that vividness and honesty about the immediate circumstances, visibly in this world, which seemed to trigger that longing which was itself what he later called Joy; and yet a complete honesty about the fact that should he go back and try and reconstruct that or get to it by picking up the biscuit tin, he'll never find it.

It sometimes seems to me that that's a particular piece of honesty that's missing in our culture. The whole purpose of the advertising industry, for example, is to surround their products with the suggestion that that joy, that sense of place and longing, will be there for us if only we make the purchase, and people are continuously buying things, finding that they 'still haven't found what they're looking for', not learning the lesson, buying again, trapped in the empty cycle of consumption and disappointment.

Lewis offers an entirely different approach. Of any good thing, any object of desire in this world, he asks us to say: 'This is a good thing, but it cannot be the whole of what I am looking for. Nevertheless, it may be a pointer, it may be a clue, it may even be a window through which I may glimpse and so regain my bearings on the "far off country".' Perhaps there's a haunting in all these passages in Lewis, of that very simple verse of George Herbert's, 'A man that looks on glass, on it may stay his eye, Or if he pleaseth, through it pass, And then the heaven espy.'[5]

So both of those passages that I've given you might be said to be passages in which Lewis suddenly has the chance of apprehending a transcendent or overarching truth and beauty through his imagination, through his aesthetic sense: 'Call it beauty', he says.

But the interesting thing about Lewis is that he doesn't leave this quest to his imagination alone; his reason is continuously alert as well. He is always trying to find out whether it can be the case that his imagination and his reason will reach the same conclusion, by different media perhaps, but nevertheless arriving at the same place. And he's not satisfied if his imagination presents something to which his reason cannot give assent. And if there is a tension between these two faculties, then he is honest enough to acknowledge and abide in that tension. If Reason appears to tell him, for example, that the world is dead and cold and pointless, that we're just a bundle of neurones and the whole thing is just a kind of concatenation of atoms in the darkness—supposing that's what his reason is saying, Lewis says, 'Okay, well, even if I'm persuaded of this by reason, my imagination says something different and I must listen to that as well.' It's this refusal to let go, this refusal to silence one voice in preference for the other . . . to choose a place in that 'apartheid' I spoke of, that post-Enlightenment divide, and be happy in it, which makes Lewis at once troubling and compelling to the modern reader. And that is because most of us, most of the time, do consent to these divisions of our culture. In the work-a-day world we accept the consensus that the world is a kind of huge, rather pointless machine, but we may as well exploit it while we're here and then, when we can't bear the bleakness of that view anymore, we go in for a bit of niche marketing of religion, we have a little lifestyle enclave somewhere, and we kind of decide to groove on that, our 'Celtic spirituality' or whatever it is that's going to keep us going, and we never say, 'Why is it that I can't bring both halves of my world together?'

Now that is precisely the question C. S. Lewis did ask, and he expressed it with particular power in a poem written just on the cusp of his conversion. It was published posthumously by Walter Hooper, who titled it 'Reason', though I think it might be better without a title, allowing the openness and the tension of the poem to speak for itself without tipping the balance between Reason and Imagination, to both of which the poem is trying to be faithful. I personally think this poem is crucial for understanding a lot of Lewis's work, and for understanding the great synthesis that I think he achieves towards the end of his life. Here he sets out the case for both Reason and Imagination, drawing on a beautifully re-imagined classical typology for Reason as Athene and Imagination as Demeter. I find it a very beautiful and interesting poem, because it is trying to be honest both to imagination and to reason. (And I think the person who helped him most in that and helped him most intellectually to engage with his imagination and trust it is Owen Barfield, who in his turn got his sense of the imagination as an instrument for genuinely apprehending truth from Coleridge.)

So I think there's a lot to be said there about his simply daring to say, 'We must allow the imagination her place not only as a genuine power in our soul against which we must not offend but as a genuine medium through which truth comes to us.' But he does it characteristically by combining it with perhaps his most forthright defence of Reason. Lewis had learned from his great tutor Kirkpatrick to be alert to false logic, to leave no room for slipshod work or for self-contradiction. As a teacher, he demanded absolute intellectual integrity. My father-in-law was one of Lewis's students at Magdalene, and has vivid stories to tell of how fierce he could be if you committed, as it were, an intellectual sin, if you said something which was shoddy and which you knew to be shoddy and which you hadn't thoroughly worked out. He was very fierce about that because he venerated the clarity of reason: as he says in this poem, 'so clear is reason'. You must not knowingly say something of which you are not, by the best of your powers of reasoning, convinced.

The contemporary Church could learn a lot from Lewis here. In my role as an academic chaplain, I'm constantly meeting students who, having attended a church as part of a genuine enquiry into the truth of things, a genuine desire to know what the faith is all about, simply find their Reason ignored or offended. They find that it's assumed that they have to check their brains at the door before they're allowed to proceed any further. Now that's a million miles away from saying (and I don't think Lewis would say) that you can reason your way into Christianity. I think what Lewis would say, along with Richard Hooker and Thomas Aquinas, is that if Christianity is true, then whilst it's not actually directly demonstrable from axiom by pure reason, and therefore requires an element of revelation, it is nevertheless not repugnant to a properly exercised reason.

So Lewis makes that point on Reason's behalf and giving the 'Enlighten-ment' its due, but he is not content to let that be the end of the story, or the only voice. We have more than one Goddess to honour, and Demeter too must have her due. And here it's worth remarking on his use of 'goddess' imagery throughout this poem. From the point of view of the subtlety of Lewis's vision and his psychological insights and the complexity of his own character and his understanding of other people's characters, this poem is remarkable. Again it gives the lie to those who want to caricature Lewis as a kind of crusty old misogynist, who had no proper encounters with women until he met Joy Davidman, and therefore didn't understand them. But here he is, in a poem that was probably written around 1929, configuring his own inner life in entirely feminine terms! 'Who will reconcile in me both maid and mother?' He is well aware that both Jung and Freud say that there is both the masculine and feminine in each person, but Lewis of course gets his insights from a much more ancient source, namely the entire tradition in western Christendom of understanding the soul as feminine. He gets it, I believe, from St Bernard of Clairvaux, who continuously speaks of himself either as a maid or as a mother, and doesn't feel his gender is compromised or challenged by that, but is rather enriched by it. It's certainly enriched by his power psychologically to use the first person singular feminine about himself.

I think you could also make a great deal out of his double image of the light and the dark in this poem, and particularly the way Lewis finds a proper place in the soul for the dark ('How dark imagining'), honest about both the fertility and the darkness of our imagination: 'Her pains are long and her delight.'

This poem, I think, sets the agenda for Lewis. It means that when he speaks of yearning, he wants to know that what he is yearning for is not simply a chimera, an emotional by-product—not something to be accounted for in this-worldly terms at all. He wants to be sure that fidelity to whatever it is that calls us in and through that experience of 'inconsolable longing' in-volves a double fidelity both to Imagination and to Reason. And I think he challenges us to the same double fidelity—a difficult challenge, since that bifurcation, that split which Lewis felt and writes about elsewhere in *Sur-prised by Joy* as well, has become even more pronounced since his death. I think our so-called postmodernism, far from transcending or healing these divisions at the heart of the Enlightenment project, is only making them worse. 'Postmodernism' and the suspicion of all 'metanarrative' just legiti-mises the idea that you can have one set of beliefs and values in this part of your life and a completely different set of beliefs and values in that part of your life, and you needn't even bother to bring them into dialogue. That, I think, Lewis would regard as offending against Athene, tainting reason itself.

When I read these things, I inevitably come back and ask myself: what about me, and what about us? Do we, as Lewis suggests, cover over, ignore and bury those moments of joy and yearning with a kind of mask of irony, dismissing them with names like 'rhetoric' or 'romanticism' or 'adolescence', or do we keep an ear open to them? Even for those people who have actually come to a position of Christian faith, that Faith itself can sometimes be the temptation; a temptation to let go of the yearning, to deceive yourself into thinking that you have already found everything you are looking for. When I was reading Lewis as an atheist and agnostic, one of my deepest fears about Christianity, and one of the things which I was fencing off about Christianity, was the notion of finality and stasis, the notion that you get this religion and that'll be the end of you—you resign yourself to God, you accept the answers, and that'd be it, the searching and adventuring and journeying of life would be over. So one of the experiences of reading Lewis for me was the discovery that this was obviously not the case, but that, rather, there was a dynamic in the faith that was a constant call to move 'further up and further in' to the Mystery.

The other image that I thought I'd just leave you with in this exploration of the notion that Lewis won't allow the value, truth and insight contained in such glimpses of heaven to stay in only one part of the world or of life, but keeps wanting them to steal over the divide, is the rather extraordinary image that he uses again in *Surprised by Joy* of the light that settles on the pages of *Phantastes* as he reads it, moving off the page into the world around him. After reading this passage, I felt it to be a really good question to ask of any work of imagination or art: However beautiful it is in its own world, does it leave my vision of the world which I actually inhabit impoverished or en-riched? Is it something from which I come away feeling more despondent about my life, sensing that by comparison with that lovely other world my world is cheap and pointless? Or does it actually enhance my vision of the world? Does something of the new vision in the book come over into my world?

This is a quite long passage but I think it's so good that it's worth having.

The evening that I now speak of was in October. I and one porter had the long, timbered platform of Leatherhead station to ourselves. It was getting just dark enough for the smoke of an engine to glow red on the underside with the reflection of the furnace.[6]

You know he's going to tell you something wonderful when he gives you these beautifully realized images, these extraordinary and vivid details. In some strange way that we can't quite account for, both in life and in fiction we remember great truths by association with vividly embodied images. We don't remember them by setting up a checklist of tick points in our mind and going through them again. We remember them because of the smell of a flower or the taste of coffee or something vivid that was going on, apparently irrelevantly, at the same time. So here this marvellous detail of the red under-side of the reflection of the furnace on the smoke of the train, so vividly re-membered, subtly prepares us for the importance of what is to follow.

> The hills beyond the Dorking Valley were of a blue so intense as to be nearly violet and the sky was green with frost. My ears tingled with the cold. The glorious week-end of reading was before me. Turning to the bookstall, I picked out an Everyman in a dirty jacket, *Phantastes, a faerie Romance*, George MacDonald. Then the train came in. I can still remember the voice of the porter calling out the village names, Saxon and sweet as a nut—'Bookham, Effingham, Horsley train'. That eve-ning I began to read my new book.[7]

And then, you remember, he describes his journey, both outwardly and in-wardly. Reading *Phantastes* is like the journey on a train: He is carried sleep-ing across a frontier and ushered, by the engagement of MacDonald's imagi-nation with his imagination, into a world which, although apparently fictional, is in fact far truer than anything else that he's encountered up to that point.

> The woodland journeyings in that story, the ghostly enemies, the ladies of both good and evil, were close enough to my habitual imagery to lure me on without the perception of a change. It is as if I were car-ried sleeping across the frontier, or as if I had died in the old country and could never remember how I came alive in the new. For in one sense the new country was exactly like the old. I met there all that had already charmed me in Malory, Spenser, Morris, and Yeats. But in an-other sense I was changed. I did not yet know (and I was long in learn-ing) the name of the new quality, the bright shadow, that rested on the travels of Anodos. I do now. It was Holiness. For the first time the song of the sirens sounded like the voice of my mother or my nurse. Here were old wives' tales; there was nothing to be proud of in enjoying them. It was as though the voice which had called to me from the world's end were now speaking at my side. It was with me in the room,

or in my own body, or behind me. If it had once eluded me by its distance, it now eluded me by proximity. . . . Thus, when the great moment came I did not break away from the woods and cottages that I read of to seek some bodiless light shining beyond them, but gradually, with a swelling continuity (like the sun at mid-morning burning through a fog), I found the light shining on those woods and cottages, and then on my own past life, and on the quiet room where I sat and on my old teacher where he nodded above his little *Tacitus*. For I now perceived that while the air of the new region made all my erotic and magical perversions of Joy look like sordid trumpery, it had no such disenchanting power over the bread upon the table and the coals in the grate. That was the marvel.[8]

Here is a light coming out from the book, from that 'subjective' work, which actually changes for the better, for the truer, the perception of the bread on the table and the coals in the grate. It is a truth which can be both transcendent, full of longing, and actually change appreciably and bring into truer focus the kind of work-a-day world that we live in. That in itself is a healing of the 'subjective'/'objective' divide.

I particularly draw your attention to Lewis's phrase 'crossing a frontier': a very interesting phrase. If, when people have stopped rabbiting on about postmodernism and decided to ask again what truth is, we're to get any kind of cultural cohesion, then we're going to need somebody like Lewis, because he has really pioneered the paths and made the passes over the frontiers that were imposed upon us in the Enlightenment. Postmodernists are blithely saying that the 'Enlightenment project' is over, but I think all they've done is capitulated to its divisions. Lewis, by contrast, has 'crossed the frontier', and discovered that the yearnings in the subjective realm and the truths to be found in the objective realm must ultimately come from the same place. So if we too are to cross such a frontier, Lewis is going to be just the person we need as a companion and guide.

And the other final thing is the extraordinary phrase that he uses to describe the light that was in the book and the light that then came to be in the room: the phrase 'bright shadow'. I think there are two ways into understanding the paradox in that phrase. One is that it implies the reconciliation that he was looking for in that poem, between Athene in her brightness and Demeter in her darkness, and the other is that much more powerful and Platonic sense that even the best 'brightness' in this world is a shadow of the brightness still to come, for which we yearn, and for which we must never cease to admit our longing.

Notes

1. This talk was given on 2 March 1999.
2. 'The Weight of Glory', in C. S. Lewis, *Essay Collection: Faith, Christianity and Church*, ed. Lesley Walmsley (London: Harper Collins, 2000), 98–99.
3. C. S. Lewis, *Poems*, ed. Walter Hooper (London: Geoffrey Bless, 1964), 27–28.
4. C. S. Lewis, *Surprised by Joy* (London: Geoffrey Bles, 1955), 22.
5. 'The Elixir', in *George Herbert: The Complete English Works*, ed. A Pasternak Slater (London: Everyman, 1995), 180.
6. Lewis, *Surprised by Joy*, 169.
7. Lewis, *Surprised by Joy*, 169.
8. Lewis, *Surprised by Joy*, 169–170.

W. H. Auden and the Inklings

Michael Piret

ONE OF THE last poems W. H. Auden ever wrote, in the posthumous volume, *Thank You, Fog* (1974), is called 'A Thanksgiving'.[1] Whether or not Auden knew he would die soon, the poem is a kind of leave-taking, a retrospective, in which he thanks a number of the literary and intellectual figures whose writings shaped him over his sixty-six years. He records his indebtedness to Hardy, Edward Thomas, and Robert Frost in his youth, to Yeats and Graves later, and to Brecht. Then he says of the war years, when he returned to the Christian faith he had abandoned in adolescence:

> *Finally, hair-raising things*
> *that Hitler and Stalin were doing*
> *forced me to think about God.*
>
> *Why was I sure they were wrong?*
> *Wild Kierkegaard, Williams and Lewis*
> *guided me back to belief.*[2]

Eleven writers are mentioned in this testimony to the great ones, written by one of the great poets of the twentieth century. Eleven writers, and two of them are Inklings: not bad going, we may feel, in this Society.

It's the nature of Auden's respect for this circle of writers that I want to talk about tonight. Chronologically there was great overlap. Auden, born in 1907, came up to Oxford—to Christ Church—in 1925, the same year C. S. Lewis was made a Fellow of Magdalen. That's also the year in which J. R. R. Tolkien was elected Rawlinson and Bosworth Professor of Anglo-Saxon; the Tolkien family moved to Oxford from Leeds early in 1926. Auden wasn't yet reading English in 1925. He began by reading Natural Science; then he dabbled in PPE.[3] It was only at the end of his first year that he switched to English, a subject for which Christ Church didn't even employ a tutor yet. He was taken on by a young tutor at another college: a kind of Inkling-to-be, at Exeter College, Nevill Coghill. When he started attending Tolkien's lectures, Auden instantly became a fan of Anglo-Saxon. 'I do not remember a single word he said', he later remarked, 'but at a certain point he recited, and magnificently, a long passage of *Beowulf.* I was spell-bound. This poetry, I knew, was going to be my dish.'[4]

A general enthusiasm for Tolkien and an appreciation of his work lasted the whole of Auden's lifetime. He was a champion of *The Lord of the Rings* from the outset, its most intellectually distinguished champion outside the circle of Tolkien's close friends. One of the more fascinating photographs that Cecil Beaton took of Auden, in 1968, shows the poet—by then a figure of veneration in literary circles, his face cragged and monumental, his fist clenched—leaning gravely on a plinth which holds a great carved bust of Dionysus. Beneath his jacket, over a shirt and tie, is a sweatshirt imprinted in large, crude, silk-screened letters with the name GIMLI.[5] (Bought, I like to imagine, off a stand in Greenwich Village at the peak of sixties Tolkien mania, when legends like 'Frodo Lives' were being painted on New York subway cars.)

Auden's popularity in the United States was enormous in the 1960s, and one of the things he did was tour. There's a delightful poem from this period called 'On the Circuit', in which he describes the relentless, exhausting air travel that was organized by his agents, and notes that the odd encounter with somebody else who loves the Inklings is one of the things that gives him a boost.

> *An airborne instrument I sit,*
> *Predestined nightly to fulfill*
> *Columbia-Giesen-Management's*
> *Unfathomable will . . .*
>
> *. . .*
>
> *Though warm my welcome everywhere,*
> *I shift so frequently, so fast,*
> *I cannot now say where I was*
> *The evening before last,*
>
> *Unless some singular event*
> *Should intervene to save the place,*
> *A truly asinine remark,*
> *A soul-bewitching face,*

> *Or blessed encounter, full of joy,*
> *Unscheduled on the Giesen Plan,*
> *With, here, an addict of Tolkien,*
> *There, a Charles Williams fan.*[6]

If Auden's first encounter with Tolkien was as an undergraduate in lectures on Anglo-Saxon, his first with Charles Williams was just over a decade later, in the summer of 1937, when they discussed an idea Auden had for compiling an 'Oxford Book of Light Verse', a project that went ahead with the approval of Williams and the Oxford University Press. Williams, in an OUP memorandum, recorded his great pleasure at meeting Auden (alongside a businesslike assessment of his proposal): 'My own inclination, subject to the judgement of the financiers, is that it would be quite a good idea to collect Auden's name. He is still generally regarded as the most important of the young poets at present, and likely to be more important if he develops. About that of course I can say nothing. He may fail as so many have failed. Even so, however, if the book were desirable and tolerable we should be no worse off, and if he really becomes a figure we should be better off.'[7]

Auden's reaction to Williams was on an utterly different plane: 'for the first time in my life', Auden said, '[I] felt myself in the presence of personal sanctity.'[8] Auden was, as Humphrey Carpenter points out, reacting to Williams as a great many people did, T. S. Eliot among them. People did find themselves in the presence of someone astonishing. Writing of Williams's 'personal magnetism', John Carey says that he 'must have been virtually radioactive with it',[9] to judge from the devotion of his admirers. Auden was overawed yet found the experience a deeply positive one, not belittling or humiliating in any sense. 'I had met many good people before', he reflected, 'who made me feel ashamed of my own shortcomings, but in the presence of this man—we never discussed anything but literary business—I did not feel ashamed. I felt transformed into a person who was incapable of doing or thinking anything base or unloving.'[10]

A couple of years after this meeting with Williams, Auden read *The Descent of the Dove: A Short History of the Holy Spirit in the Church*—a reprint of which he would eventually supply with an introduction. He was going through a sea-change, and his quest for truth was drawing him to explore religious faith. He wrote to tell Williams 'how moved he was' by *The Descent of the Dove*, and he seems to have been led by that book to read Kierkegaard.[11] (Remember that 'Wild Kierkegaard,' along with Williams and Lewis, had a part to play in guiding him 'back to belief.')[12] There were many other personal and intellectual factors that led him to adult faith. His brother-in-law

Golo Mann, writing of this period of transition, mentions the importance of Reinhold Niebuhr's *The Nature and Destiny of Man*, even though 'Fundamentally', Mann wrote, 'Auden never allowed himself to be led by others; he picked out of books what he needed for himself and digested it to an extent which justified him, subjectively, in claiming it as his very own.'[13] Contemporary events, too—those 'hair-raising things / that Hitler and Stalin were doing'—posed urgent questions that pointed him towards faith: 'Why was I sure they were wrong?'[14] Mann recalls Auden saying, around 1938–1939, that 'the English intellectuals who now cry to Heaven against the evil incarnated in Hitler have no Heaven to cry to; they have nothing to offer and their protests echo in empty space.'[15]

He was longing for a criterion, a base of moral objectivity on which outrage at Hitler and Nazism could be reasonably grounded. This longing is of a piece with the kind of Christianity that C. S. Lewis was about to articulate publicly in his broadcast talks (though whether those programmes could possibly have made their way to Auden in New York on the BBC Overseas Service I do not know). It is too easily assumed, because of Auden's extremely liberal sexual behaviour, that he would be liberal in theology, thoroughly modernised, unorthodox, avant-garde. In fact his attraction to traditional dogma was deep and strong, inclining decidedly towards the toughness that he admired in George MacDonald; indeed he seems to query MacDonald's unorthodoxy with regard to 'the ultimate salvation of the Devil', while still commending him warmly not in spite of his toughness, but because of it. Like Lewis, Auden had no time for innovations in theology which threw out 'the Christian doctrines of God, Sin and Grace' in favour of 'some vague emergent "force making for righteousness" or a Pelagian and secular belief in "Progress".'[16] It could be that a sense of underlying guilt about his own wide-ranging sexual conduct predisposed him towards an un-reconstructed traditionalist view of sin: as Humphrey Carpenter puts it, 'he expected a very high level of sinfulness in himself', and so 'like Augustine he put tremendous emphasis on the grace of God as the saving power, rather than on any natural goodness or good works in Man.'[17] 'We are not, any of us, very nice', he writes at the end of his essay, 'Heresies'.[18] Lewis provides what could be read as a generalised commentary on Auden's perspective in *The Problem of Pain* (1940) as he identifies basic elements of religious belief: 'The moralities accepted among men may differ . . . but they all agree in prescribing a behaviour which their adherents fail to practise. All men alike stand condemned, not by alien codes of ethics, but by their own, and all men therefore are conscious of guilt. The second element in religion is the consciousness not merely of a moral law, but of a moral law at once approved and disobeyed.'[19]

Our relation to such a law was, for Auden as for Lewis, part of the existential background in response to which religious faith makes an authoritative claim on us. A poem called 'The Hidden Law' (dated 1940, the year of his return to the church) shows this law to be everywhere, pervasive yet strangely disregarded. Silently present alongside the physical laws of the universe, the 'Hidden Law' cannot be captured within our political systems or pinned down by our 'legal definitions.' It does not interfere when we defy it; it 'answers nothing when we lie'. Yet our acts of disobedience, our attempts at evasion, our forgetfulness of its demands, come at a cost. They are in themselves 'the ways we're punished by / The Hidden Law.'[20] In a closely related poem of the same period, 'Law Like Love,' he says,

> . . . all agree
> Gladly or miserably
> That the Law is
> And that all know this. . . .

Turning away from the impulse to define the Law, he chooses a simile instead—what he calls a 'timid similarity'—and it is a profoundly Christian one. The Law, he says, is 'Like love':

> Like love we don't know where or why,
> Like love we can't compel or fly,
> Like love we often weep,
> Like love we seldom keep.[21]

The explorer reaching this pass is on the frontier of belief. The consciousness of a deep Law 'at once approved and disobeyed', so central to Lewis's apologetics, was also clearly at the forefront of Auden's thinking as he was about to make his leap of faith. A God, or something very like him, was looking absolutely necessary if one was to cry out coherently 'against the evil incarnated in Hitler'. Before long, to quote Mann again, Auden 'drew his own conclusions, which were the product both of reasoning and of his own very strong force of will.' Something peculiar started to happen. 'On Sundays he began to disappear for a couple of hours and returned with a look of happiness on his face', Mann recalled of that period in New York. 'After a few weeks he confided in me the object of these mysterious excursions: the Episcopalian Church. And in the Church he remained for thirty-three years.'[22]

It's tempting to go down side-alleys and talk about other affinities between Auden and Lewis as Christians: both adult converts, both with a passion for poetry and myth which left them no less convinced about the importance of doctrine and dogma. (Auden would counter the view that 'the interpretation is more important than the fact' of the Resurrection by asking, 'It does make a difference if it really happened, doesn't it?')[23] On the subject of liturgical reform, both were conservatives at heart, and would have endorsed the manifesto of any Prayer Book Society. Lewis might have been the more progressive of the two—at least accepting the necessity of modest changes from time to time—but he felt the Church would have to produce another Cranmer, or someone like Cranmer, if the Prayer Book were to be adequately revised.[24] Auden's conservatism was more pronounced. Anne Fremantle notes that just before his death, he provocatively 'declared that the Book of Common Prayer should now be used only in Latin, since there is a perfectly respectable translation extant, instead of being transliterated into contemporary jargon.'[25] Orlan Fox recalls that Auden 'began to attend Greek Orthodox services in later years to hear the mass in an ancient language.'[26] He was appalled by the Trial Liturgies of the Episcopal Church in the 1960s, and faulted the Roman Catholics in the wake of Vatican II for having 'made a cacophonous horror of the Mass.' He goes on to say, 'We had the extraordinary good fortune in that our Book of Common Prayer was composed at exactly the right historical moment. The English language had already become more or less what it is today, so that the Prayer Book is no more difficult to follow than Shakespeare, but the ecclesiastics of the sixteenth century still possessed a feeling for the ritual and ceremonious which today we have almost entirely lost. Why should we spit on our luck?'[27] No surprise that he once wrote (and often repeated), 'I like to fancy that, had I taken Anglican Holy Orders, I might by now be a bishop, politically liberal I hope, theologically and liturgically conservative I know.'[28]

In addition to these affinities, another intriguing resemblance between Auden's faith and Lewis's suggests itself, in Auden's apprehension of a particular 'signpost' experience, one which had, for him, a significance comparable to Lewis's experience of Joy. Alongside his reaction to Hitler, alongside his sense of 'a moral law at once approved and disobeyed', alongside his need for expressions of piety and prayer that would 'stay put',[29] there was a momentary experience that had opened him up to another dimension, a reality beyond, something which passed quickly but was felt on the pulses and never forgotten. Lewis's accounts of Joy are too well known to need repetition here; but Auden's experience is less well known, and his account of it bears quoting at length. It had little or nothing to do with nature, which was in many ways a curiously closed book to him, in comparison with what it meant to Lewis. (As a walker, for example, Auden was said to take no notice of his surroundings.

In his student days, his favourite walk in Oxford was reportedly past the gas-works, along 'the dingiest part of the river towpath'[30] —this, to him, was beauty—though on the whole he wasn't much for walking at all. His friend James Stern recounts his typical response to the question, 'Wystan, it has stopped raining, shall we go for a walk? . . . The look of horror: "A *walk*? What on earth *for*?"')[31] It was in a human encounter—not an encounter with nature—that Auden was to taste a sensation Lewis might have described in Milton's words, one of 'enormous bliss'.[32]

This is what Auden wrote about his experience, which is recorded as an account of 'The Vision of Agape', in his preface to *The Protestant Mystics*. (It should be noted that Auden, like Lewis, did not regard himself as a 'mystical' person.)[33] Without identifying himself as the author, he presented the experience as 'an unpublished account for the authenticity of which I can vouch':

> One fine summer night in June 1933 I was sitting on a lawn after dinner with three colleagues, two women and one man. We liked each other well enough but we were certainly not intimate friends, nor had any one of us a sexual interest in another. Incidentally, we had not drunk any alcohol. We were talking casually about everyday matters when, quite suddenly and unexpectedly, something happened. I felt myself invaded by a power which, though I consented to it, was irresistible and certainly not mine. For the first time in my life I knew exactly—because, thanks to the power, I was doing it—what it means to love one's neighbor as oneself. I was also certain, though the conversation continued to be perfectly ordinary, that my three colleagues were having the same experience. (In the case of one of them, I was able later to confirm this.) My personal feelings towards them were unchanged—they were still colleagues, not intimate friends— but I felt their existence as themselves to be of infinite value and rejoiced in it.

> I recalled with shame the many occasions on which I had been spiteful, snobbish, selfish, but the immediate joy was greater than the shame, for I knew that, so long as I was possessed by this spirit, it would be literally impossible for me deliberately to injure another human being. . . . And among the various factors which several years later brought me back to the Christian faith in which I had been brought up, the memory of this experience and asking myself what it could mean was one of the most crucial, though, at the time it occurred, I thought I had done with Christianity for good.[34]

It would be quite wrong to imply an equivalence between Auden's 'Vision of Agape' and Lewis's Joy. The differences are obvious and numerous. Auden's experience lasted for hours and seems never to have been repeated; it had a distinctly moral dimension, focussing on his relationships with other people; it was more about insight and fulfillment than about the 'unsatisfied desire' which Lewis associates with Joy. But it struck him with the same 'sense of incalculable importance', and he might well have felt it true to say, with Lewis, that 'in a certain sense everything else that had ever happened to [him] was insignificant in comparison.'[35] Both men looked back and identified these phenomena, years later, as pointers on a journey towards faith which had made a uniquely significant impact long before either of them imagined they might have anything to do with God. Richard Davenport-Hines writes of Auden's experience, 'This was the moment when Auden had the first glimpse of the numinous object of his quest.'[36] It was a quest he undertook not just for the sake of poetic development; it was a quest he undertook simply as a human being, searching for an absolute, for the ultimate ground of reality.

If there is a single word or idea that can focus for us the nature of Auden's affinities with the Inklings and his attraction to them, I think it is exactly this idea of the *Quest*. For him it was a quest for meaning amidst chaos, a quest to ground moral instinct and judgement in metaphysical reality, a quest for authentic love and faith, a quest to transcend self-regard, and imprisonment within the limits of present apprehension as it can shut down around us. The genre of the Quest was of signal importance to him, and his devotion to it accounts in great part for the seriousness and depth of his admiration for Tolkien. He had read *The Lord of the Rings* as it came out, and Carpenter notes that he was so keen to read and review *The Return of the King* that he obtained a set of galley proofs from Tolkien.[37] His reviews for the *New York Times* were among the early endorsements of the books which Tolkien had in mind when he wrote in a letter, 'I am . . . very deeply in Auden's debt in recent years. His support of me and interest in my work has been one of my chief encouragements. He gave me very good reviews, notices and letters from the beginning when it was by no means a popular thing to do. He was, in fact, sneered at for it.'[38] Edmund Wilson was one of those who sneered, clearly feeling that Auden's respect for Tolkien's work was odd enough to need special pleading: 'he no doubt so overrates *The Lord of the Rings* because he reads into it something that he means to write himself.'[39] Whether or not Auden had such designs, he certainly did read into *The Lord of the Rings* much of who he was, coming up with a stylised, quite individual assessment of how it all works. This was most fully articulated in his essay on 'The Quest Hero', published in *The Texas Quarterly* in 1961.[40]

To put Auden's reading of Tolkien into context, we must remember his preoccupation with continual transcendence of the present, continual development of the self into something new and beyond what it was before. And we need to understand that he was in the habit of seeing himself in quest stories. Carpenter says, 'Later in his life he liked to point out that in fairy-tales it is the youngest of the three brothers'—that is what he was—'who succeeds in the quest and wins the prize. "I, after all, am the Fortunate One," he wrote, "The Happy-Go-Lucky, the spoilt Third Son."[41] So it is not surprising to find him gravitating towards the mythology of Tolkien's books, where the *arete* of the hero is inapparent.[42] As is the case with youngest sons, so too in a story where hobbits win the day: after all, who could, on the surface of it, be more unlikely heroes? Neither is it surprising that he should frame the Quest as a literary mimesis of our subjective experience.[43] There are many things he admired about *The Lord of the Rings*—including Tolkien's 'gift for topographical description', 'his gift for naming and his fertility in inventing incidents'[44] —but it was what he regarded as this mimetic correspondence with particular aspects of 'our subjective experience of life'[45] that was the focal point of his praise. After laying out the 'essential elements' belonging to typical Quest stories, Auden enumerates the ways in which they are mimetic of inner reality. They give expression, first, to the purposive nature of our actions; secondly, to our consciousness of 'time as a continuous irreversible process of change', which 'translated into spatial terms' will be seen as 'a journey'. Thirdly, they illustrate our individuality and our uncertainty, as self-consciously unique persons 'confronting an unknown future', not knowing whether we will succeed in the end or not. Finally, they give expression to 'contradictory forces' within ourselves, some good and some evil, 'continually trying to sway [the] will this way or that.'[46] Thus the Quest, and by extension Tolkien's Middle-earth, becomes a ground on which the struggles of the psyche—indeed of Auden's own psyche—get played out. Through it we learn about the mistakes made by Evil because of its inability to imagine Good; about the nature of irrational cruelty and the 'necessarily unstable' alliances of Evil with Evil; and we learn about the fruits of victory as well, bittersweet as they are, since in a good Quest story, as in our historical experience, 'the best solution involves loss as well as gain.'[47]

Tolkien raised a suspicious eyebrow at Auden's critical approach to *The Lord of the Rings*. He was 'very grateful' for Auden's glowing *New York Times* review in 1956, but he also wrote a long critique of it (evidently for himself only).[48] What made him particularly uneasy was the suggestion, which could indeed be drawn out of the 1956 review, that *The Lord of the Rings* was an attempt, on Tolkien's part, somehow to write in symbolic terms about his own inner life. 'I believe', Tolkien stated, 'that it is precisely because I did *not* try, and have never thought of trying to "objectify" my personal experience of life that the account of the Quest of the Ring is successful in giving pleasure to Auden (and others). . . . The story is not about JRRT at all, and is at no point an attempt to allegorize his experience of life—for that is what the objectifying of his subjective experience in a tale must mean, if anything.'[49] It seems unlikely, though, that Auden ever regarded *The Lord of the Rings* as an allegory 'about JRRT'. Certainly by the time he came to write his essay on 'The Quest Hero', his real focus was on the way in which the tale helps to illuminate (for all of us) the nature of our subjective experience more generally. It is helpful here to remember the precise distinction Tolkien himself makes, in his Foreword to *The Lord of the Rings*, between *allegory* and *applicability*: 'I cordially dislike allegory in all its manifestations, and always have done so since I grew old and wary enough to detect its presence. I much prefer history, true or feigned, with its varied applicability to the thought and experience of readers. I think that many confuse "applicability" with "allegory"; but the one resides in the freedom of the reader, and the other in the purposed domination of the author.'[50] Auden was in a way simply exercising his freedom as a reader. Whether that exercise of freedom was on Tolkien's wavelength or not, Tolkien had left plenty of scope for it, and the opportunity taken by Auden had profound resonance for him personally. It helped a major poet make meaning of a life full of contradiction: a mixture of freedom and constraint, good luck and mistakes, intellect and passion, humour and happiness, and also tragedy. *The Lord of the Rings* didn't only make its way into his poetic vocabulary (where we will find 'Middle-Earth' in his 'Ode to Terminus' and 'A New Year Greeting', and 'the Dark Lord' in the famous anthem set to music by William Walton, 'The Twelve').[51] It was part of his personal journey, towards that ultimate truth in the light of which all shall be judged, a journey full of celebration and absurdity, not without grief and exhaustion, and not without encouragement and grace from beyond.

I'll end with the closing lines of Auden's fine quest poem, 'Atlantis' (1941), a product of that pivotal time when the world was struggling, as he was, for a vision of peace and sanity amidst war and overwhelming chaos. But first, I want to mention a trivial but steady source of comic frustration I had when I was an active member of this Society. We had a canon of seven authors then; perhaps it is still the same. The 'seven' were Lewis, Tolkien, Williams, Dorothy Sayers, Chesterton, MacDonald, and T. S. Eliot. Eliot?—I always thought. Why Eliot any more than Auden? If this talk has accomplished anything, I hope it has convinced you that Auden is a bit more relevant to this circle of writers than you thought he was before I began. To my mind the idiom of

'Atlantis' (like most of Auden's verse) is more contemporary than Eliot's, let alone that of Tolkien or Lewis, and maybe his air of contemporaneity is one reason why he didn't make the canonical 'seven'. But the Quest is timeless, and its object is the Ancient of Days.

The reader is addressed as one embarking on a journey, setting off for Atlantis. We are exhorted to persevere on the Quest, gaining wisdom and experience as we travel, and to 'Stagger onward rejoicing' in the face of exhaustion, desolation, or despair. If at the end of our journey, we should be 'allowed / Just to peep at Atlantis / In a poetic vision', we are told (in words echoing those of Simeon in Luke's Gospel) that we should

> *Give thanks and lie down in peace,*
> *Having seen your salvation.*
>
> *All the little household gods*
> *Have started crying, but say*
> *Good-bye now, and put to sea.*
> *Farewell, dear friend, farewell: may*
> *Hermes, master of the roads,*
> *And the four dwarf Kabiri,*
> *Protect and serve you always;*
> *And may the Ancient of Days*
> *Provide for all you must do*
> *His invisible guidance,*
> *Lifting up, friend, upon you*
> *The light of His countenance.*[52]

Notes

1. This talk was given on 30 April 1996.
2. W. H. Auden, *Collected Poems*, ed. Edward Mendelson (New York: Random House, 1976), 671.
3. Philosophy, Politics, and Economics.
4. 'Making, Knowing and Judging', in W. H. Auden, *The Dyer's Hand and Other Essays* (London: Faber and Faber, 1963), 41–42; cf. Humphrey Carpenter, *W. H. Auden: A Biography* (Boston: Houghton Mifflin, 1981), 55.
5. See photographs 63 and 64 (pp. 167 and 168), in *W. H. Auden: A Tribute*, ed. Stephen Spender (New York: Macmillan, 1975).
6. Auden, *Collected Poems*, 548.

7. Quoted in Carpenter, *W. H. Auden*, 223–224.

8. See Auden's entry (pp. 32–43) in *Modern Canterbury Pilgrims: The Story of Twenty-three Converts and Why They Chose the Anglican Communion*, ed. James A. Pike (London: Mowbray, 1956), 41.

9. 'Oxford's Beer and Baccy Brigade', in John Carey, *Original Copy: Selected Reviews and Journalism 1969–1986* (London: Faber and Faber, 1987), 193.

10. Auden, *Modern Canterbury Pilgrims*, 41.

11. See Carpenter, *W. H. Auden*, 285.

12. Auden, 'A Thanksgiving', *Collected Poems*, 671.

13. Golo Mann, 'A Memoir', in *W. H. Auden: A Tribute*, 101–102.

14. Auden, 'A Thanksgiving', ll. 13–16.

15. Mann, 'A Memoir', 102. Cf. Auden's account of his return to belief, in *Modern Canterbury Pilgrims* (p. 40): 'Unless one was prepared to take a relativist view that all values are a matter of personal taste, one could hardly avoid asking the question: "If, as I am convinced, the Nazis are wrong and we are right, what is it that validates our values and invalidates theirs?"'

16. See 'George MacDonald', in W. H. Auden, *Forewords and Afterwords*, selected by Edward Mendelson (New York: Vintage Books edition, 1974), 272.

17. Carpenter, *W. H. Auden*, 300.

18. Auden, *Forewords and Afterwords*, 48.

19. C. S. Lewis, *The Problem of Pain* (London: Centenary Press, 1940), 9–10.

20. Auden, *Collected Poems*, 209.

21. Auden, *Collected Poems*, 208–209.

22. Mann continues: 'I have no doubt that his decision was good for him, for his soul, for his way of life, for his work. It also made him even readier to help others, and with a readiness to help which was methodical, slightly severe, and protestant in spirit'; in *W. H. Auden: A Tribute*, 102.

23. See Ursula Niebuhr, 'Memories of the 1940s', in *W. H. Auden: A Tribute*, 108.

24. See C. S. Lewis, *Letters to Malcolm: Chiefly on Prayer* (London: Geoffrey Bles, 1964), 17: 'Cranmer may have his defects as a theologian; as a stylist, he can play all the moderns, and many of his predecessors, off the field'.

25. See Fremantle, 'Reality and Religion', in Mann, *W. H. Auden: A Tribute*, 89. Fremantle refers to a contribution he made to the American edition of *Vogue* magazine, which appeared days after his death in the Autumn of 1973; cf. Edward Mendelson, *Later Auden* (London: Faber and Faber, 1999), 519, 559.

26. Fox, 'Friday Nights', in *W. H. Auden: A Tribute*, 176.

27. See 'Liturgy, Reform of', in W.H. Auden, *A Certain World: A Commonplace Book* (London: Faber and Faber, 1971), 226.

28. See the entry on 'Bishops', in Auden, *A Certain World*, 38.

29. The words are from Lewis's *Letters to Malcolm* (p. 13): 'Thus my whole liturgiological position really boils down to an entreaty for permanence and uniformity. I can make do with almost any kind of service whatever, if only it will stay put'.

30. Carpenter, *W. H. Auden*, 58.
31. Stern, 'The Indispendable Presence', in *W. H. Auden: A Tribute*, 125.
32. Quoted in Lewis, *Surprised by Joy: The Shape of My Early Life* (London: Geoffrey Bles, 1955), 22. The reference is to *Paradise Lost*, Bk V, l. 297.
33. Auden to Anne Fremantle, editor of *The Protestant Mystics*: 'I am not mystical' (*W. H. Auden: A Tribute*, 90). Cf. Lewis in *Letters to Malcolm* (p. 86): 'You and I are people of the foothills . . . I do not attempt the precipices of mysticism'.
34. 'The Protestant Mystics', in Auden, *Forewords and Afterwords*, 69–70.
35. Lewis, *Surprised by Joy*, 23, 22.
36. Richard Davenport-Hines, *Auden* (London: Heinemann, 1995), 133.
37. Carpenter, *W. H. Auden*, 379. For Auden's review, see 'At the End of the Quest, Victory', *New York Times Book Review* (22 January 1956).
38. To Robert H. Boyer (25 August 1971), in *The Letters of J. R. R. Tolkien*, ed. Humphrey Carpenter with the assistance of Christopher Tolkien (Boston: Houghton Mifflin, 1981), 411–412. Tolkien continued, 'I regard him as one of my great friends although we have so seldom met except through letters and gifts of his works' (p. 412).
39. 'Oo, Those Awful Orcs!' (1956), in Edmund Wilson, *The Bit Between My Teeth: A Literary Chronicle of 1950–1965* (London: W. H. Allen [1965]), 326–332, see 329.
40. Auden, 'The Quest Hero', *Texas Quarterly*, vol. 4, no. 4 (Winter 1961), 81–93; quotations here are from the essay as reprinted in *Tolkien and the Critics: Essays on J. R. R. Tolkien's The Lord of the Rings*, ed. Neil D. Isaacs and Rose A. Zimbardo (Notre Dame: University of Notre Dame Press, 1968), 40–61.
41. Carpenter, *W. H. Auden*, 3. The poem is 'Danse Macabre' (1937), in *Collected Poems*, 129–131.
42. See Auden, 'The Quest Hero', 46: 'The youngest son, the weakest, the least clever, the one whom everybody would judge as least likely to succeed, turns out to be the hero when his manifest betters have failed'.
43. See Auden, 'The Quest Hero', *passim*, e.g., 42, 44, 48, 54.
44. Auden, 'The Quest Hero', 52.
45. Auden, 'The Quest Hero', 44.
46. Auden, 'The Quest Hero', 44–45.
47. Auden, 'The Quest Hero', 57–58, 60.
48. Printed in *The Letters of J. R. R. Tolkien*, ed. Carpenter, 238–244.
49. Tolkien, *Letters*, 239.
50. J. R. R. Tolkien, Foreword to *The Fellowship of the Ring*, 2nd ed. (Boston: Houghton Mifflin, 1965), 7.
51. See 'Ode to Terminus' (1968), ll. 24–25, 'A New Year Greeting' (1969), l. 8, and 'The Twelve' (1965), part 1 (Auden, *Collected Poems*, 608, 628, 612).
52. Auden, *Collected Poems*, 245–246. For Simeon's words, see Luke 2:29–31: 'Lord, now lettest thou thy servant depart in peace, according to thy word: for mine eyes have seen thy salvation, which thou hast prepared before the face of all peoples. . . '.

9

The Lewis Diaries: C. S. Lewis and the English Faculty in the 1920s

Tom Shippey

I HAVE BEEN reading Lewis's 1922–1927 diary, *All My Road Before Me*, and I have to confess that I read it with a certain thought in mind, and a certain position to decide.[1] I had been sent it in the page-proof stage, with the suggestion that it should be reviewed for the *London Review of Books*; and it was fairly clear that the intention was to link the diaries with the (then-recent) A. N. Wilson biography of 1990, with its claims of a long-lasting sexual relationship with Mrs Moore, and hints of Lewis as a masochist. So I read the diaries wondering, 'Is this going to be of interest to a large audience? Can I make a scandal out of it?' But my conclusion was, 'No, it's not going to work. If I try to do this, it will be sheer invention.' So I rang up *LRB* and said 'No go'.

The conclusion I drew from the diaries was indeed that Andrew Wilson was quite wrong in his interpretation of Lewis. I don't think anybody could be conducting the kind of relationship Wilson was talking about, and writing up a diary every day, and keep any hint of it out. There would be some trace, and there wasn't. Having considered that, it struck me further that Wilson, like so many biographers of literary people these days, doesn't like writing about books, or at least, not the books their subjects are interested in, and this is a disqualification. If you're writing about people who are interested in books, and you aren't, then there's an evident gap between the two of you. There was therefore room for another kind of biography, which would centre on books.[2] The most interesting thing in this diary (covering 1922–1927) was indeed a bookish matter, namely, Lewis's conversion from doing Classics and Philosophy to doing the School of English and, eventually, in 1925, getting his fellowship in English in Magdalen College. He told us a great deal about that, and what he says about it still has a kind of modern relevance. But I couldn't find anybody saying very much about it, so I thought it was, perhaps, a subject worth consideration partly for its own sake—I think it has an interest in intellectual history—and partly also as a kind of explication of the Lewis biography.

So, that is the subject of my paper, and how I came to it. There was a scandalous interest in the diaries which I decided was not relevant and not there. Instead there was a kind of bookish interest, and now I'm going to talk about that.

This period starts with Lewis doing his exams in Greats and Philosophy, getting through those, finding there was no appropriate fellowship available, and being persuaded to do English Schools in one year, and go on and apply for an English fellowship—something which you couldn't think about doing now, though it seemed quite possible then. Speaking as someone who's been teaching English at universities for about twenty-five years, it strikes me that things were very different then. One thing I noticed straight away was that, although Lewis read every day—and he seems to have read very fast—it was curiously sporadic. If I'd been supervising him, I'd have said 'Don't you think it'd be a good idea to concentrate on a period for a bit, or even an author? Why not read about someone this week and somebody else next week, instead of reading whatever you feel like?' The curious thing is that Lewis had a very good idea of what he ought to read in total, as if someone had given him an approved reading list (which they hadn't). But then he seems to have dotted round: one day he was reading *David Copperfield*, and the same day he's reading Elizabeth Browning's *Sonnets from the Portuguese* (311). He was clearly reading both of them for a purpose, but he wasn't comparing them with each other. It seems rather that he got a pile of books and he picked one up, and he picked another one up, and he read them till he'd finished, and he made notes on them, but he doesn't seem at any point to have been reading in order to write a paper, or reading in a directed kind of way. I do notice that, very early on, he'd got out George Saintsbury's 1898 *Short History of English Literature* and made a table for himself, a list of a couple of hundred major works of English literature chronologically, and he went through checking them off. But he didn't start, as I imagine I would have, at number one, and worked to 200; he picked them out from any point. There's never any suggestion that he was trying to work through an author or a period. Nowadays at Oxford they'd say, 'OK, this year you're going to do the nineteenth century', and give you a list, but Lewis didn't do that kind of thing. He was trying to do what would now be a two- or three-year job in one year. Even so, if I was doing that I'd try to work through it period by period, but he didn't. It is striking that he worked in that different way.

The other thing which comes over is his opinions of the teaching he got, and he approached the whole thing clearly with a prejudice against it. He thought that English was a pretty third-rate School. This was a common opinion, which you can see for instance in Waugh's *Brideshead Revisited*, when the protagonist, who decides to take English, is approached by his cousin, and told that third-rate people do English and he should do something respectable instead. Well, Lewis started off thinking that. He says in 1922, when he's talking to A. J. Carlyle, 'We then discussed my idea of taking English if I do not get the Fellowship. He said I should get private tuition for the Anglo-Saxon. . . . He said he didn't know who my regular tutor would be, but that most of them were "good literary men, you know, but a bit foolish"' (115). Just over the page, Lewis comments on this. He finds himself in the Examination Schools, where lectures are held, having just bought a gown at the extortionate price of 32/6d, and says there was the usual confusion at the Schools, moving from one room to another; 'I had thus plenty of time to feel the atmosphere of the English school which is very different from that at Greats. Women, Indians and Americans predominate, and—I can't say how—one feels a certain amateurishness in the talk and look of the people' (120). That puts them in their place! This is a snobbish reaction: he thinks that moving from *Literae Humaniores* to English is a come-down.

Well, that was his first reaction, but his reactions didn't improve very much. For quite some time, he was obviously rather appalled by what he was asked to do. His tutor in Old English, Betsy Wardale, is mentioned early on: 'Miss W., in her cap and gown, looks a very odd figure: quite a good lecture, but her voice is not strong enough and the strain of listening is tiresome. She drew a distinction between the pessimism of O[ld] E[nglish] literature and the comparative cheerfulness of the Icelandic' (123). As time goes on his comments become both more detailed and more depressing. 'I then bicycled to [St] Margaret's Road and did my tutorial with Miss Wardale. I think this old lady will not be much use: she is too much interested in phonology and theory of language, delightful subjects no doubt, but life is short' (125). Nervousness increases as time goes by: he says 'I cycled to Miss Wardale. She startled me by promising to give me for next week a paper on all the phonetics and laws of mutation wh[ich] she has been talking about and wh[ich] I have not been listening to!' (129). Possibly being irritated by being given this paper, he says a couple of weeks later, 'I went to the library of the English Schools and read Wyld's most elementary book (I forget the title)[3] by way of preparing for Miss Wardale's paper' (130). He then goes off to begin his essay, and says, 'I went to the Schools library. Here I puzzled for the best of two hours over phonetics, back voice stops, glides, glottal catches, and open Lord-knows-whats. Very good stuff in its way, but why physiology should form part of the English school I really don't know' (130). Lewis is still trying, but he always says 'but . . .'. His complaints run on like this, but they run into disaster in the end. Lewis says, when he finally gets to the exams (and this is, of course, a year later, June 1923): 'Began Schools today. Old English in the morning. The translation and literary questions were alright but I could make no serious attempt at the grammar despite all my painful memorising and did the worst paper I have ever done since I came up' (243). He then did the traditional thing by saying the examiners weren't being fair. He went round to Miss Wardale and said something along the lines of 'I wasn't prepared for that question'. 'I saw Miss Wardale and went over my language papers. She thought them "un-expected" and had been making representations to Craigie', who was then the Professor of Anglo-Saxon. 'His question, "Give the definite forms of the adjec-tive" was unintelligible to her' (247). Lewis couldn't have been trying very hard, but I have to say that the question does beat me rather. I think Craigie means the strong adjective, because those are the forms you do not use with the definite article. (If you've got the definite article you don't need the definite form of the adjective as well, so then you use the weak forms.) However, I can see that in an examination the word 'definite' there leaves you thinking, does it mean 'adjectival forms used with the definite article' or 'without the definite article'. At that point you toss up, but what I'd have done is given them both. Lewis found all this troublesome, it worried him from the start, and went right through to what he thought was a disaster at the end. Though it seems, and this is remarkable in itself, as if nobody else could do any better. After all, Lewis got a First, and either he thought he'd made a mess of it and he hadn't, or everybody else did too, as often happens.

The other experience he had—and this I found rather irritating—is that he keeps on talking about H. C. Wyld, mentioned above. Lewis goes to the library and gets Wyld's book out to mug up for Miss Wardale's paper. He re-gards Wyld as the authority. Now, somewhere in my fairly recent travels I have been in a study with somebody, and that somebody pulled off the shelf a copy of one of Wyld's books (his *History of Modern Colloquial English?* his *Short History of English?*—one or the other) and opened it up and showed it to me. It was done with something of a raised eyebrow, so obviously it must have been one of my literary colleagues, saying in effect, 'This guy's on your side [i.e. language not literature], so what have you got to say about this?', and that's the only thing I can remember. But inside the fly-leaf of this book was a long poem in heroic couplets, entirely abusive of Wyld. The whole thing had clearly been written in one of Wyld's lectures, commenting on the lecture as the poem was written, and it was a pretty good poem! What's irritating is that

I've forgotten who it was, and I've been ringing people up and asking if they've got a copy, and would they mind looking in the fly-leaf. They all say it wasn't them, so either I dreamt it all, or it's someone I've forgotten. The point is, I can almost remember the end of the poem. It ends up something like 'That fearful cad and bounder H. C. Wyld'.[4]

This is obviously what Lewis thought, too. Wyld irritated Lewis really badly. He starts off saying things like: 'I went to the lecture by Wyld on the History of the language. He spoke for an hour and told us nothing I haven't known these five years: remarking that language consists of sounds, not letters, and its growth did not depend on conscious changes by individuals, that two and two make four, and other deep truths of that kind' (120). As time goes by it becomes more personal. 6 November 1922: 'In the morning to Wyld's lecture. I was very much impressed by his abuse of the privilege of monologue. He said of a certain word, "Some of you superfine young gentlemen may pronounce it so—if you ever deign to mention such a vulgar thing. I don't care if you do. I pronounce it so." This is not the only occasion on which I have noticed a similar hectoring strain' (133).

Actually, I know the kind of thing Wyld is talking about here; I've heard it mentioned before. There are certain English pronunciations which are shibboleths: You know, Book of Judges, chapter 12—Gileadites and Ephraimites, all confused, coming back through the pass, and the Gileadites set up a block and tell everyone who comes through, 'Say shibboleth'. The Gileadites all say 'shibboleth', and the Ephraimites all say 'sibboleth' and are immediately killed! A 'shibboleth' is a mode of speech which tells you whether somebody is an insider or an outsider. There are many shibboleths in English, and I've been taught most of them at some time or another. A classic one is whether one uses a short or long vowel in words like 'class' and 'bath'. Though there is no mention of it in the little biographical note at the end of the *Diaries*, one of Wyld's books was *The Best English: A Claim for the Superiority of Received Standard English* (1934), and I'm told that Wyld used to argue that the long vowel of Received Standard just *sounded* better: to which the right answer would have been to say, 'So, Professor, English would be a better language if we agreed that the opposite of "thin" was "fart", is that correct?' No doubt no-one would have ventured to do so. Still, that's the kind of thing Wyld was talking about and Lewis objected to: though I do not know what particular deviation from Received Standard might have been heard among 'superfine young gentlemen' in the 1920s. Nowadays, public school boys at Oxford commonly pretend to talk 'Estuary English', deliberately using 'Non-U' forms out of inverted snobbery.

I'd add that the whole idea of 'U' and 'Non-U' forms comes from another professor of English Language, Alan S. C. Ross, who used to be a colleague of mine. I admired him very much because of the money he made out of this kind of thing! He decided he was short of money, he'd got to make some, he'd write a book about—what could he write a book about which would make him a lot of money? Answer: class! So he wrote a book about 'U' and 'Non-U' forms and made a mint. Wyld was doing the same kind of thing, but without Ross's forgivably commercial motive, and Lewis really found this very hard to take. As I've said before, there was a kind of snobbish reaction in Lewis, and he reacted badly to people he regarded as fakes. He thought Wyld was a linguistic fake. He was talking to someone else who agreed with him about Wyld. Wyld, he said, 'had been heard to boast that he enjoyed frightening people at vivas: and at some minor university where he'd been, female candidates usually left in floods of tears. He was, in fact, an ordinary bully, and while professing a purely scientific attitude towards rival pronunciations, he was morbidly class conscious. A snob who liked to picture himself as a country gentleman of the old school and piqued himself on saying "wesskit"' (133). Note that Tolkien's Gaffer Gamgee also says 'wesskit' for 'waistcoat': in English, as has often been noted, old working class and old upper class tend to use the same pronunciation. It is the middle classes who use spelling or foreign pronunciations, like (to give two examples), 'forehead' for 'forrid' and 'garAGE' for 'garridge'.

All this continues to irritate Lewis, and he doesn't leave it at that. After this he always refers to Wyld simply as 'the Cad': 'I set off after breakfast to the Cad's lecture'. Lewis discusses the lecture and again, the thing that strikes him is 'the Cad' 'boasting of his victory in discussion over one unnamed who had lectured somewhere on the pronunciation of English. "I had him in the hollow of my hand", said the Cad' (137). This still goes on over a matter of two weeks. 'After breakfast went to the Schools for the Cad's lecture. He distinguished himself this morning by doing what I've never seen or heard of a lecturer doing. He suddenly turned on a man sitting in the front row, and exclaimed "Do you understand that? Could you give an explanation of that?" The man very naturally made no answer. "H'ngh!", grunted the Cad, "You weren't listening, were you? I'd advise you to listen if I were you". It's really ridiculous how angry this little incident made me for the rest of the day' (139). And it obviously did make him angry. A friend tells him 'this sort of thing was quite common. He once turned upon a girl in the front row who was turning the pages of her notebook, and bellowed "Haven't you found the place yet there? I'm not going to lecture in this Sunday School way". I begin to understand why the Greats School was called *Literae Humaniores*' (139–140). Lewis means that those reading Classics were more humane, i.e. more civilised, than people in the inferior School of English.

As said above, Lewis is doubtful about the utility of what he gets off Betsy Wardale, who is teaching him Old English, and actively dislikes H. C. Wyld, who is teaching him English Language. But there is something more than personal in all this. What I've been talking about are the people who've been teaching Old English and English Language, but actually Lewis thinks that such failings are widespread at Oxford, and not only in the people who are doing English Language but also the people who are doing English Literature. He is now at the Library and is worrying about his phonetics (this damn paper for Betsy Wardale) and trying to master the laws of i-mutation. 'While I was there, a stout youth came in and began to talk to Simpson, who was pasting in book plates at my table'. Simpson, actually, was a don of almost fantastic age—I think he lived to be 97—and he resigned his fellowship in 1936 when he was 71, so at this stage he must have been 57 and still had 40 years to go as the editor of Ben Jonson. Lewis comments, 'the rule of silence apparently does not apply in this library', for the stout youth asked Simpson if Walter Raleigh, the previous professor, 'had not been preparing a book on Chaucer before his death. Simpson said, "No, he funked it. And he was quite right. He'd have been caught out on the scholarship. Now he once suggested to *me* that we might collaborate on a book on Chaucer. I would have done the scholarship and he would have done the appreciation".' Lewis then comments angrily, 'God above! Polonius and Ariel, Wagner and Euphorion would be well mated to this! Simpson droned on beside me till he drove me nearly mad, and I went out and bought pressed beef' (130–131). The thing that stands out here, I think, is the feeling that there is a total split between scholarship and appreciation. You do the scholarship, I'll do the appreciation—they don't of course have any connection with each other. And also, what is the point of scholarship? It's to make certain you can't be 'caught out'. But it doesn't actually teach you anything; it's just a minefield; it's really like the i-mutation in phonetics, which Lewis had been writing this damn paper on.

Lewis, then, gives a very negative view of the Oxford English School—and to be fair to him and the people he's talking about, he does actually remark on his own faults, and the faults of his student colleagues. He says they make a bad audience (and I agree with him there: Oxford audiences are bad audiences). Lewis had been lunching with G. S. Gordon, the Merton Professor of English Literature (which shows Lewis was pretty well-connected), and 'Gordon had been talking about the difference between Oxford and a Scotch audience in a lecture: here we sat looking bored, whether we were or not. There, they stamped with their feet when they were displeased, and loudly applauded every good point. We agreed that the Scotch was the best practice. It would certainly do Simpson [etc.] a lot of good' (131). So Lewis did point out the difficulty of lecturing to people such as himself; but his reactions to the English Faculty remain solidly negative.

As I read through, it amazed me how long all this has lasted. They were still recommending Betsy Wardale's *Chapters on Old English Literature* in my time, forty years later, and Wyld's books as well were still absolute standards (indeed I've still got them). But behind this relatively comic account, I think there is a major intellectual disaster. Something went very badly wrong during this interwar period, and Lewis was confirming it to me. It very much marked his life, and it marked Tolkien's life. Biographers have a habit of underestimating the importance of work. You spend most of your active life working, and once you've done it you may well forget most of it, because it isn't very memorable, it's become a routine. It does, though, mark you more than anything else. People don't like to write about it, and they don't like to write about it in fiction, but though they write much more about what they do in their private lives, they probably put much more emotion into their working lives—more things happen! Greg Benford, in a science fiction novel called *Timescape*, did actually try to discuss what happens in someone's working life. He tried to give an account of a Cambridge PhD viva, and remarked to me (as another academic) that PhD vivas are extremely tense and strained events. Everybody is anxious, not just the candidate, and there are tactics and ebbs and flows, which you must understand—especially if you are a supervisor in a viva and have to try and protect your candidate without appearing to do so. How do you do that? Simple. You ask them a hard question to which you know they know the answer. Then they can take off. But if you do this too often, the other examiners will realize you are shielding your candidate, so you must also give the candidate an occasional one to which he does not know the answer, but where he might make some kind of attempt at it, without looking too rehearsed. We agreed such situations were interesting, but he said 'Try to write that in fiction . . . ?' It's difficult to do because it depends on exact knowledge, which your reader does not share. Benford said he tried to do it in Chapter 20 of his novel—but he conceded that the result was much more boring in fiction than in real life.

My point is that people are very marked by work, but it is very difficult for biographers to write about this because it demands a background of knowledge which is not shared (in Lewis's case, usually a knowledge of particular books and texts). Just the same, can you write a biography whilst ignoring all this? That's what biographers do, but I can't help thinking it's wrong. Biographers of Tolkien and of Lewis write as if the two men didn't spend eight hours a day, five days a week, and a lot more time besides, thinking about work. Now, behind these entries in the diary (and unperceived by A. N. Wilson), there is a major intellectual disaster which Lewis had to live with for forty years, and Tolkien for fifty years, and of which I am sure they were very conscious. That disaster is the separation of language and literature teaching, and the failure of language teaching. This is still a topical subject in Oxford, and they tell me matters are much improved, but I don't believe it. I think we have inherited a failure whose roots are back in Lewis's time. I also think Lewis realized what was going wrong, and it was acute of him to notice it. At an early stage, he is talking to Miss Wardale, who will soon be grimly teaching him phonetics and causing him to ask, 'Why is physiology part of the English school?' But rather before that, I think on their second meeting, he says, 'She spoke of Classical education and said that for us English, who have no grammar of our own, it [Classical education] was a necessary introduction to the study of language.' Lewis comments, 'I thought this perfectly true'—of course he had had an excellent education in Classics—but it's quite as wrong as anything he might have heard from Wyld on pronunciation. Nevertheless, that's the kind of thing that people used to say, and still do say. George Orwell repeats it, more or less, in his astonishingly ill-informed section on 'The English Language' in his essay on 'The English People'. A common view? It couldn't be held by any non-native speaker of English—they know better—but it is widely held by speakers of English, and what we seem to mean by it is that English has no morphology, or very little morphology. It doesn't have word endings. If you're doing Latin or Old English you have to learn the word endings. (That's what Craigie set the question about: 'What are the definite forms of the article?'—word endings.) But modern English has very few word endings and that, to some minds, is grammar; therefore, 'English has no grammar'. That is a major intellectual mistake, but it seems to be being made here by someone who is lecturing on language.

Meanwhile, the thing that gets Lewis down about this, and a further part of the disaster I'm talking about, is the feeling that there are two areas of study. One is phonetics, which is absolutely regular, totally rigorous, and something which must be memorised. The exam is a very difficult memory test. Once you've done the definite forms of the adjective, the examiner is liable to say 'just discuss the changes in forms of Class 2 strong verbs, will you?' (That was indeed a question set in Oxford in my time. I remember standing up at the examiners' meeting and saying, 'That's not a good question, the changing forms of Class 2 strong verbs, there aren't enough of them to make a decent reply!') The question was still set, but none of the two hundred-plus candidates chose to write an answer on it: the whole issue had become ancient lore, set because things like that always were set. Meanwhile the other area of study, over there somewhere far away from the phonetics and the morphology, was literature: wishy-washy stuff, generalisations about pessimism and optimism, themes, riddles, that kind of thing. And in between the two, between the scholarship/phonetics and the appreciation/literature, nothing. That was the major error.

Talking on another occasion about Tolkien, I discussed what he meant by philology, and I pointed out that philology has different meanings in England and America, and different meanings over the years. If you look up 'philology' in the Oxford English Dictionary, you get rather unhelpful entries, and have to look up 'comparative philology' before you realize what they mean. But Tolkien, I'm sure, thought there was an important discipline called philology, which extended over the whole linguistic sphere, and furthermore was a vital part of literary appreciation. But he couldn't persuade anybody to take that broad view of philology, nor could he persuade people to take a broader and more realistic view of grammar. Wyld's *Growth of English*, Wardale's *Old English Grammar*—these are all phonetics and morphology, with a little bit of syntax thrown in. Apart from that, nothing except the enormous expanse of 'literature', which is regarded as not rule-bound and largely inscrutable to analysis. Quite different subjects, no connection between them, you do this one, then you do that one, there is no way you can put them together. I repeat that the disaster was that philology remained, for most of its teachers and its students, stuck at the level of phonetics. It refused the challenge of looking at grammar, of taking a wider view of language and extending that to literary appreciation. Philology lost the middle ground. In Lewis's time it had already lost it: Lewis already perceived it as a split Faculty, and the split has never been healed. It goes on, in a way, into the present day, though many things have changed—notably, the defeat of the language side and a near-100 percent takeover by the literary critics. The disaster stayed with Tolkien and Lewis from the 1920s till they died, and I am sure they were both extremely conscious of it and extremely depressed about it one way or another. It's something they spent their career lives fighting against, but they were not successful.

Some of this shows up here and there in what Lewis says, and in some of his more positive remarks about the English Faculty, but you have to comb through to find them. There's just the odd remark of 'that was a good lecture, and that was the way that you ought to do it'. For instance, he once mentions Professor Onions, one of the lexicographers on the Oxford English Dictionary: 'I went to school at 10 o'clock to hear Onions on Middle English. . . . Onions gave a delightful lecture, the best part being the quotations which he does inimitably. Once he repeated nearly a whole poem with much relish, and then observed "That wasn't what I meant to say". A man after my own heart' (184). I'd add that Onions, like Tolkien, was another Brummy and had, they've told me at Oxford, an extremely thick Birmingham accent, so he had not done what Wyld did, which was to promote himself up the social ladder. In fact, the one thing I can remember about Onions—and this is pure oral memory—is that he never talked about the main road, he always called it the 'orse road', i.e. the opposite of the pavement, and he continued to say this long after everyone else had dropped the phrase. Anyway, Onions repeated the whole poem just because he liked it, and Lewis instantly appreciates that and picks it out, but it doesn't happen very often. In another example, he comments on Nevill Coghill with some appreciation: 'he seems an enthusiastic, sensible man without nonsense, and a gentleman, much more attractive than the majority' (189). Lewis still feels the English Faculty, on the whole, are not gentlemen, they're of a lower social class.

Another thing I picked out which is more difficult to interpret is that in the background of all this there is the madness of his lodger, Dr Askins (Mrs Moore's brother), who is going crazy, Lewis thinks—though he later retracts the suspicion (207)—as a result of syphilis. Askins is ranting on all the time about having deserted a woman whom he got pregnant, and who wrote to him for assistance, only for him to turn his back on her. Lewis is very offended at this and thinks this is the action of a cad, rather like Wyld but sexual rather than verbal, so to speak. And then somebody tells him that the woman was a common prostitute, and Lewis seems relieved to hear it. Meanwhile, Askins himself is going mad, having delusions of hell fire, and Lewis is trying to talk him out of it. He reports that '[a]bout an hour later we were hauled up again. Mary said the dope had apparently had no effect. After another ghastly struggle . . . we got him to take a second dose. In bed again about six. The light was coming in at my window and a lot of birds were singing—sane, clean, comfortable things.'[5] Then he gets up in the morning and tends to the patient. 'Afterwards I did the *Bruce* passage in Sisam—good, honest stuff' (216). I suggest that at this stage Lewis is using his course therapeutically. Notice the way he talks about things which are the opposite of madness and sexual horror. He is withdrawing from the horrors of the night and into books, and the books he likes are those that do not present this kind of struggle or torment of doubt to him—in this case, Barbour's fourteenth-century heroic poem about the deeds of Robert the Bruce. He likes that because it is a withdrawal from what has been going on in his own life.

There is, then, a drive in Lewis towards some forms of literature, even Middle English literature, but I'm not really clear what Lewis's selections were based on. He's certainly not getting any guidance from the Faculty, it's something he has to work out for himself. What I'm suggesting is that Lewis was trying to invent a subject for himself, and that's where, in fact, his later career went. He wrote on areas which he thought other people weren't doing. He was trying to combine the study of language and literature. He was trying to write in a literary way about matters normally regarded as not the business of the literary people, about materials which you had to do the language course to understand. He worked that out for himself and very successful it was, but he was trying to fill a gap, and succeeding by personal effort—as did Tolkien in his own private and personal way. But the fear they had was that they did this by their own efforts and without official backing, and so in a way without future success. As teachers and then professors, they filled in an academic gap. But then they died, and the matter was once again dropped, and the gap is still there.

How did the gap seem to Lewis in, say, 1925? In 1925, he actually got the Fellowship at Magdalen, and the way he saw it and puts it is that on one side you've got people like Wyld, pedants, the kind of people who give pedantry a bad name. And on the other side there are people he dislikes just as much, people he regards as Sitwellites, people who are affected, purely literary, who have no interest in rigorous study, and who are usually monoglots, having no interest in a language other than their own. He resents them intellectually, and also I think socially. That's the choice he seemed to have in front of him, but he refused the choice and tried to do something down the middle, which was non-official and non-institutional. I think this struggle has never been resolved, and to me, the weak spot was abandoning grammar. Phonetics is not a subject which leads you on to the study of literature, nor is morphology, though it may be necessary. A subject which does lead you on from language studies to the study of literature is grammar. If you understand grammar, you can then comment on how sentences and paragraphs are laid out, and you can go on into the study of style and the means of expression. It wasn't a subject within English Studies then, and it isn't now. There is indeed a science of 'stylistics' now, but that's a relatively modern invention which, once again, hasn't caught on. This struggle has never been resolved, but it's a subject which Lewis and Tolkien spent their lives on. It's still a topical subject. You have furious partisans on one side or the other, and both positions are not really very attractive or sensible.

Partisanship, furthermore, doesn't do people much good. If you spend all your life fighting for your side, you end up lacking in candour and lacking in depth. Both Tolkien and Lewis were mixed up in this, and if one did an intellectual biography of this, my impression is that one would see that they took turns. Sometimes Lewis would be saying 'let's try and get on with these people' and Tolkien would be saying 'no no, let's try and destroy them all'. Then Tolkien would say 'I'm tired of this, let's try and get on with them, give the guy doing the syllabus a ring', and Lewis would say 'no, I'm fed up with this, I'm not going to co-operate with them at all'. I think that happened over decades during their joint existence. There was certainly one point, I think, in 1934, when Tolkien wrote his piece on the English School, in which he was trying to propose some kind of armistice, and Lewis said 'no, we don't want an armistice, forget it'. Later on it was a different matter, I think, for Tolkien had become a hardliner and Lewis was saying, 'I've had enough of this, I'm going to Cambridge', which of course he did. I can't help thinking they were both embroiled in a struggle which didn't do either of them any good, which wasted a great deal of time and ended in failure.

How does it show up in Lewis's work? Well, I think Lewis had what we would now call a judgemental streak. It shows up in the diaries. He's very quick to label people as 'the Cad' or 'the Bitch' or 'the Beast' (Mrs Moore's husband), and having made an enemy he likes to keep it up. He doesn't like to lose enemies just like that, and is capable of keeping up a grudge. But, as happens with partisans, this was reciprocated. Wilson says that Lewis was deeply unpopular at Oxford and that there were many people who disliked him very much, quoting one elderly don at Magdalen—he doesn't say who it was—who says Lewis was the most evil man he'd ever met. Why? I don't know. Quite possibly it was the feeling that Lewis was denying Faculty boundaries. Along with that, he may have been felt to be disloyal to his own School. One remark he made which is often quoted was that there are 'three kinds of people: the literate, the illiterate, and the B-Litterate'. It's an in-joke about the strange and anomalous Oxford B.Litt. degree (a Bachelor's degree, but only taken by graduate students), which Lewis obviously felt was a waste of time, but which even in the 1970s was regarded as one of the glories of the Faculty. Cracks like that, and if Lewis thought of a joke he was not one to keep it to himself, made him unpopular within his own small world.

Another factor is that the account in *That Hideous Strength* of university life is seriously wounding. Lewis presents college life as a series of interlocking cliques with an outer and an inner circle, and then an inner inner circle, but you can see that he's describing it from life. Faculty life, as he sees it, contains too many bitter, stupid, pointless, trivial, immediately forgettable wrangles in which you waste your energy and your spirit. That's what's happening to Mark Studdock (who is turning into a wraith) until events drag him out of it. If nothing else, partisanship wasted a lot of Lewis's and Tolkien's time, and it meant, I fear, that they were unable to leave any institutional mark. They left, of course, a very deeply personal mark which they weren't expected or supposed to, and which has, further, not contributed to their Oxford popularity. It's very embarrassing when you've been patronising someone for donkey's years to discover they're the most popular writer of the century, and them having loads of money doesn't help! So the matter isn't yet dead, and in a minor way the saga or vendetta continues. I repeat that though Lewis and Tolkien left deep personal marks, through their off-campus writing, they didn't leave institutional marks. What they stood for, what they believed in, was not taken up, it was dropped, and not much progress was made from the state of affairs in 1922. The idea of a language/literature split has remained very powerful.

So how do you react to this kind of thing? Well, you withdraw, don't you? If you can't get on in your job, then you mark time and you drift off. In a sense, both Lewis and Tolkien did that. Tolkien retired within himself to write his books (unknown to his colleagues, and still very largely not appreciated by them), and Lewis went off to Cambridge where he thought he'd find a better audience—which, as it happens, included me. His series of lectures on Spenser—were they late 1962 or early 1963?—was the best-delivered course of lectures I'd ever heard. I hardly needed to take any notes (though I did), because I could have written out what he said from memory, he said it so clearly. That set of lectures did come out as a book posthumously, *Spenser's Images of Life* (1967), reconstructed from Lewis's notes by Alistair Fowler, but I'm sure the book could have been quite adequately reconstructed from my notes as well. And not only was the delivery outstanding (though the lectures were given sitting down, because Lewis said he wasn't strong enough to deliver standing), the content was genuinely helpful as well: no trace of grandstanding, just a conscientious desire to help undergraduates with a difficult topic. So I'm personally grateful for Lewis's move to Cambridge. But just the same, both Lewis and Tolkien, I believe, saw the split I've been talking about, tried to patch it up, weren't successful, were punished for it institutionally, and drifted off. That's the way I see their intellectual biography, and you can see the start of it in Lewis's diaries from 1922 to 1927, where, as I've been saying, he reacted badly to the Oxford English syllabus and Faculty, and in my opinion justifiably.

The last thing I will say is that reading his diaries has explained some things to me because, although I admire Lewis and Tolkien very much, there are times when both of them get on my nerves. Why was Lewis in particular so sharp-edged? Now I realize it's because they had to live through this kind of thing; they were really emotionally challenged. And that emotion was a professional emotion, a work emotion, and those are acute, bitter, and difficult for outsiders to understand. They realized they were not winning the argument, they were losing it, and would not hand on what they believed in to the next generation. They were being shoved out. If there was an element of obsession in them, it came as a result of this experience. One thing I do feel sure about is that they may not have managed to leave a direct intellectual succession, but they did deserve to. English studies in universities have been the poorer for allowing their legacy to be inherited off-campus.

Notes

1. This talk was given on 8 November 1991.
2. Author's note: Now, in 2014, we are a lot better served, especially by Michael Ward, *Planet Narnia* (New York: Oxford University Press, 2008), *The Cambridge Companion to C. S. Lewis,* ed. Robert MacSwain and Michael Ward (Cambridge: Cambridge University Press, 2010), and Alister McGrath, *C. S.Lewis: A Life* (Carol Stream, IL: Tyndale House Publishers, 2012—though there is still more to be said.
3. Author's note: It could have been one of several, all very much the same: *The Growth of English* (1907), *The Historical Study of the Mother Tongue: An Introduction to Philological Method* (1907), *A Short History of English* (1914), or *A History of Modern Colloquial English* (1920), and see comment below on *The Best English* (1934).
4. Author's note: The poem was, as I recall, so witty, and so metrically skilful, that now (in 2014) I wonder uneasily whether Lewis might have written it. Alas, neither memory nor inquiry have served to trace it.
5. Author's note: This is, incidentally, a very literary reaction. Sir Lancelot is similarly comforted by birdsong when in the depth of despair—but only in Sir Thomas Malory's English *Morte D'Arthur*, not in the otherwise very similar French source of the passage.

10

It All Began with a Picture: The Making of C. S. Lewis's Chronicles of Narnia

Walter Hooper

HERE IS ONE of the most arresting sentences C. S. Lewis ever wrote: 'At every tick of the clock, in every inhabited part of the world, an unimaginable richness and variety of "history" falls off the world into total oblivion.'[1] This comes from Lewis's essay on 'Historicism', in which he argues against the attempt to discover the finger of God in those very few fragments of history that had survived. 'Is there a discovered law', he asked, 'by which important manuscripts survive and unimportant perish? Do you ever turn out an old drawer . . . without wondering at the survival of trivial documents and the disappearance of those which everyone would have thought worth preservation?'

But I mustn't sound too pessimistic, standing as I am only a short distance from the Bodleian Library's fine repository of C. S. Lewis letters and papers, none of which is trivial. Even so, my theories about the Origins of Narnia have depended almost entirely on what has come to light when a few old drawers have been turned out. Here is what I mean. What I take to be the oldest Narnian fragment consists of four sentences scribbled on the back of the manuscript of *The Dark Tower*, which incomplete story was going to be a sequel to *Out of the Silent Planet* and was most likely written in 1939. Lewis never wasted paper, and used the surface of any piece of paper that was handy. I think we may conclude that after abandoning *The Dark Tower*, the back of the manuscript was used for whatever ideas came to Lewis at the beginning of World War II.

The governments of Europe had been watching with horror the rise of Adolf Hitler, and Britain and France did all they could to appease German territorial demands. But when the Germans marched into Poland on 1 September

1939, Lewis's brother, Warnie, was called back into service, and England prepared for battle. On the 2nd of September thousands of children from schools in and around London were sent out of that great city. Many were sent to Oxford, and four young girls from London arrived at the home of C. S. Lewis and his friend, Mrs Moore. 'Our schoolgirls have arrived', Jack Lewis wrote to Warnie on 2 September, 'and all seem to me . . . to be very nice, unaffected creatures and all most flatteringly delighted with their new surroundings.'[2] Lewis wrote to his brother every week, and every letter contained news of the children. They were not always the same, but some left as others arrived. There is not one sour note from Lewis about the children. In fact, one gets the impression that he enjoyed their company. It therefore does not seem unlikely that those four sentences I mentioned earlier were written when some of the children were staying at The Kilns. Those sentences are:

> This book is about four children whose names were Ann, Martin, Rose and Peter. But it is most about Peter who was the youngest. They all had to go away from London suddenly because of Air Raids, and because Father, who was in the Army, had gone off to the War and Mother was doing some kind of war work. They were sent to stay with a kind of relation of Mother's who was a very old Professor who lived all by himself in the country.[3]

Three of the children's names were changed, but the resemblance of this fragment to the opening paragraph of *The Lion, the Witch and the Wardrobe* is obvious. Did he write any more at that time? When Roger Lancelyn Green and I were working on our biography of Lewis in the early 1970s we assumed that Lewis abandoned whatever plans he had for a children's story at the beginning of the war. The next piece of evidence about *The Lion* that we knew anything about came in Chad Walsh's *C. S. Lewis: Apostle to the Skeptics* (1949). Walsh visited Lewis in the summer of 1948, and in a passage about what he was doing at that time, he said Lewis 'talks vaguely of completing a children's book which he has begun "in the tradition of E. Nesbit".'[4] I was led to imagine that Lewis had started *The Lion, the Witch and the Wardrobe* in 1939, stopped, and then started again in 1948. However, a few years after that connection was made, the Wade Center came into possession of two letters to Mr and Mrs E. L. Baxter of Kentucky. In one, dated 10 September 1947, Lewis said: 'Don't the ordinary fairy tales really already contain most of the Spirit, in solution? . . . is not Redemption figured in *The Sleeping Beauty*? . . . what about Geo. MacDonald's *The Princess & the Goblins* [sic], *Curdie & the Princess*, *The Wise Woman*, and *The Golden Key*? . . . I have tried one myself but it was, by the unanimous verdict of my friends, so bad that I destroyed it.'[5]

My first guess was that Lewis completed the story he started in 1939, read it to the Inklings, decided it was no good, and destroyed it. But the fact that Roger and I were so quick to assume the 1939 beginning was the same story Chad Walsh mentioned swore me off such 'Historicism'. Far too much of the 'unimaginable richness and variety of "history"' has fallen off the earth to allow for anything except fairly wild, improbable, guesses.

Let us begin instead with the events just preceding what we know about *The Lion, the Witch and the Wardrobe*. By the time Chad Walsh's book was published in 1949, Lewis's home-life was in crisis. Some of you will know that when he went to war in 1917 he promised his friend, Paddy Moore, that if he died he—Lewis—would look after his mother. Mrs Moore had been his daily care since 1919, and by 1949 she was elderly and an invalid. Lewis spent nearly every available minute at home looking after the woman he now called his 'mother'. Mrs Moore's goddaughter, Vera Henry, was also there helping to look after her. Friction between them broke out into open quarrels, and Lewis had to act as peacemaker.

Meanwhile, his friend Don Giovanni Calabria of Verona pressed Lewis to continue his apostolate of writing. Lewis replied on 14 January 1949, the exhaustion and a sense of futility showing through. 'As for my own work', he told Don Giovanni,

> I would not wish to deceive you with vain hope. I am now in my fiftieth year. I feel my zeal for writing, and whatever talent I originally possessed, to be decreasing; nor (I believe) do I please my readers as I used to. I labour under many difficulties. My house is unquiet and devastated by women's quarrels. . . . My aged mother, worn out by long infirmity, is my daily care. Pray for me, Father, that I ever bear in mind that profoundly true maxim: 'if you wish to bring others to peace, keep thyself in peace'.[6]

Besides caring for Mrs Moore, Lewis was worried about his beloved brother, Warnie, who in February 1949 had trouble with alcoholism and was in hospital for several weeks. It was almost certainly at about this time, when Lewis's spirits were very low, that he began dreaming of lions. 'All seven of my Narnia books and my three science fiction books', he said,

> began with seeing pictures in my head. At first they were not a story, just pictures. The *Lion* all began with a picture of a faun carrying an

umbrella and parcels in a snowy wood. This picture had been in my head since I was about sixteen. Then one day, when I was about forty, I said to myself: 'Let's try to make a story about it'. At first I had very little idea how the story would go. But then suddenly Aslan came bounding into it. I think I had been having a good many dreams of lions about that time. Apart from that, I don't know where the Lion came from or why he came. But once He was there He pulled the whole story together, and soon He pulled the six other Narnia stories in after him.[7]

Lewis possibly dreamed about Aslan in February, when things seemed almost as bad as they could get. His young friend, Roger Lancelyn Green, who came to know Lewis when he attended his lectures, was living in Oxford and was just beginning to devote himself to writing about children's literature. He dined with Lewis at Magdalen College on the 10th of March 1949, and after dinner they went to Lewis's rooms where he read aloud the first two chapters of *The Lion, the Witch and the Wardrobe*. Lewis had not finished the story, but Roger remembered thinking that 'he was listening to a book that could rank with the great ones of its kind.'[8]

Lewis was finding his way into a completely new world. He always wrote with an old-fashioned nib pen which you nip into an ink well about every half-dozen words. This suited him perfectly. He loved the wetness of ink and the scratch of the pen across the paper. He told me that in writing he always 'whispered the words aloud' because 'it is as important to please the ear as it is the eye'. I think he must have remained at his desk for long periods because when he saw Roger Lancelyn Green again at the end of March 1949 he had finished *The Lion, the Witch and the Wardrobe*. Roger said he protested that Lewis had brought Father Christmas into the tale, for he felt his presence broke the spell. But Lewis felt he should be there. Lewis nearly always had a tussle with his publishers and friends over the titles to his books, but Lewis never called this story anything but the famous title it bears today, *The Lion, the Witch and the Wardrobe*.

The first time Lewis mentioned the story to Roger, he said he'd read the story to Tolkien, who disliked it intensely. Roger ran into Tolkien shortly afterwards who remarked: 'I hear you've been reading Jack's children's story', said Tolkien. 'It really won't do, you know! I mean to say: "*Nymphs and their Ways, The Love-Life of a Faun*". Doesn't he know what he's talking about?'[9]

You must not be upset by this. Tolkien didn't like a lot of things! Only a man of very singular tastes could have given us such a great work as *The Lord of the Rings*. Besides the fact that none of the Inklings had literary tastes as vast as that of C. S. Lewis, Tolkien did not like mixing various mythologies, and he was unhappy with Lewis's theological audacities. He told me that his main objection to the Narnian stories was that the Christian elements were 'too obvious'. I should point out that, despite the fact that Tolkien didn't like the Narnian stories, he did not think they should be off-limits to everyone else. Mrs Tolkien sent copies of the stories to their grandson.

Before going on to discuss the other six Narnian stories, I feel compelled to bring in something that has been growing in my mind for the last dozen or so years. When I was editing Lewis's diary covering the years 1922–1927, one thing seemed to me more and more obvious. Lewis had always been brilliant, as an atheist as well as a Christian. Before his conversion he could write well, and he was more ambitious than at any time in his life. But apart from two—his early volumes of verse—nothing happened. I believe the whole thing can be summed up in five words: *Lewis had nothing to say*. It really does appear that when Lewis cared more about God than being a writer, God *gave* him things to say. I use the word 'gave' advisedly, but I think God *gave* Lewis and Tolkien—sub-creators both—the books we love so much. If I seem to be claiming too much, let me say that I meant the same thing Lewis meant and said in a letter to Professor Clyde Kilby: 'If every good and perfect gift', Lewis said, 'comes from the Father of Lights[10] then all true and edifying writings, whether in Scripture or not, must be *in some sense* inspired.'[11]

I think this is borne out by some of the comments he made shortly after the publication of *The Lion, the Witch and the Wardrobe*. 'In a certain sense', he said,

I have never exactly 'made' a story. With me the process is much more like bird-watching than like either talking or building. I see pictures. Some of these pictures have a common flavour, almost a common smell, which groups them together. Keep quiet and watch and they will begin joining themselves up. . . . But more often . . . there are gaps. Then at last you have to do some deliberate inventing, have to contrive reasons why these characters should be in these various places doing these various things.[12]

While the first Chronicle of Narnia seemed to pour straight from Lewis's pen without interruption, he found a problem awaiting him in the next story, one which involved 'deliberate inventing'. As Lewis told Roger Lancelyn Green, he wanted to discover what had gone before the Pevensie children met the White Witch, and how the lamp-post came to be standing on the edge of Narnia.

So Lewis began a story about a boy, Digory, who could understand what the trees and animals said. However, when he cut off a branch from the oak tree to help Polly, the girl next door, in the building of a raft, he became deaf to the trees and animals, and they to him. Digory is grieved when he finds that, because of this violation, he has lost the gift to understand the rest of creation. At this point he has a visit from his elderly godmother, Mrs Lefay, who is obviously endowed with strange powers. She is a grumpy but delightful old lady who, looking closely at Digory says: 'You look exactly like what Adam must have looked five minutes after he'd been turned out of the Garden of Eden.'[13]

Sadly, none of the complete manuscripts of the Narnian stories have survived. During the three months I was with him in 1963, I asked Lewis what he did with his manuscripts. You can imagine how my heart sank when he said, 'After writing a book, I turn the manuscript over and write another work on the other side. I then throw it away.'

Perhaps, after all, the finger of God *was* at work because various Narnian bits and pieces escaped 'falling off the world into total oblivion'. The longest is 'The Lefay Fragment' which is published with the other Narnian fragments in a little book called *Past Watchful Dragons*. In June 1949 Lewis read 'The Lefay Fragment' to Roger Lancelyn Green, who was afraid Mrs Lefay, as a character, was wrong for what Lewis had in mind. Lewis agreed, and that story—which would eventually become *The Magician's Nephew*—was set aside.

But Narnian pictures kept coming. When Lewis wrote to his American friend, Vera Mathews, on 17 September 1949, Lewis told her that 'a good idea for a (children's) story . . . arrived this morning'[14]—in other words, the idea for *Prince Caspian*. When you read the final volume of Lewis's *Collected Letters* you will be surprised at how many titles Lewis and his friends had to consider— *Drawn into Narnia, A Horn in Narnian* amongst them—before they settled on *Prince Caspian*. Lewis knew exactly how this story should go, and it was completed by December 1949, when he asked Roger Lancelyn Green to read it.

Roger brought his report along to Magdalen College on 31 December when Lewis had a luncheon party to meet Pauline Baynes, who had illustrated the first story and was to do the others as well. You could hardly imagine anyone as humble as this twenty-two-year-old woman. She'd come to Lewis's attention through the illustrations to Tolkien's *Farmer Giles of Ham* (1948). Things had been moving fast. Lewis signed a contract for *The Lion, the Witch and the Wardrobe* with the publisher, Geoffrey Bles, on 18 August 1949. Bles got in touch with Miss Baynes, and her illustrations were completed by the middle of December. And so when she met Lewis for the first time at Magdalen on 31 December it was because he wanted to thank her personally. One of the things he loved in her illustrations was 'the wealth of vigorous detail',[15] and he looked forward to their collaboration on the other stories. Pauline told me later that 'all I could think of was whether I was saying and doing the right thing' and that 'I distinctly remember him picking the chestnuts out of the Brussels sprouts with his fingers and saying it was a pity to waste them at the end of the Magdalen lunch!'[16]

I doubt if Pauline Baynes told Lewis of her first reaction to *The Lion, the Witch and the Wardrobe*, but she told me, and before I mention it I think I should first say a few words about what Lewis and Tolkien meant by imagination. By this time Lewis had made Tolkien's theory of 'sub-creation' his own, and he made a clear distinction between Fantasy and Imagination. He believed that Fantasy, or wish-fulfillment, when directed onto something which purports to be 'real life' is compensatory, and 'we run to it from the disappointments and humiliations of the real world: it sends us back to the real world undivinely discontented. For it is all flattery to the ego.'[17] *Imagination*, on the other hand, takes us right out of ourselves—to Middle-earth, to Malacandra, to Narnia. It is an *addition to life*, and affords a view of reality from many angles.

Along with this we should consider this passage from another of Lewis's essays. 'Why', he asked,

> did one find it so hard to feel as one was told one ought to feel about God or about the sufferings of Christ? I thought the chief reason was that one was told one ought to. An obligation to feel can freeze feelings. And reverence itself did harm. The whole subject was associated with lowered voices; almost as if it were something medical. But supposing that by casting all these things into an imaginary world, stripping them, of their stained-glass and Sunday school associations, one could make them for the first time appear in their real potency? Could one not thus steal past those watchful dragons?[18]

Lewis could have Pauline Baynes in mind. She told me that while drawing the picture of Aslan enduring all the 'awfulnesses' at the hands of the White Witch and her dreadful creatures, she was crying all the time, 'How could they *do* this to Him?' It was difficult to draw these things when it was breaking her heart and tears were falling on the picture. Pauline said that it was after she posted the illustrations of *The Lion, the Witch and the Wardrobe* to Geoffrey Bles that the truth struck her. Now she knew why she was crying for Aslan: she was weeping for the Crucified Christ.

By the end of February 1950, *Prince Caspian* was in typescript and the manuscript of the third story, *The Voyage of the 'Dawn Treader'* was ready for

Roger Lancelyn Green to read. Lewis also asked the children of his friend Frederick Lawson, Professor of Comparative Law, to read *Prince Caspian*. They were very enthusiastic about it.

At the end of March 1950, illustrations for *The Lion* were coming in and being discussed at the Tuesday morning Inklings meetings. Roger Lancelyn Green was in the Bird and Baby pub on the 22nd of June when proofs of *The Lion, the Witch and the Wardrobe* were being handed round and read by the Inklings. The next month Roger spent most of one day reading what he thought the most enthralling story of the four he had so far seen—*To Narnia and the North*, finally called *The Horse and His Boy*.

It was after reading the first part of *The Horse and His Boy* in manuscript that Lewis was to see less of his best critic. Roger Lancelyn Green had to leave Oxford and move up to Cheshire to take over the running of an estate that had been in his family for a thousand years. His weekly meetings with Lewis came to an end, but he visited him every term, and when he was staying with Lewis in November 1950 he read part of the manuscript of what was then called *Night Under Narnia*, and which became *The Silver Chair*. When Roger was back in Oxford again in March 1951 he finished reading *The Silver Chair*. In case you are confused, while *The Silver Chair* was the fifth story to be written, it was the fourth to be published.

Although nothing can persuade me that *The Lion, the Witch and the Wardrobe* is not the best of the seven, I am one of the many readers charmed by Puddleglum in *The Silver Chair*. I came to know Lewis's gardener, Fred Paxford, the first time I visited The Kilns, and when I moved in for a while as Lewis's secretary, I saw a good deal of him. Although Lewis did not usually enjoy talking about his own works, he made a big exception with the Narnian stories. It was not, however, like an admirer talking to an author about his work, but two admirers talking about something both liked. I said Puddleglum was my favourite character. 'Mine, too', said Lewis, and this led to him telling me what I should have guessed—Puddleglum was modelled on Paxford. By this time I had come to know his Puddleglumish character. If you thought the sun would come out, he was sure it would rain. It you thought it was going to be warm, he was sure it would be cold. At the same time, he seemed one of those rare beings that, for all his gloomy outside, believed in his heart that things would turn out right. I didn't need to know him a long time to realize that he was one of the most generous and unselfish men I've ever met. If I were God, I would want him near me.

As far as I could tell, Paxford almost never went anywhere—except to do the shopping. This was a pity. So far as I could see the only Christian doctrine he was certain of was the Second Coming. This explained why there was always so little tea, coffee, sugar, and most other things in the house. 'What would we do', he asked, 'with all those things if the World comes to an end? We don't want a lot of extra *sugar* on our hands!'

But Lewis's example of Paxford's Puddleglumish character says even more about the man. He told me that Joy's great ambition was to go to Greece, and before they realized that her cancer had returned, Roger Lancelyn Green and his wife June had urged them to join them in a trip to Greece. However, by the time of the trip, April 1960, Joy's cancer had returned, and Lewis was very apprehensive about the trip. He told me that he and Joy were in the taxi, about to leave for the airport to fly to Greece, when Paxford came to see them off. Leaning through the window of the car, he said, 'Well, Mr Jack, there was this bloke just going on over the wireless. Says an airplane just went down. Everyone killed—burnt beyond recognition. Did you hear what I said Mr Jack?—*burnt beyond recognition!*' 'And on that note', said Lewis, 'we flew to Greece.'

There is hardly a page of the Chronicles in which some incident does not have behind it a profound truth. I am thinking of that great scene in *The Silver Chair* when Puddleglum, Prince Rilian, and the children are the prisoners in the Underworld kingdom of the Witch. She has used every artifice in her power to persuade them that they have dreamed up Aslan, and even the world outside. Fighting the enchantment, they do their best to recall the world above, the sun, and Aslan. 'There never was such a world', the Witch says, strumming on her musical instrument.

> You have seen lamps, and so you imagined a bigger and better lamp and called it the *sun*. You've seen cats, and now you want a bigger and better cat, and it's to be called a *lion*. Well, 'tis a pretty make-believe, though, to say truth, it would suit you all better if you were younger. And look how you can put nothing into your make-believe without copying it from the real world, this world of mine, which is the only world.[19]

The sweet, heavy smell of the enchantment grows stronger. 'Thrum, thrum, thrum'. Then at great pain to himself, Puddleglum stamps out the fire and says with a clear head:

> Suppose we *have* only dreamed, or made up, all those things—trees and grass and sun and moon and stars and Aslan himself. Suppose we have. Then all I can say is that, in that case, the made-up things seem a good deal more important than the real ones. Suppose this black pit

of a kingdom of yours *is* the only world. Well, it strikes me as a pretty
poor one. And that's a funny thing, when you come to think of it. We're
just babies making up a game, if you're right. But four babies playing
a game can make a play-world which licks your real world hollow.
That's why I'm going to stand by the play-world. I'm on Aslan's side
even if there isn't any Aslan to lead it. I'm going to live as like a Narnian as I can even if there isn't any Narnia. So, thanking you kindly for
our supper, if these two gentlemen and the young lady are ready, we're
leaving your court at once and setting out in the dark to spend our lives
looking for Overland. Not that our lives will be very long, I should
think; but that's a small loss if the world's as dull a place as you say.[20]

In 1963 Nancy Warner, mother of Lewis's pupil, Francis Warner, mentioned to Lewis that one of her sons, a philosopher, had remarked on Lewis's
use of the 'Ontological Proof' or Argument in *The Silver Chair*. Lewis said in
reply: 'I suppose your philosopher son[21] . . . means the chapter in which Puddleglum puts out the fire with his foot. He must thank Anselm and Descartes
for it, not me. I have simply put the "Ontological Proof" in a form suitable for
children. And even that is not so remarkable a feat as you might think. You
can get into children's heads a good deal which is quite beyond the Bishop of
Woolwich.'[22]

The philosophers here will explain this better than I, but simply put, the
'Ontological Proof' or 'Ontological Argument' comes originally from the *Pro-
slogion* of St Anselm of Canterbury (1033–1109) and can be formulated as
follows: (1) 'God' is the greatest being which can be thought. (2) It is greater
to exist in reality *and* in thought than in thought alone. (3) Therefore, 'God'
exists in reality *and* in thought. Lewis has Puddleglum use this Proof or Argument in the passage I quoted above from *The Silver Chair*. What a tribute to
Paxford. When I mentioned that Lewis had made him a character in one of
his stories, he said, 'Well, Sir, I reckon Mr Jack will lose money on *that* book!'

After the publishers decided to publish *The Silver Chair* fourth, they returned to *The Horse and His Boy*. Again, it took a long time to find a title for
what Lewis had originally called *Narnia and the North* and half a dozen other
names before the matter was settled.

Meanwhile, Lewis was turning back towards the story he intended should
follow *The Lion*, and which would describe the beginnings of Narnia—why
the lamp-post stood in 'Lantern Waste', and how the White Witch came to be
there. Starting again on *The Magician's Nephew*, and using only the names
Digory and Polly from 'The Lefay Fragment', he began writing. When Roger
Lancelyn Green went to stay with him at the end of May 1951, he found that

half of the new story was written. When Roger was in Oxford at the end of October he found Lewis had written three-quarters of it.

According to Roger, Lewis had decided to make the first humans in Narnia a countryman, Piers, and his wife from the dying world of Charn. Piers was based on Piers Plowman from Langland's Middle English poem of that title. Roger found Piers not only long-winded, but out of harmony with the rest of the book, and Lewis was persuaded to drop this scene. Revisions continued until Lewis lent the revised typescript to Roger Lancelyn Green in February 1954. He was very pleased, and found the completed *The Magician's Nephew*, at last, a single unit, besides being 'irresistibly gripping and compelling'.[23]

Lewis had reason to value the enormous help he received from Roger Lancelyn Green during the writing of the first six Narnias, and I can't help but feel it a great pity that he wasn't around to chronicle the writing of *The Last Battle*. But Lewis seems to have encountered few problems in writing about the end of Narnia. If I had been Tolkien, I think I'd have been happy to get Frodo back to the Shire and stop. And I'd be tempted, if I were Lewis, to take us to the end of *The Silver Chair* and stop. For this reason, I can't admire them enough for unwinding *upwards*, you might say, taking their creations to a daring level. The theme of this final volume is, as Lewis said in that important letter to Anne Jenkins, 'The coming of the Antichrist (the Ape). The end of the world and the Last Judgement.'[24] The depth and majesty of the book will remind some of us of Michelangelo's great wall-painting. It is very tempting to mention the debt to Plato's ideas about the world as a 'Shadowland' and much else found in *The Last Battle*. But I, too, am familiar with those splendid new books by Marjorie Mead, Leland Ryken, and Peter Schakel and I know they cover these matters much better than I could.

Let me instead end with two comments about Lewis and his Narnias. First, in one of the first critical works I read about Lewis, the author lamented that he did not write 'a purely *human* story.' There is hardly a day I do not think about this. I'm sure the answer is that when you know God and know, as Lewis said, that He is 'the ultimate source of all concrete, individual things and events',[25] and you know, the whole history of Salvation—you can't pretend the Lord of all life is just not there. A 'purely human story' has to have God in it or it's not human.

My second comment is not easy to make, but I think it important and I would be grateful if you would consider it. Many of you will know that the Church's understanding of the doctrines of Christianity took many centuries to develop. That 'development' is the subject of a very important work by John Henry Newman called *An Essay on the Development of Christian Doctrine* (1845). Newman points out that, although the truths of the Gospel are 'communicated to the world once for all by inspired teachers' those truths are not 'comprehended all at once by the recipients' and that 'longer and deeper thought' are necessary for the 'full comprehension and development.'[26] What did he mean? He meant that the Apostles, Peter, Paul and the others, received the *fullness* of Christian truth, such as the nature of Christ, the nature of the Father, the nature of original sin and so on, but that a full and accurate *understanding* of these doctrines took a long time. For example, the Church's understanding of Adam's fall—Original Sin—was not developed until the time of St Augustine of Hippo in the fourth century. In other words, the doctrine of Original Sin was, as Newman said, 'held implicitly' at the beginning of the Church before 'asserting itself' and becoming 'fully developed'. It follows that if St Augustine had been able to ask the Apostles about his theory of Original Sin, they would have said, 'Yes, this is what we meant'.

You are, no doubt, aware that most of those who write stories set in imaginary worlds either omit any reference to Christianity altogether, or else make up a different religion for their creations. When it comes to 'matching' the religion of his imaginary worlds with Classical Christianity, I expect Lewis is unique. When we get to Malacandra in *Out of the Silent Planet* we find that the inhabitants of that planet know a lot of things about Christ and God the Father we don't know, but which are perfectly compatible with what we do know. Most important of all, Lewis has not imagined anything that contradicts one word of the Gospel. He does the same with Narnia. He asks us to consider what this imaginary country would be like if the Son of God became incarnate there in the form of a Lion, as He became incarnate here in the form of a Man. I maintain that what happens in those seven stories is a true 'development' of the Christian Gospel, and that if you showed the Chronicles of Narnia to St Peter and St Paul, and asked 'Is this what you meant?' they would say, 'Narnia is not a real place, but, Yes: *this* is what we meant'. Of course Lewis intended for the Christian parallels to be fairly obvious, but *repeating* things from the Gospel is not the same as *continuing* that Gospel into another world.

Finally, there is, I believe, one sure way of finding out whether the Narnian stories are an authentic development of the Everlasting Gospel. You will remember that at the end of *The Voyage of the 'Dawn Treader'* Aslan tells Lucy and Edmund that they are too old to come back to Narnia, and so must remain in this world. They are heartbroken. 'It isn't Narnia, you know', sobbed Lucy.

'It's *you*. We shan't meet *you* there. And how can we live, never meeting you?'
'But you shall meet me, dear one', said Aslan.

'Are—are you there too, Sir?' said Edmund.

'I am', said Aslan. 'But there I have another name. You must learn to know me by that name. This was the very reason why you were brought to Narnia, that by knowing me here for a little, you may know me better there.'[27]

If you have come to know Aslan's name in this world better as a result of visiting Narnia, then C. S. Lewis has been successful in his attempt to extend the Gospel to another world, and we are all of us greatly blessed.

Notes

1. C. S. Lewis, *Christian Reflections*, ed. Walter Hooper (London: Geoffrey Bles, 1967; Fount, 1998), 'Historicism', 136–137.

2. C. S. Lewis, *Collected Letters: Volume II, Books, Broadcasts and War 1931–1949*, ed. Walter Hooper (London: HarperCollins, 2004), 270.

3. Roger Lancelyn Green and Walter Hooper, *C. S. Lewis: A Biography* (London: Collins, 1974; Revised and Expanded Edition, HarperCollins, 2002), ch. 11, 303.

4. Chad Walsh, *C. S. Lewis: Apostle to the Skeptics* (New York: Macmillan, 1949), 10.

5. C. S. Lewis, *Collected Letters: Volume II*, 802.

6. C. S. Lewis, *Collected Letters: Volume II*, 905–906.

7. C. S. Lewis, 'It All Began with a Picture . . . ', in idem, *Of This and Other Worlds*, ed. Walter Hooper (London: Collins, 1982; Fount, 2000), 64.

8. Green and Hooper, *C. S. Lewis: A Biography*, 307.

9. Green and Hooper, *C. S. Lewis: A Biography*, 307.

10. James 1:17.

11. Letter to Clyde Kilby of 7 May 1959, in C. S. Lewis, *Collected Letters: Volume III*, 1045.

12. C. S. Lewis, 'On Three Ways of Writing for Children', in *Of This and Other Worlds*, 53–54.

13. Walter Hooper, *Past Watchful Dragons: The Narnian Chronicles of C. S. Lewis* (New York: Macmillan, 1979), ch. V, 64.

14. C. S. Lewis, *Collected Letters: Volume II*, 980.

15. Letter to Paul Baynes, 17 December 1949, in C. S. Lewis, *Collected Letters: Volume II*, 1009.

16. Walter Hooper, *C. S. Lewis: A Companion and Guide* (London: HarperCollins, 1996), 407.

17. Lewis, 'On Three Ways of Writing for Children', in *Of This and Other Worlds*, 50.

18. Lewis, 'Sometimes Fairy Stories May Say Best What's to Be Said', in *Of This and Other Worlds*, 59.

19. C. S. Lewis, *The Silver Chair* (London: Geoffrey Bles, 1953), ch. XII, 153.

20. Lewis, *The Silver Chair*, ch. XII, 155.

21. Martin Michael Warner (1940–), Senior Lecturer in Philosophy at the University of Warwick since 1990. He is the author of *Philosophical Finesse: Studies in the Art of Rational Persuasion* (Oxford: Clarendon Press, 1989).

22. Letter to Nancy Warner, 26 October 1963, in *C. S. Lewis, Collected Letters: Volume II*, 1472.

23. Green and Hooper, *C. S. Lewis: A Biography*, ch. 11, 314.

24. Green and Hooper, *C. S. Lewis: A Biography*, ch. 11, 324.

25. C. S. Lewis, *Miracles: A Preliminary Study* (London: Geoffrey Bles, 1947; Fount, 1998), ch. 11, 90.

26. John Henry Newman, *An Essay on the Development of Christian Doctrine* (South Bend, IL: University of Notre Dame Press, 1989 [1854]), Introduction, section 21, 29–30.

27. C. S. Lewis, *The Voyage of the 'Dawn Treader'* (London: Geoffrey Bles, 1952), Ch. XVI, 222.

PART II

Memoirs

Memories of C. S. Lewis
by His Family and Friends

II

The Lewis Family

Joan Murphy

I. Jacks as a Child

Jacks was almost a twin of my father, Joseph T. Lewis.[1] His father and my grandfather were brothers, and they grew up in Belfast and lived very close to each other, about a five- or ten-minute walk away. The two little boys, Jacks and Joey, who were actually only six or seven weeks between them, grew up together, and I remember Jacks saying to me once, 'your father was my first friend', and I'll never forget that.

Jack's mother and my father's father died within a month of each other when the boys were about eight years old, and I think this brought them both together. My grandmother then looked after the two little boys, because Jack's father, Uncle Al, was devastated by the death of his wife, and really didn't know what to do with these two boys; so my grandmother used to look after them. She had five children, so two more weren't really too much trouble to her.

Jacks and my father also shared a governess, Miss Harper. Miss Harper was my governess afterwards, and she was a funny little person. She was a very staunch Belfast Presbyterian. And she was small. She taught me everything except Latin and French, and I suppose she must have taught the boys the same. She would stop in the middle of a lesson if the Spirit moved her—as it did frequently—and give you a long sermon. Now you can just imagine what this did to two rather high-spirited nine-year-old boys. They were having lessons in what was known as the breakfast room. There was a sort of side serving table there at which the children sat, and there was a desk in the corner which Miss Harper used. The boys used to get a bit bored—especially with the sermons. 'You're not as bad as your father was', she used to say to me. 'Your father and Jacks used to run round the table and jump from the chairs if they didn't like what I was telling them'. So she used to bribe them. She used to say if they behaved themselves for the first half of the day and did their work, she would give them a treat. She would take them to the bottom of Cypress Avenue to where the steam train went. Both the boys were absolutely mad about trains—they themselves had a little train set. And they would be allowed to walk down there and see the train go across. The train driver was called Jack, and that's where Jacks's name comes from. He hated the name Clive, and so he took this name unto himself and remained Jacks for the rest of his life. I don't know anybody who ever called him Clive.

The family by that stage had moved to a very much smarter house. Uncle Al had become the town solicitor, and he had moved out to the outskirts of Belfast to a big house. I don't know whether you've ever seen photographs of it, but Little Lea was a really big house. And my memory of that house, visiting there many years after, was that it was full of books. There were books everywhere. You walked up the stairs and there would be piles of books on the stairs going up. Uncle Al was a voracious reader, and once he became a widower he really just retreated into his study and read. And I think that explains a lot of why the boys—Warren and Jacks—became so close to each other, and also why they took themselves up to the top of the house—rather like the Brontës—and created their own little world up there.

II. Albert Lewis

I can only remember Uncle Albert [C. S. Lewis's father] as a child. I was three when Uncle Al died, but children can remember things, and I can't stop thinking he was a dreadful old man. My father was a doctor and he used to go and visit Uncle Al with great regularity on a Sunday and sometimes I was taken with him and I can remember going into this dull, dark great house and being really rather frightened.

He was a very dominant, even domineering man. He ruled everybody, but I wonder now if a psychiatrist and psychologist wouldn't say that he had an awful inferiority complex, because Aunt Flora was a very clever woman, I think—she had a degree in mathematics, which was not usual for a woman at that time—and she came from a rather well-connected Presbyterian clergyman's family. The Hamiltons were an old family in Northern Ireland, while Uncle Al's family—well, Jacks once told me that I was descended from an itinerant Welsh boiler maker, and I think that that's the truth. The Lewis family came from North Wales; they went to Liverpool in the ship trade, and then moved to Cork and later to Belfast, to the shipyards. There they set up a ship-building firm called MacIlwaine and Lewis, which later became Harland and Wolff.

When my great-grandfather, Richard Lewis II, was putting his sons to a trade (he put them all to trades that would help with the business), he sent my grandfather to become a naval architect, Uncle Bill and Uncle Dick into the rope works to learn about the rope trade, and Uncle Al as an apprentice to a solicitor; he was to look after the business end. Now I have a feeling that all his life Uncle Al felt a bit inferior to the Hamiltons, and that this was some of the reason for his extraordinary behaviour, because the Lewises never, although they were a long time out of Wales, lost their Welsh feeling. Their houses were always called after the Welsh villages that they came from. My grandfather's house was called Sandycroft and another house that he owned was called Harden; the house that my great grandparents lived in was called Ty Isa, which means 'the red house' in Welsh; and the house that they had in Larne was called Tigh na Mara, which means 'a house by the sea' in Welsh. In spite of the fact that they'd been out of Wales for some time, they kept this highly emotional Welsh sort of feeling, and they were always quite liable to show their feelings and to weep and things like that, which would not be right for an upright Hamilton to do, I don't think.

Uncle Al was a very dominant man. When my grandfather died, he took over my grandmother lock, stock and barrel, and the managing of all her affairs, as well as those of the children. This will give you an idea of what sort of man he was. My eldest Aunt, Martha, was a great beauty, and had many suitors, two of whom were particularly strong. One ended up the Governor of the Bank of Ireland and the other ended up the town solicitor of Belfast (which was, actually, what Uncle Al became). But in those days Uncle Al didn't think they were good enough for Aunt Martha. My grandmother was told that she was to forbid these two young men in the house, and she did; and the poor woman in the end married a clergyman who was—I beg your pardon, gentlemen—regarded as perfectly eminent, but turned out to be a dreadful bully, and she had the most dreadful marriage. In short, Uncle Al was a man who, I think, had no idea how to deal with young people. And if he dealt with his nieces like that, how did he deal with his own sons?

Uncle Al died in 1929, and that is my first real memory of Jacks, because Jacks came over when his father was ill. My father was looking after him, and Jacks came over to Ireland and stayed part of the time with us and part of the time at Little Lea. I can just remember the great fun when he came into the house and they used to tell us stories. When Uncle Al's funeral was over, all the family had come. Brothers and aunts from Scotland—the lot—came to our house, because they were all going to go to the boat, and Uncle Bill went out of the room for something and apparently I said, 'Well, I'm glad that old man is gone because he was horrid', and I can remember Jacks picking me up and putting me on his knee and saying, 'Out of the mouth of babes and sucklings comes the truth'.

III. Holidays with Jacks

In the 1930s we had a house in Newcastle, in County Down, and we used to go there for the summer, and Jacks and Warnie used to often come over and stay at Kilkeel, which is a little further south.

I remember one particular visit: We were to meet at a special place called the Bloody Bridge, where there'd been a battle, and to have a picnic. We met at the Bloody Bridge and went down onto the sea, and we found a lovely promontory of rocks with pools and just the sort of thing any child would love. This was 1934—I would have been eight and my sister six, and my cousins (there were three boys) around that age, too—and we found these pools and we all had boats, little yachts that kids have, and we had the most smashing time. I can remember Jacks telling us stories about those boats having adventures—they sailed across the sea and got to the other side—and then he made us make up stories. He never let you get off lightly, we knew we had to do some work—we had to decide where our boats were going. And my cousins' boats were all submarines and things like that, and I had an Armada ship and that pleased Warnie. Warnie decided that I was a historian, that I did much better stuff than the others. That was the famous year that Mrs Moore came to Ireland and we had a tea party in my Aunt Martha's house, and she came and took tea with my grandmother, and all I can say is children do *feel* things. Nothing in the family was said, everybody was very polite, but you felt a funny sort of atmosphere, and she only came the once. But with Warnie and Jacks we had our picnics and walks on the beach, and Jacks used to go and walk round the links with Daddy when Daddy was playing golf. I don't remember him ever playing golf, but I know that they used to go and walk with Daddy when he was playing.

Those visits were something I could remember; it was a feeling that they were great fun. I remember sitting in the back of my father's car one day, with Daddy and Warnie in the front, and Beth and me sitting in the back with Jacks between us, all of us telling stories to each other and making them up, and that was the thing that he encouraged us to do more than anything else—to make up stories. Many years later, he advised when I was starting teaching that you must never just say to children, 'be frightened', you must frighten them; and that was the sort of thing that he was going on and on about.

Jacks also had an *enormous* sense of fun or jokes (there's a family word for it, which is 'wheezers'). I remember a car trip with him and Warnie through the nearby Mountains of Mourne, with Jacks singing appallingly out of tune all sorts of Irish songs. You can just imagine that to two little girls of eight and six this was a marvellous thing—it was a highlight of our summer when Jacks and Warnie came to stay for a week or ten days and looked after us.

IV. Letters to Prison

Well, with the coming of war the holidays stopped, and my father went into the army and was taken prisoner at Tobruk, and Jacks wrote to him every single week when he was a prisoner of war. Every single week, no matter what he was doing, he wrote to Daddy. Now whether those letters all got through or not, of course we don't know, but Daddy said that the letters that did come through were some of the greatest comfort he had, and he would never forget that. Now, they weren't letters about anything deep or religious or academic; they were just chatty gossipy letters about what was going on in Oxford, what he and Warnie were doing, how they were managing, various things like this. He also told him about this marvellous creature he had invented, called Screwtape; he told him lots of things about Screwtape, and I think when he got desperate, he used to write a little bit of Screwtape into the letters. Unfortunately, of course, when Daddy was repatriated he wasn't allowed to bring them with him. He had to destroy them all. But Daddy said they were the most uplifting things. I think that that says something about Jacks that not all the books can say: what a very understanding man and what a very kind man he was.

V. Last Memories

In the 1950s, I used to have to come to Oxford to do some work at the Bodleian. My eldest son, David, was then a small child, and I'd no one to look after him. So I used to bring him over and take him down to Magdalen; we'd have our lunch there, and Jacks and Warnie would look after him for the afternoon. Once I said to David, 'What did you do?' 'Well', he said, 'we'd go for walks, we'd see the deer, and Jacks tells me stories.' And I said, 'What sort of stories?' He said, 'Ghost stories.' I said, 'Ghost stories?' And he said, 'Yes.' He said, 'Have you ever heard of anybody called'—this was a five-year-old boy—'anybody called Oscar Wilde?' So I said, 'Vaguely. He went to Daddy's school you know. Yes, I know him. Yes.' 'Well', he said, 'you know his ghost haunts Magdalen.' I said, 'No.' 'Oh yes it does. You know that bit along by the chapel by those old funny figures?' he said. 'The ghost's there. Walks up and down there.'

The last time I saw Jacks was when he and Joy came to visit Belfast. They stayed at Crawfordsburn, at a little inn on the loch, and we had an *enormous* luncheon party, and we were laughing and joking and having a marvellous time, and they were reminiscing, and Jacks turned to Joy and pointed to me and said, 'This is the only other party card-carrying leftie in the family', because I had been to the Soviet Union. I remember Joy as being great fun. And she was a very great and good influence on the end of his life, someone who made it happy, which is a thing that, in many ways, his life had never really been before, I think.

When I began to think about this talk and wrote down things that I wanted to say, I noticed that there were two words that became dominant in my memory, and they kept coming up and coming up again: the first was *encouragement* and the second was *laughter*. Those are two things that I remember most about Jacks.

They were sunny days and I loved him. I didn't see him very often, but Warnie and Jacks coming together to visit us was always an event, and always a happy one.

Note

1. This is an aggregate of two overlapping talks, given on 6 May 1986 and on 21 November 1995. 'Jacks' is the Lewis family children's distinctive (and consistently used) name for C. S. Lewis.

12

Recollections of C. S. Lewis

George Sayer

I WAS UP in the 1930s, and English was not then a popular subject at Magdalen College.[1] Actually, I can think of only two other pupils in my year who read English. Lewis was not well known; he'd written nothing of any importance, nothing that most people knew. But he had a growing reputation as a lecturer—in fact he was one of the only three lecturers in the Oxford English Schools whose lectures were, I think, worth going to. He made up his workload by taking pupils from other colleges, notably from Univ, but also pupils from Magdalen in Political Economy or Philosophy. Tutorials in those days weren't shared.[2] With Lewis one often had two a week, one in Literature and the other in Language. He was remarkable in teaching the whole field of English Literature from Old English *Beowulf* right down to as far as one was allowed to go in those days, namely Keats, as well as doing all the language work, the philology. I don't think anyone does this now.

It was formidable being alone with Lewis. He sat on a sofa at one side of the fireplace and the pupil on the other. If the student had not done his essay, he would be sent away at once—Lewis could be quite fierce. I remember a delightful but odious, very lazy friend of mine in Magdalen who had to leave the college altogether after a year because he didn't do the work or didn't do it sufficiently well. Lewis expected his pupils to work. The fact that he didn't work was the reason why Lewis had fallen out with John Betjeman ten years earlier. He did find Betjeman irritatingly affected, but his main objection, I'm quite sure, was Betjeman's laziness.

All his English pupils, I think, agreed that he was a conscientious tutor. Some found him too conscientious. He was most anxious that English should not be a soft option, and gave a lot of attention to the less popular and less easy aspects of the subject, such as Old English grammar. 'How do you scan line four?' was quite a common question from Lewis, and one I found difficult to answer very often. He was also insistent on the accurate use of words. Questions like 'What exactly do you mean by "sentimental"?' or 'How are you using the word "romantic"? What do you suppose it meant 200 years ago?' were common questions from Lewis. If you failed to give a clear and convincing answer (and I usually failed), the question might be followed by the cutting remark, 'Wouldn't it be rather better, Sayer, if you're not sure of the meaning of that word, not to use it at all?'

Except in pursuit of accuracy, he tried to avoid impressing his pupils with his own views. Thus, I was his pupil for two years before I realized that he was a Christian or, for instance, that he held the Restoration Dramatists in contempt. He set out to help the pupil form his own views, develop the strength of his own views, if they were at all reasonable. This was his object in arguing against the pupil when the essay had been finished. He hoped to stimulate the pupil into finding ways of supporting his opinions. With his best pupils— I wasn't one—I think it worked rather well and could be a lively and mutually enjoyable, hammer-and-tongs discussion, but not many had the competence or the ability to argue with Lewis in this way.

He didn't always set essays. I wish he always had. I remember being told to translate a passage of about thirty or forty lines of Anglo-Saxon poetry into rhyming couplets and another passage into Spenserian stanzas. After I'd read my very feeble versions, he read me his, incomparably better, which he said he'd rattled off before breakfast that morning.

From what I've said, he must seem to be a most destructive tutor. It wasn't the case. The great feature of his teaching was his obvious delight in and enthusiasm for many of the books that we were studying, and his ability to communicate this enthusiasm. He had wide taste: Writers he loved best included Spenser, Milton, Wordsworth, Jonson, but he was also an enthusiastic champion of lesser known writers such as Gower, Gavin Douglas, Tyndale, Hooker, Sydney, Herbert, Traherne, Scott, and Crabbe. He was helped in this advocacy, and indeed in all his teaching, by his ability to quote from memory many of the best passages. If you were his pupil, you had the enjoyment of an anthology of the best and most interesting passages, splendidly declaimed in his rich and powerful voice, with its slight and to my mind rather delightful northern Irish accent.

He gave end of term parties, or at least end of year dinners, for his pupils. A. N. Wilson gives an account of them in his biography. I wish he'd told us the source, because his account is quite different from my memory of them. Wilson writes that 'the idea of the evening was primarily to get drunk, and this was a matter about which Lewis was exuberantly insistent.'[3] Certainly there was plenty to drink on the table, and one was invited to help oneself, but there was no pressure to get drunk, and I really can't think of anyone who did. The story is too hard to believe for another reason, which comes from Lewis's private life. One of his greatest anxieties was his brother, who was an alcoholic. It seems to me very unlikely that he would want to encourage pupils to become alcoholics like his brother, and I've every reason to suppose that he much disliked the sight of drunken people.

Again, Wilson tells us that 'the conversation had to be what he called "bawdry". "Nothing above the belly or below the knee . . . ".'[4] He then quotes part of a sentence from a letter Lewis wrote to Warren Lewis, his brother, in December 1931: 'Bawdy ought to be outrageous and extravagant. . . .'[5] He doesn't quote the rest of the passage, in which Lewis states that 'bawdy must have nothing cruel about it' and 'must not approach anywhere near the pornographic.'[6] Just as I cannot recollect any drunkenness at any of these dinners, so I cannot recollect any bawdiness, and of course nothing in the least pornographic. I can think of at least one occasion when he had an opening for bawdy. 'Gentlemen, remember', he said. 'Let's drink to my pupil Jones who cannot be with us today because he was married this afternoon.' But all he added was, 'and where he is now our chaste minds may not follow him.' It was spoken seriously and I don't remember a titter.

He showed, in fact, when I was there, considerable concern for my moral welfare. I was, I think, a very difficult and trying pupil, extremely naïve and uncertain of myself, and probably very easily led astray. There is a story that can illustrate this. I went one Saturday in the summer term to a play in Stratford. My companions were two American Rhodes Scholars. After the play we had a drink in a pub and each of them pocketed an ashtray as a souvenir of our trip. The landlord, who'd become rather fed up with people—perhaps especially Americans who pocketed ashtrays and other things—complained to the police, and when we arrived at the railway station we found them waiting for us. They took us to the police station and took our fingerprints and so on, and we were summoned to appear before the magistrate the following Wednesday. Acting on advice, I went and asked Lewis for a testimonial of good character. He gave it to me and asked me to go and tell him what had happened at the magistrates' hearing. I did, and I told him that the case had been dismissed under the First Offender's Act, on payment of a fine. Then I remarked that I thought I'd been very unlucky because I'd done nothing, and because a lot of fuss had been made about almost nothing. 'I don't agree', he said, 'I'm very glad you were caught. You were aiding and abetting a theft. You should have told your American friends not to be so childish. What, anyway, are you going around with Americans for? Surely you can find better friends?' I remarked that I was thinking of going on a bicycling tour in the summer with —, a man in University College, also a pupil of his. 'You could do better', he remarked, '— has great merits, but I'm afraid he's too much interested in that which lies between the navel and the knee.' Such a man could not be described as a corrupter of his pupils' morals. If anything, he was, do you think, a little puritanical?

When the war was over, I went to live in Malvern, Worcestershire. One day in the summer holidays, I was astonished to meet in the town Lewis with his brother Warren and Tolkien. They'd been lent a house there for a few days. They invited me to walk with them and to act as their local guide. Before they left, I invited the two brothers—Tolkien had to go back to Oxford—for a meal at our house. In the course of it Jack, as he now bade me call him, said how much he enjoyed Malvern and wished he could come more often. My wife asked if he'd care to come to us for a weekend. He said 'yes', and there began a series of visits which lasted until not long before his death. It is to them that I am indebted for most of the knowledge I have of him, and which I've tried to bring together in *Jack: C. S. Lewis and His Times*.[7]

Notes

1. This talk was given on 23 October 1990.
2. Traditionally (and continuing to and beyond George Sayers's time), students were supervised by a single tutor, who would teach them all or most subjects (or 'papers', in Oxford terminology). In addition to weekly tutorials (that is, one-on-one meetings with their tutor, in which they discussed a previously set and written essay), students would attend lectures organized centrally by their Faculty and usually delivered at the Examination Schools.
3. A. N. Wilson, *C. S. Lewis: A Biography* (London: Collins, 1990), 131.
4. Wilson, *C. S. Lewis: A Biography*, 131.
5. Wilson, *C. S. Lewis: A Biography*, 131. Also C. S. Lewis, *Collected Letters, Volume II: Books, Broadcasts and War 1931–1949*, ed. Walter Hooper (London: Harper Collins, 2004), 27.
6. Lewis, *Collected Letters, Volume II*, 28.
7. George Sayer, *Jack: C. S. Lewis and His Times* (London: Macmillan, 1988). A second edition was issued as *Jack: A Life of C. S. Lewis* (Wheaton, IL: Crossway Books, 1994).

13

C. S. Lewis as a Parishioner

Ronald Head

CLIVE STAPLES LEWIS—with Mrs Moore, his adopted mother, and her daughter, Maureen—came to live in Headington Quarry at The Kilns as early as 1930.[1] Although the house itself was not very large—being rather like a bungalow with an upper story added, a kind of chalet—it then stood well back from Kiln Lane, in a piece of ground some eight acres in extent. The house acquired its name from two old brick kilns standing on the land not far from the house—brick-making, of course, was a local industry at Headington Quarry during the nineteenth century, particularly in that period after the actual quarries themselves had been worked out. The little estate comprised a tennis court, a wood, and a pool—dignified by the name of a 'lake'—where the poet Shelley is said to have meditated. This secluded haven remained the Professor's residence until his death.

The house itself, of course, can still be seen much as it was, except that a brick garage has been substituted for the former wooden structure.

C. S. Lewis's brother, Major Warren Hamilton Lewis—always called 'Warnie'—arrived at The Kilns on retiring from the Army in 1932, and became part of that remarkable household presided over by Mrs Janie King Moore. After the Major's death, the property was sold by Mrs Moore's daughter Maureen—by then known as Lady Dunbar—and other houses were built on part of it—and that complex is what you now see at the end of Lewis Close.

I never, in fact, knew Mrs Moore, as she died in 1951—the year before I arrived here—and was buried in the churchyard in a grave occupied by another Mrs Moore[2]—who as far as I can ascertain was not even a relative.[3] The operations of my predecessors have always amazed me.

Headington Quarry village itself did not finally become part of the City of Oxford until 1929—and that part of my parish where The Kilns is situated still remains in the county of Oxford, and not in the city.[4] Even the construction of the Eastern By-Pass road about 1960 failed to destroy the country character of that little estate. The village character of Headington Quarry itself, which still persists, was of course very, very much stronger in the 1930s, particularly in its ecclesiastical aspect.

The Professor and the Major, as they were known in Quarry itself, found themselves at home in a community which took these two eccentric men just as they were found. My parishioners knew little about them and had no idea who they were. They looked like countrymen, walked around in old clothes, smoking pipes, visiting public houses, and fitted in happily with the local scene.

Now you will realize that I speak of 'them' and not of 'him'—because I knew them together. My conversations were usually with two men, who, when seen apart, seemed to share a striking likeness, although one did not notice this so much when they were there together. Their conversations sparkled, and seemed to deal with any subject with equal brilliance.

They were Irish-born—being Ulstermen—and of course one noticed at certain times what one might call that Irishness of character. (It is a fact carefully noted on their tombstone that they were born in Belfast.) All of this was of course enjoyed by me in a different manner from other people, as I knew them as parishioners—parishioners who, however much they treated the Vicar as an equal, never forgot who he actually was.

The Major was at one stage my Churchwarden—previously, for many years, the correspondent of the Headington Quarry Church School Managers, of which the Vicar was the Chairman. In those early days, the Major also acted as the Professor's secretary, dealing with the vast correspondence from America and elsewhere. He always seemed to be sitting in the little room at the end of the passage down there at The Kilns banging away at the typewriter.

Before the Professor's departure to Cambridge in 1954, they probably walked through the churchyard and my garden at some time on most days in Term. I therefore often met them. My garden is not a public place—or is not supposed to be! But we had an understanding concerning this particular perambulation.

When I came to Headington Quarry, the Professor, originally agnostic, had already long before returned to the Church's fold; the Major, I believe, had never actually left it. When the Lewis establishment first appeared at The Kilns, Father Wilfrid Thomas was Vicar, a Catholic-minded priest in a village which had been influenced by the Oxford Movement in various ways at least since 1867. Nevertheless, it was, interestingly enough, a village which had strong Methodist connections, antedating the Parish Church which had not been erected until 1849. A new Vicar of low-Church outlook was instituted to the Benefice by the evangelical Bishop Strong of Oxford in 1936, and this incumbent remained until 1947, when the return of the pendulum began with my predecessor in 1947, and reached the status quo ante on my appearance later on.

People have often asked me what C. S. Lewis might have heard from the Parish pulpit all those years, and I must confess that the theology must have been different at different stages. But the brothers Lewis are not likely to have ever heard much of it. The Professor did not like organ music, so their appearance at sung services was not so frequent—and the modern mode of sermons at said Masses would not even yet have reached Holy Trinity. But the brothers Lewis appeared at 8.00 a.m. Holy Communion on Sundays without fail, unless they were away.

It was during the period of the 1939 War that the Professor—already known widely for *The Screwtape Letters*—became famous as a Christian apologist on account of his broadcast talks and lectures to the Forces, leading up to the publication of *Mere Christianity* and other works of that kind. As far as I can tell, this fact remained unknown to the great majority of the faithful at Quarry, or they entirely failed to realize that this brilliant expositor was the man sitting concealed by a pillar in the aisle. My parishioners in general, at that time, had not read either the science fiction, *Out of the Silent Planet*, or the children's stories. There were, of course, some, like Miss Griggs and Mrs Barnes-Griggs at Tewsfield, who had read everything; but they were quite exceptional.

I first met the Professor by Shelley's pool at The Kilns after I had, in fact, been visiting Mrs Barnes-Griggs and Miss Griggs, the two elderly sisters-in-law living at Tewsfield whom I have just mentioned. Tewsfield was a house which then shared a common drive with The Kilns before it passed by the wood and the lake to the house. Therefore the ladies met the Professor and the Major continually, often held their hands at various stages, and knew all about them.

I'd already met the Major in Church, and I believe that the first thing I ever said to the Professor was not what you would imagine one would have said, but was, 'You must be the Churchwarden's brother'. We then promptly retired back into The Kilns, to the study at the end of the passage, to drink strong tea in large mugs or cups, and engaged in cheerful talk about all kinds of things.[5]

My predecessor had already warned me that the brothers would not talk about their books. The Major also, of course, had a literary flair of an historical kind, concentrating on seventeenth- and eighteenth-century France—a subject on which he possessed very considerable knowledge.

At that period, when I first met them, the house was rather dark and dowdy; the walls were lined with books; old, large, comfortable chairs were scattered around; the 1939 blackout curtains, impregnated with the smell of tobacco, still hung about the windows. The ménage consisted of the general handyman/gardener/spare cook and everything else—namely Fred Paxford—together with a Mrs Miller, who performed as cook on a daily basis, a dog—a poodle which should have been shorn, but wasn't—and several cats, who were also in evidence. It was indeed a man's world, in which it was easy to settle down once one got used to the Professor being addressed as 'Jack' and the Major being called 'Warnie'.

C. S. Lewis was appointed Professor of Medieval and Renaissance Literature at Cambridge in 1954. From then on, during term-time, he spent weekdays in Cambridge and weekends in Oxford, going backwards and forwards in a taxi—he couldn't drive. He had attempted this at one stage long, long before, but I'm afraid it ended in failure. Holidays, which they spent during the vacations, included the usual trips to Ireland—the Major going from time to time to Drogheda and to Cork.

When at home, the Professor came to Holy Communion on Sundays and major Saints' Days in the week; daily of course in Holy Week. The brothers adjusted the Sunday evening mealtime to come to Evensong and Address in Lent, probably regarding the organ music, if not the address, as a suitable mortification for their time. They always sat in the same place—a separate pew for two by a pillar in the aisle, strategically placed so that they could see the altar and the pulpit and not be seen. They left the Church immediately after the Blessing, before anyone else could move.

The only difficulty was that they were strangely clumsy with their hands, and sometimes dropped walking sticks, and could not quietly manage the bogus mediaeval door latch. I solved that one once by ensuring that the Verger—we had that kind of labour in those far-off days—open the door for them.

It's interesting to reflect that, in some respects, they seemed almost shy. In any case, they were not prepared to engage in conversation at that point. They vanished back into The Kilns and firmly shut the door.

For all kinds of reasons, Headington Quarry Parish Church is a religious entity and not a social one. There were not many social events; but those few which took place could usually rely on the presence of the Major and the Professor happily talking to those around. Both were also well known in the Masons Arms, the public house which is just by the Church gate.

C. S. Lewis—who, as I have said, became known to his intimates as Jack—usually arrived early to Church services, and would sit there quietly reading the Psalms or other parts of the Prayer Book. The 1662 Prayer Book is still used at Quarry; in any case, the regurgitations of the Liturgical Commission were not available during the Professor's lifetime. I've often thought that *Meditations on the Psalms*[6] in some respects occurred in my Church.

The marriage of the Professor to Mrs Helen Joy Gresham—an American Jewess and the authoress of *Smoke on the Mountain*—took place very privately in the Oxford Registry Office in 1956, and [she] was blessed by Father Peter Bide in hospital in 1957 when she was thought to be dying. I had myself ministered to her in the Churchill Hospital, where I was Chaplain, although she had principally been a patient in the Wingfield Hospital in the next Parish. Mrs Lewis made a remarkable recovery, and I then found myself communicating her with him at The Kilns. At first she had a bed in the drawing room, where often she and the Professor could be found playing Scrabble in Latin or in Anglo-Saxon. Their conversations sparkled in a notable way.

She was, I may say, the first American lady of learning I had ever met; a rather intimidating experience, which one got used to in time when one got used to the voice, the bulging eyes, and the diabolical spectacles she used to wear.

Her health so improved that she could get about, and occupied another room on the ground floor. I believe one of the first excursions they ever took out after her return from death's door was a visit in my car to the Vicarage for tea, when she demonstrated her pianistic accomplishments by playing with me duets on two pianos.

Her arrival at The Kilns presaged a revolution indeed. The house was done up: the furniture re-upholstered, refurbished; the blackout curtains disappeared; and many improvements occurred, not exactly in a flash, but fairly quickly.

Her boys, David and Douglas, were home at holiday times. They all came to Church together.

As is well known, unfortunately, this remission of her malady was of limited duration; after a visit to Greece, her condition deteriorated rapidly, and she died on the 13th of July 1960. She was cremated privately—the service, at which I was present, being taken by Dr Farrer, the Warden of Keble. She is commemorated by a plaque set up in one of the cloisters at the Oxford Crematorium.

Life at The Kilns could not, in any respect, return to what it was before. The two Lewis brothers now had a pair of teenage boys—David and Douglas Gresham—as a constituent part of their household. They went through various interesting and curious rearrangements, but on the whole, I think, it worked out much better than one might have thought.

Professor Lewis was indeed bereft, as any reader of *A Grief Observed* must know—and, as always in circumstances of this kind, one wondered how his health would stand up to such a strain. In 1961 he was not so well; I communicated him at home on several occasions. In the following year, 1962, in some respects he seemed better; he was still travelling to and from Cambridge, but on the whole did not seem so active. Major Lewis, who was older, seemed in a little better state, and went off to Ireland for long periods.

The domestic administration of The Kilns went on much as before. That was about the time of the *Honest to God* controversy. Conversations with the Professor naturally touched on such matters as the Bishop Robinson's observations and things of that kind, also on prayer, matters theological arising out of sermons, and so forth. *Letters to Malcolm*, number 12, reports on an actual conversation on prayer with me. The Professor was what one would call properly and strictly orthodox—like the old Church of Ireland, which is much sounder and more united in theology than the Church of England. His writings, like his conversation, were designed to support the faith and to fortify the faithful, a thing not notable in twentieth-century theology: too frequently it tends to do the opposite and is designed for that purpose.

I always felt that conversations with the Professor were purposeful, never mere chatter or pleasant nothingness. He was a very logical thinker, not allowing anyone to get away with slipshod argument. I am told he was a terror to his pupils, but of course I really don't know much about that.

It was about this time in 1963 that Father Hooper, then a layman, appeared from 'the plantations of the colonies'.[7] I believe they had been in touch with one another by correspondence over quite a period. He was very knowledgeable about the Professor's writings, as you all know. And they clearly took to each other immediately, appearing in church together and so forth. It was much later that he came to me as a Vicar.

The Major again was away in Ireland, and not well.

In July 1963 the Professor was seriously ill indeed in the Acland Home and the Radcliffe Infirmary. Father Hooper took me down to Keble to confer with Dr Farrer in these moments of crisis. It was not possible to get the Major back; he also was in hospital. Happily, the Professor—after being anointed by Father Michael Watts, the Precentor of the Cathedral—recovered, and in time returned to The Kilns with a male nurse temporarily and Walter Hooper permanently added to the household.

Lewis's heart attack, and its complications, led to his resignation from the Cambridge professorship. I then began communicating him at home on a fortnightly basis—which situation continued until his death.

The Major had recovered and was back again.

In the nature of the case there was a period when I had long conversations with the Professor—covering, of course, the usual field of spiritual matters, questions concerning the faith, the problems besetting the Church, dangers of change, revision of services, and so forth. He had a solid preference that the prayers of the Church should be familiar so that one should be free to meditate on them, to sink into them, to take them as one's own. Hence his interest in the quotations from the Ancient Fathers—Augustine on the Psalms and so forth—which often coloured my observations in church.

He was a man of deep devotion (for example, when receiving Holy Communion), and a man of long-standing affection—he never failed to put Mrs Moore's name on the list of the faithful departed on All Souls' Day. He was a very humble man, self-effacing, never speaking of his remarkable talents, or of his service to other people.

One could note his care in answering letters. Those he received, after he read them and dealt with them, I think he'd usually throw them away. Of course I remember his generosity in giving money away; not, I believe, so much to institutions, but rather to individuals he could help . . . scholars, clergy, all sorts of people.

His death was, on the whole, unexpected. I'd only communicated him a few days before, when he seemed to me much the same, nothing notably amiss. Yet he died suddenly on Friday the 22nd November 1963 at half-past five. Later that evening, the Major was running about looking for me, forgetful that it was the anniversary day of the Parish Church's consecration in 1849. I was actually presiding over a Parish party, unaware both of the death of the Professor and the assassination of President Kennedy in Dallas on the same day.

The Professor's funeral took place in the Parish Church, and he was buried in the churchyard. No announcement had been made about it. The Major was prostrate, and indeed, not there. He had previously said that there should be no flowers, but the foot of the coffin, and subsequently the grave, was graced by a sheaf of flowers brought by Dr Nicholas Zhernof. The Professor's body had been received in Church the night before, and I said a requiem on the day of the burial—Tuesday the 26th.

His memorial service took place in Magdalen College Chapel on the following Saturday, the 30th. His tombstone, bearing the quotation from *King Lear*—'Men must endure their going hence'—was not laid out exactly as one could have desired, as the Major seemed unable to realize that when he died, something more would, in fact, have to be added on. Happily, the Major lived for another ten years, which gave plenty of time to solve that particular problem. (Clergymen are always faced with this problem that they have to try and make inscriptions on tombstones read sensibly from beginning to end.)

The Professor's grave has become a place of pilgrimage for many people, particularly those from across the Atlantic. There is no actual memorial to him in the Parish Church, but perhaps some day something might actually arrive.[8]

Notes

1. The editors would like to thank Rev. Tim Stead and the Wardens of Holy Trinity Church Headington Quarry, Oxford, England, for permission to include this memoir by the Rev. Canon R. E. Head, given at the C. S. Lewis Society on 11 February 1986. Through the assistance of Ms Helen Day and Mr Adrian Wood the church provided a transcript of a later version of the same talk given by Rev. Head. The second talk, entitled 'Two People of the Foothills', was given at Holy Trinity Church, Headington Quarry on 7 July 1988 and was recorded by Mr Kim Gilnett, transcribed by Ms Valerie Baker, and typed out by Mr Stephen Jones. Slight variations are present between the two versions and several minor additions from the later version of the paper have been included here.

2. Mrs Alice Hamilton Moore is described on her tombstone as 'widow of Dr Robert Moore of Bush Hills, Ireland'.

3. Author's note: Consultation of the Burial Register, however, revealed the interesting fact that the Irish Mrs Moore, buried earlier in 1939, was also recorded as resident at The Kilns. One can only conclude that she may have been an inherited resident in The Kilns itself, or lived in the bungalow—sometimes described as the Summer house—which then stood on the grounds.

4. The area known as Risinghurst where The Kilns is located was integrated into Oxford City in 1992.

5. Variant in second talk: 'We were sitting there among the books beside the ancient gramophone, with its vast trumpet.'

6. C. S. Lewis, *Reflections on the Psalms* (London: Geoffrey Bles, 1958).

7. Author's note: Father Walter Hooper was present at this society meeting, and a round of laughter followed this good-natured comment.

8. In 1991 an engraved window featuring themes from the Chronicles of Narnia was added to the church building near the pew where C. S. Lewis and his brother regularly sat.

14

Marrying C. S. Lewis

Peter Bide

HOW DID I come to marry Lewis and Joy?[1] I had come up to Oxford in 1936, at the age of 24, to read English. After I took my degree in 1939, I kept up with Lewis during the war when I was a Royal Marine. When I came through Oxford I used to go and see him, and later on, when I was ordained, I continued the habit.

My first parish was Hangleton on the edge of Hove. As well as having this tiny mediaeval church in the middle of a down, with great fields round it, I had care of the local 'fever hospital', as we used to call it in those days. In 1954 I think it was, we had a terrible epidemic of polio, and people were streaming into the hospital. I had people dying between the ambulance and the hospital—about the only time I'd been grateful for a motorbike. I had a scooter, one of those small Italian jobs. I was once in the hospital holding a woman's hand, and I said, 'You don't know me' and she said, 'Oh yes I do', and my heart sank. She said, 'You're the clergyman on the Vespa.' So that was much better to me than having a collar on, it was an immediate sign of recognition. She died, poor thing. But I had many people to look after, and I had lots of experiences with different ones, too many to retell to you now.

But there came an afternoon when the Bishop of Lewes came to baptise my latest child, and after the baptism I came out of my tiny church and somebody said, 'Do you know that the Gallagher's boy is seriously ill?' Now the Gallaghers were Roman Catholic Irish who had just come to live in my parish. I said, 'No I didn't know he was ill, but I'll go and see him as soon as I've got rid of the Bishop.' And so we went home and had tea, and then I got on my scooter.

Now this is a very difficult story for me to tell, and I shall undoubtedly end up in tears, but you will forgive me for that. I went down to the Gallagher's, and it was clear from the beginning that something very serious was going on because there they all were, with Mrs Gallagher at the centre, handkerchief in her hands, and all the local Irish community round about her in a tiny room. I said to her, 'What's the matter, Mrs Gallagher?' and she said, 'Michael's up in the hospital and they say he's going to die.' 'Well', I said to her, 'there's one thing I can say about that; the doctors haven't got the gift of life and death. Only God has the gift of life and death, and what you've got to do is to relax your fear and your distress in so far as you can, and rest on the mercy of God. Meanwhile I'll go and see him.'

I got on my scooter and I went up the half-made road to the hospital. And as I went, it was as if a little green man was sitting on the handles, babbling away in my ear: 'What the hell do you think you're going to do? Have you got your bones with you? Why don't you take those out and throw them round? You're going to see this boy? What can you do about it?'

Well, I didn't turn around and go back; I don't know why, but I didn't. I got to the hospital and I put on my gown and my mask and went into the room where this boy was. And it was absolutely clear that something very serious was happening to this child, because the sister was sitting in the room with him, an unusual thing for a sister to do. There was nobody else there, but she was sitting there with him, and I went up to the bedside and there he lay. His face was the colour which I had come to associate with death, a sort of leaden, blue-y white. His eyes were wide open and turned up so only the whites were visible. He was flailing the pillow with his hands. If there was ever a child dying, it was this boy; and at the same time, as I saw this, I had this sort of feeling that this was a crux. Something about my whole vocation hung on it.

I didn't touch the boy. I went down on my knees beside him and I said some simple, naïve, corny prayer like, 'Lord, look at this Thy child, if it be Thy gracious will, let him recover in the name of the Father and the Son and the Holy Ghost. Amen.' Then I got up and I turned to the sister and said, 'Well, now I hope he'll be all right.' And she looked at me as if I was mad—not unnaturally, not unnaturally: I thought I was mad myself. And I went back and I got ready for that evening.

Now there were two churches in this parish. I only had one of them, but the vicar made quite unreasonable demands on me as far as the other one was concerned. This was Lent, and I was giving a whole series of Lenten evening lectures on the nature of faith, such as most of you have suffered under at some stage or another. The preceding week, I had been discussing the healing of Jairus's daughter, which makes a very good story for discussing the nature of faith and what is involved in faith. And I said to this group, 'I'm sure that since last week, in your prayers and thoughts, you have been concerning yourself with the nature of faith. Now here is Michael Gallagher. If you will rest on everything that you have learnt in this church, all the many blessings that have come to you through sacrament and worship, and put Michael's welfare at the heart of this, then he will get better.' I heard myself say this, and of course it was a terrible thing to say. I was putting all these people's faith at risk, and equally well I'd drawn a blank cheque on the Holy Spirit, which is not in my judgement a very good thing to do. But I went on with what I had to say to them that particular evening, and when I got onto my scooter again, I went straight up to the hospital.

When I got into the ward, the night sister was on duty. I can remember her face very well. I said to her, 'How is he?' and she said, 'I don't know why, but he's getting better.' Two days later, the chief physician at the Children's Hospital in Brighton rang up the 'fever hospital' and asked what the result of the autopsy was, and was told he was sitting up in bed having his breakfast.

Now, I found this theologically extremely puzzling. I had visited all sorts of other patients in this hospital: I'd prayed for them, I'd laid hands on some of them, and they'd died. Why was Michael (who incidentally turned out a right tearaway) selected from all this? It really worried me. It may not worry you, but it worried me like nothing else, and the next time I went up to see Jack Lewis, I discussed it with him. We went over the top of Shotover, as we nearly always did, and I told him how I found this incomprehensible.

I don't think he'd got any special answers to this—I don't even remember what he said about it, to tell you the truth. But this is the basis on which he sent for me later on.

When Joy was diagnosed as having a sarcoma, he wrote to me and said would I be kind enough to come up and lay hands on her? Well, how could I say 'no'? He was a friend of mine and this was a terrible situation, and of course I had to say 'yes'. So I went.

When I got there, up to the quarry where he lived, Jack said, 'Peter, what I'm going to ask you isn't fair. Do you think you could marry us? I've asked the Bishop, I've asked all my friends at the faculty here, and none of them will.' He said, 'It doesn't seem to me to be fair. They won't marry us because Joy was divorced, but the man she married in the first place was a divorced man, so in the eyes of the church, surely there isn't any marriage anyway. What are they making all this fuss about?'

Well, I must admit that I had always thought that the Church of England's attitude to marriage was untenable. They rested everything upon the promises given in the marriage service, and said that they couldn't possibly be repeated elsewhere. However, there was one exception. If the man turned out not to be able to consummate the marriage, then a Decree of Nullity would go through the courts and be recognized by the church. This made the whole thing collapse in my view. I mean, if you promise for better or worse, and non-consummation isn't for worse, I don't know what is.

On the other hand, I went to a minor public school, and a public school is a terrible place not least because it gives you a lasting fear of authority. 'The headmaster wants to see you.' And that lasts all through life—I've never got rid of it totally. And so the fact that there were church laws by the dozen which forbade me to do anything of the sort really worried me. I mean it worried me because it wasn't something that I just thought was a superficial thing, something I could just push to one side. I wasn't in my own parish, I wasn't in my own diocese. What right had I to go charging into a situation like this which everybody else had refused to have anything to do with?

Well, I know you'll probably find this a rather corny thing, but after long cogitations—and it took me the best part of an hour—I said to myself, 'What would He have done?' and then there wasn't any further answer at all. Of course He would have married them, wouldn't He? Would He have regarded the law and everything else above the expression of love which this woman had made both towards the church and Himself and to her future husband? And so I married them in the hospital, with Warnie and the ward sister as witnesses. I laid hands on Joy, and she lived for another three years.

I don't understand this, I never have done; but that is the story, and what you see in *Shadowlands* has little or nothing to do with it. It made me very cross that there have been about six different treatments of this episode in the course of the last ten years and nobody has ever come and asked me what happened. It strikes me as absolutely extraordinary. A. N. Wilson went all the way to America to talk to somebody who had talked to me: an expensive journey, when he could have walked down the road and found me himself. It's a very odd thing, but now you know what the truth is. My own wife died of cancer about a year before Joy Lewis, and I wrote to him and told him about it, of course, and he said, 'There's nothing I can say Peter. Eat a lot', he said, '... eat a lot. It's the best form of comfort.'

What happened after the wedding was rather alarming. The first thing that I did the next day was to go down to Bishop Carpenter's house—Bishop Carpenter was the bishop in Oxford in those days—and tell him what I'd done. I went over it quite properly, and at the end of it he said, 'Well, I'm not going to give you a penance. You go home and tell your bishop.' Well, I loved George Bell with a passion, and the idea of going and telling him something which I thought wouldn't please him at all was very, very difficult. But I went home and I rang up George's secretary and said, 'Could I come and see the bishop?' 'Oh', she said, 'he's been trying to get hold of you for the last 24 hours. He wants to see you.' So I thought, 'Oh Dear.'

But when I got there, he had no idea why I wanted to see him, and I sat in front of him. He had wonderful lucid blue eyes, which entirely transfixed you.

And he said, 'Peter, what did you think you were doing?' His main point was that they had been married in the registry office, and since the church recognized the marriage of the registry office, why was this remarriage in any sense necessary? I, for my part, found it very odd that he didn't see that a woman who believed she was dying wanted to have the sacramental act of the church, the blessing of God on her marriage. It seemed to me very odd that the bishop shouldn't see that. Anyhow, having said all this, he said, 'Ah well, you won't do it again will you Peter?' Well, I couldn't really envisage a situation where I would ever do it again, so I said, 'No, my Lord.' We called our bishops 'my Lord' in those days. And he said, 'Ah, good.'

Now on the way from Hangleton to Chichester, you pass a parish called Goring-by-Sea, one of the plum parishes in his diocese. 'Go look it over', he said, 'it's yours if you'd like it.' That's why he had wanted to see me. I did find out afterwards that my beloved wife had been to see him—while I was away, totally unknown by me—and said, 'Bishop, take him out of there or take him out in a box.' The fact is that I was working 14 hours a day, seven days a week, and she knew there was only a certain end to this. But that was George. I've known some wonderful people in my life, and Jack Lewis and George Bell were two of the greatest.

Note

1. This talk was given on 24 January 1995.

Memories of the Socratic Club

Stella Aldwinckle

I. The Story of the Patched Shirt

St. Hilda's has been reconstructed so I don't suppose any of you know the old entrance to the main house with the enormous hall that ran from the front door and around the corner past a long staircase and ending in a double JCR.[1] We were booked to have our Socratic meeting in that double JCR. I got there at about ten past eight for an eight-fifteen meeting. When I opened the door, there were so many people around the door you could hardly get in, and when you got inside, you couldn't move at all. Someone asked the Bursar whether she could let us move into the dining room, because the double JCR had been full for a long time and the hall passage was absolutely packed with people. So all the paraphernalia were moved, and then the crowd surged into this dining room, and still there was standing room only. The only people who got seats were the two speakers and myself as chairman up on the dais. It was stiflingly hot, of course. And after about ten minutes Professor Joad[2] peeled off his jacket (very sensibly), and looked much better. So I leant over to C. S. Lewis, who was the other speaker, and I said to him, 'Why don't you take off your jacket also?' And he leant back to me and said in a whisper, 'Because my shirt is patched.'

It's a funny story, but I also felt very moved by it, because here was a man who must have been earning thousands of pounds a year, and yet he has his shirt patched so that he could give the money away.

II. The Socratic Club

The objective of the Socratic Club was to have an open forum for both atheists and Christians. It was a very lively club, and we used to go on talking under the street lamps until two or three in the morning.

Some people, of course, were much readier with their questions than others, and sometimes, I think, freshers would be a bit nervous about piping up. But I can remember as though it was yesterday, I was in the chair and people were sitting (as always) on the floor, and on my right, sprawled on the floor, was a young fresher. He joined in the discussion rather a lot, and I thought to myself: that young man is going far. His name was Bernard Williams.[3]

Over the years, the club became more technical. I suppose that was because we had so many dons: we hardly ever had a paper from someone who wasn't a don or a professor. They got interested in strictly philosophical questions, and that's how it started drifting. I think it's a great pity myself; it might have been a good thing to ask some undergraduates who weren't reading philosophy to present papers. But of course it was a pleasure to have such distinguished speakers. Austin Farrer was one of the outstanding ones. Mascall[4] used to come a lot, and Dorothy Sayers, too, came and gave us a paper.[5] Among Lewis's fellow Inklings, Owen Barfield came and gave us a paper, just the one.[6] And I think Charles Williams did, though I'm not absolutely certain of that.[7] Our furthest traveller came from France: the philosopher Gabriel Marcel.[8] He came and talked to us, but I must admit that we didn't have to pay all his fare, because we were sharing him with someone else.

I know that many people appreciated the Socratic very much. In fact, Professor Grensted,[9] who was professor of Christian philosophy at Oriel, reckoned that the Socratic Club was the most important thing that had happened in Oxford during the war. He judged it was so important to have tackled the issues: to bring out agnosticism and atheism instead of having a rather hush-hush attitude to it, as it had been before the war. Between the wars, it was very much the case that people with an attitude of that sort hid it. But I think the climate is changing now, because of the threat of nuclear war. People changed rather from being cocky agnostics to being rather listless ones.

III. C. S. Lewis at the Socratic Club

C. S. Lewis himself always came. He came to every meeting, eight meetings a term, unless he was actually ill or had to attend something in London. His support was simply wonderful.

In meetings, he was never ever dogmatic or domineering. He would listen sympathetically to the other person's point of view and would comment helpfully, not antagonistically. Because, you see, we weren't debating. In a debating society you are out to score points and to win the votes. But we were Socratic, that is, we wanted to get to the truth of things, and to follow the argument in good faith and good temper wherever it went.

IV. The End of the Socratic Club

The Socratic Club lasted for more than twenty-five years. In fact, we had a sherry or claret party for our twenty-fifth anniversary, to which Elizabeth Anscombe came. But the intellectual climate changed very much over the years. Agnosticism grew a great deal, and people developed the habit of having very small little meetings in their rooms, simply inviting a few friends. So the club dwindled, and when Lewis got a professorship at Cambridge, it fell off, partly because he wasn't there. Basil Mitchell, our second president, then still at Oriel, carried on very eloquently, but of course he had not exactly the gifts that C. S. Lewis had had that made such a difference to the meetings. At our last discussion about the club, he said, 'Oh well, I don't think the climate is any longer suitable or inviting to support such an endeavour. We'd do better to close it down.' And I agreed with him. Then he murmured something about 'perhaps in the future there might be a time when we could begin again.'

Notes

1. This is a condensed version of a Q&A given on 24 January 1984. A JCR or Junior Common Room is a campus space set aside for undergraduate socializing.
2. C. E. M. Joad (1891–1953), English philosopher and broadcaster.
3. Sir Bernard Williams (1929–2003) became one of the most significant English moral philosophers of the twentieth century. Williams began his career as a Prize Fellow at All Souls College, Oxford, and was later Knightbridge Professor of Philosophy at Cambridge, Provost of King's College, Cambridge, Deutsch Professor of Philosophy at the University of California, Berkeley, and White's Professor of Moral Philosophy at Oxford, before returning to All Souls for his final years.
4. Eric Lionel Mascall (1905–1993), University Lecturer in Philosophy of Religion at Christ Church, University of Oxford.
5. 'Poetry, Language, and Ambiguity' on 3 June 1954 (with Austin Farrer).
6. 'The Nature of Meaning' on 11 February 1952.
7. 'Are there Any *Valid* Objections to Free-Love?' on 2 March 1942.
8. 'Theism and Personal Relationships' on 16 February 1948 (with L. W. Grensted).
9. L. W. Grensted, D. D. (1884–1964), Nolloth Professor of the Philosophy of the Christian Religion at Oriel College, University of Oxford.

Memories of the Inklings

16

The Inklings

Walter Hooper

MY GUESS IS that if you had fifty speakers lecturing on the origin of the Inklings, each would begin somewhere different. But in the end I think all fifty would admit that the friendship of C. S. Lewis and J. R. R. Tolkien is at the very heart of that remarkable group, whose influence is being felt nearly everywhere on the planet. Rather than behave like a dog following his tail round and round, trying to decide where to plop down, I'm going to say that the beginning of the Inklings was probably the first meeting of Lewis and Tolkien in 1926.

I should perhaps remind you that Professor Tolkien went up to Exeter College, Oxford, in 1911. After taking a First in English in 1915, he went straight into the Lancashire Fusiliers. Shortly after his marriage to Edith Bratt in 1916 he fought in the Battle of the Somme. While convalescing afterwards he began writing *The Simarillion*, the myths and legends of what became known as 'The First Age of the World'. After being demobilized from the army in November 1918, Tolkien moved to Oxford to work on the Oxford Dictionary. In 1920 he went to the University of Leeds as Reader in English Language, and in 1924 he became Professor of English Language. Tolkien returned to Oxford in 1925 as the Rawlinson and Bosworth Professor of Anglo-Saxon. He was to remain in Oxford for almost the rest of his life.

Lewis, six years younger than Tolkien, came up to University College in 1917, but after a few months he was gazetted into the Somerset Light Infantry and sent to France. By the time he reached the front lines in 1918 and took part in the battles around Arras, Tolkien was back in England. Lewis returned to Oxford and took up his scholarship at University College in January 1919. He worked tirelessly for the next five years, which ended in 1923 when he took his third First class degree. The next two years were spent looking for a fellowship in Philosophy. In the end he accepted with joy and relief a fellowship in English at Magdalen College. His college rooms were number 3 on Staircase 3 of New Building.

The School of English was still in its infancy. Although it was recognized as a subject as far back as 1899, and given its own Chair in 1904, it remained a part of the Modern Languages Board until 1926, when a separate English faculty board was established. The faculty was still small in 1925, and it seems likely that Lewis and Tolkien would have seen one another during that important year when both joined it. But there is, so far as I know, no record of their having met until that English faculty tea on 11 May 1926, when Lewis recorded in his diary: 'To Merton for the "English tea" at 4.' After describing some of the questions raised during the meeting, he said: 'Tolkien managed to get the discussion round to the proposed English Prelim. I had a talk with him afterwards. He is a smooth, pale, fluent little chap—can't read Spenser because of the forms—thinks the language is the real thing in the school— thinks all literature is written for the amusement of *men* between thirty and forty—we ought to vote ourselves out of existence if we were honest. . . . No harm in him, only needs a smack or so.'[1]

Thank God I never showed Lewis's diary to Tolkien! But why did Lewis think he needed 'a smack or so'? Probably because he and Lewis were on different sides of a debate between the Language and the Literature camps of the English School. On one side were the philologists, who considered literature later than Chaucer to be insufficiently challenging to form the basis of a degree course. On the other side were enthusiasts for 'modern' literature— which meant literature from Chaucer up to the nineteenth century. Some of these 'literature' people considered the study of Anglo-Saxon and Middle English word mongering and pedantry.

What Tolkien wanted was not merely linguistic courses in themselves, but to base linguistic studies on literature, whether Anglo-Saxon or mediaeval. Lewis voted against Tolkien's ideas at the time, but when Tolkien was successful in revising the syllabus and putting it into operation, Lewis saw how well it worked and in a few years time he gave it his full support.

But going back to that meeting in May 1926, Lewis was not sure what to make of Tolkien, and it's as well to remind ourselves of what Lewis later said in his autobiography about him: 'At my first coming into the world I had been (implicitly) warned never to trust a Papist, and at my first coming into the English Faculty (explicitly) never to trust a philologist. Tolkien was both.'[2]

We may presume that they talked to one another whenever they met, but what really brought them together was the Icelandic Society which Tolkien founded in 1926. This was a club of dons who met regularly to read Icelandic sagas in the original. Lewis joined the club the following year and in a letter to his boyhood friend, Arthur Greeves, of 26 June 1927, he said: 'I am realising a number of very old dreams . . . above all, learning Old Icelandic. We have a little Icelandic Club in Oxford called the "Kólbitar": which means (literally) "coal-biters", i.e. an Icelandic word for all cronies who sit round the fire so close that they look as if they were biting the coals. We have so far read the Younger Edda and the Volsung Saga. . . . *You* will be able to imagine what a delight this is to me, and how, even in turning over the pages of my Icelandic Dictionary, the mere name of a god or giant catching my eye will sometimes throw me back fifteen years into a wild dream of northern skies and Valkyrie music.'[3]

Before Lewis got to know Tolkien intimately, something greater than the Inklings, and which made the Inklings possible, occurred. After a long struggle to keep God out of his life, God came in anyway. The passage from *Surprised by Joy* is very familiar: 'You must picture me alone in that room in Magdalen', said Lewis, 'night after night, feeling, whenever my mind lifted even for a second from my work, the steady, unrelenting approach of Him whom I earnestly desired not to meet. That which I greatly feared had at last come upon me. In the Trinity Term of 1929 I gave in, and admitted that God was God, and knelt and prayed: perhaps, that night, the most dejected and reluctant convert in all England.'[4]

But, as Lewis said, his conversion was to Theism. He still did not understand how Christ fitted into Christianity. The main effect of this conversion was that, with the greatest relief, Lewis lost nearly all interest in himself. He became, as he said to one of his correspondents: 'a room to be filled by God and our blessed fellow creatures, who in their turn are rooms we help to fill.'[5] Lewis shared with Pope John Paul II what the Pope called the 'Law of the Gift'—'self-giving, not self-assertion', as the road to human fulfillment.[6] It is the old, old story of the seed which must fall into the ground and die because only by dying will it bring forth fruit.[7] By transcending oneself, living for others, one becomes free of self-centredness. Lewis's self-giving was the most radical I've witnessed, and as I've said before, he was the most converted man I ever met.

Soon after his conversion, Lewis showed what a changed man he was in his tender treatment of his father, who died on 25 September 1929. Back in Oxford, Lewis wrote to Arthur on 3 December 1929 about events in Magdalen College. 'I have got rather into a whirl', he said, 'as I always do in the latter part of the term. . . . One week I was up till 2.30 on Monday (talking to the Anglo-Saxon professor Tolkien who came back with me to College from a society and sat discoursing of the gods & giants & Asgard for three hours, then departing in the wind & rain—who cd. turn him out, for the fire was bright and the talk good?)'[8] He mentioned Tolkien again to Arthur on 30 January 1930. 'Tolkien', he said, 'is the man I spoke of when we were last together—the author of voluminous unpublished metrical romances and of the maps, companions to them, showing the mountains of Dread and Nargothrond the city of the Orcs.'⁹

A few months later, Lewis was writing about two more potential Inklings. 'Since writing the last sentence', Lewis said in a letter to Arthur Greeves of 29 July 1930, 'I have come into College to entertain two people to dinner & spend the night. As they did not leave till 3 o'clock . . . I am feeling rather morning-after-ish! One of them is a man called Dyson who teaches English at Reading. He is only in Oxford for a few weeks and having met him once I liked him so well that I determined to get to know him better. . . . He is a man who really loves truth. . . . Have you observed that it is the most serious conversations which produce in their course the best laughter? How we roared and fooled at times in the silence of last night—but always in a few minutes buckled to again with renewed seriousness. . . . The other man was Coghill of Exeter.'¹⁰

With the introduction of Hugo Dyson and Nevill Coghill, the Inklings are on the point of numbering four. And at this point I find myself in difficulty. I had the privilege of knowing all the Inklings mentioned so far, but I am conscious of just how vulgar it must sound for someone so astronomically inferior to them to claim friendship. But I am going to risk being vulgar because all the Inklings, except Christopher Tolkien, have died, and it makes sense that this Society would invite someone to speak to you who knew some of those giants, even if not well.

Now, on with our story! Hugo Dyson had much in common with Lewis and Tolkien. He fought in World War I, and like Tolkien was educated at Exeter College, albeit shortly after Tolkien had taken his degree. Hugo Dyson was a tutor in English at Reading University—about 20 miles from Oxford—from 1925 until 1945, when he moved to Oxford as Fellow of English at Merton College. Writing to his brother Warnie on 22 November 1931 about Hugo, Lewis described him as 'a burly man, both in mind and body, with the stamp of the war on him. . . Lest anything should be lacking, he is a Christian and a lover of cats.'¹¹ The best description of him comes from Warnie who, after meeting him in 1933, said that he 'gives the impression of being made of quick silver: he pours himself into a room on a cataract of words and gestures, and you are caught up in the stream—but after the first plunge, it is exhilarating.'¹² When I met him thirty years later, he was less burly, and walked with a stick, but his presence and conversation were still like quicksilver. He's the only man I know who, if he knew what it was, would find e-mail too slow.¹³

Nevill Coghill, a year older than Lewis, was the enormously talented translator of Chaucer, who was the Merton Professor of English Language and Literature from 1957 to 1966. He and Lewis had studied English together as undergraduates. Coghill played a vital part in the Oxford University Dramatic Society. Richard Burton had been his pupil, and he is the one who introduced him to the stage. This charming and courteous man did not attend the Inklings meetings regularly, but he made a difference when he *was* there.

If I seem to be making too much of Lewis's conversion in a story of the Inklings, it is because I am convinced that the Inklings would not have happened without it. We come, then, to the all-important question of how Christ fitted into it. Lewis wrote to Arthur on 22 September 1931 with the news that Dyson had dined with him on the evening of 19 September, and spent the weekend. Tolkien was there, too, and Lewis said the three of them had a 'long, satisfying talk' which began with a stroll in Addison's Walk, was interrupted at 3 in the morning when Tolkien went home, and continued for another hour. Arthur pressed for information about that 'long, satisfying talk' and on 18 October 1931 Lewis explained what happened. 'What had been holding me back', said Lewis,

> has not been so much a difficulty in believing as a difficulty in knowing what the doctrine *meant*: you can't believe a thing while you are ignorant *what* the thing is. My puzzle was the whole doctrine of Redemption: in what sense the life and death of Christ 'saved' or 'opened salvation to' the world. . . . What Dyson and Tolkien showed me was this: that if I met the idea of sacrifice in a Pagan story I didn't mind it at all: again, that if I met the idea of a god sacrificing himself to himself . . . I liked it very much and was mysteriously moved by it: again, that the idea of the dying and reviving god . . . similarly moved me provided I met it anywhere *except* in the Gospels. The reason was that in Pagan stories I was prepared to feel the myth as profound and suggestive of meanings beyond my grasp even tho' I could not say in cold prose 'what it meant'. Now the story of Christ is simply a true myth: a myth working on us in the same way as the others, but with this tremendous difference that it *really happened*: and one must be content to accept it in the same way, remembering that it is God's myth where the others are men's myths: i.e. the Pagan stories are God expressing Himself through the minds of poets, using such images as He found there, while Christianity is God expressing Himself through what we call 'real things'. Therefore it is *true*. . . . The 'doctrines' we get *out* of the true myth are of course *less* true: they are translations into our *concepts* and *ideas* of that wh. God has already expressed in a language more adequate, namely the actual incarnation, crucifixion, and resurrection.[14]

Compared to the years of World War II, when Lewis furnished the English-speaking world with a small library of theology, the 1930s are almost without incident. They were years of reflection, when Lewis was *receiving*, not giving. Lewis's theories of literature probably began taking shape at this point. When he was still an atheist, he said, 'The two hemispheres' of his mind 'were in the sharpest contrast. On the one side a many-islanded sea of poetry and myth; on the other a glib and shallow "rationalism". Nearly all that I loved I believed to be imaginary; nearly all that I believed to be real I thought grim and meaningless.'[15] On the eve of his conversion he wrote in a poem, 'Oh who will reconcile in me both maid and mother'[16]—that is, Reason and Imagination. With his conversion they were reconciled, and in 1931 he wrote to T. S. Eliot about his belief in 'imagination as a truth-bearing faculty.'[17] Put another way, Reason is a way of Telling, while imagining is a way of Showing. Lewis was good at both: sometimes Reason—telling—worked best; sometimes Imagination—showing—worked best.

At the same time, Lewis took exception to the belief, expressed in 1930 by E. M. W. Tillyard, that we should not be concerned with what *Paradise Lost* is about, but 'the true state of Milton's mind when he wrote it.'[18] Replying to what he called 'The Personal Heresy', Lewis insisted that '[t]he poet is not a man who asks me to look at *him*; he is a man who says "look at that" and points; the more I follow the pointing of his finger the less I can possibly see of *him*.'[19] What the reader should hope to get from literature, he maintained, is 'a voyage beyond the limits of [the author's] personal point of view, an annihilation of the brute fact of his own particular psychology rather than its assertion.'[20] Or, as he was to put it years later, 'an enlargement of our being'.[21] Except for his steady work on *The Allegory of Love*, which he began in 1928, Lewis wrote very little at this time except a few religious poems. It was probably these that he read to Tolkien while Tolkien read aloud stories from *The Silmarillion* and the material that went into the Appendixes of *The Lord of the Rings*.

The Inklings as a group was taking shape. Shortly after that remarkable evening that began in Addison's Walk, Lewis wrote to Arthur on 22 November 1931: 'It has become a regular custom that Tolkien should drop in on me of a Monday morning and drink a glass. This is one of the pleasantest spots in the week. Sometimes we talk English school politics: sometimes we criticise one another's poems: other days we drift into theology or "the state of the nation": rarely we fly no higher than bawdy and "puns".'[22] 'My happiest hours', Lewis was later to say, 'are spent with three or four old friends . . . sitting up till the small hours in someone's college rooms talking nonsense, poetry, theology, metaphysics over beer, tea, and pipes. There's no sound I like better than adult male laughter.'[23]

Two years before this, a gifted young man, Edward Tangye Lean—brother of the film director David Lean—had matriculated at University College. While being tutored by Lewis, he formed a club actually called 'The Inklings'. Its members met for the very purpose of reading aloud unpublished compositions, and Lewis and Tolkien were invited to join. While all this was going on, Tangye Lean edited a university magazine and published two novels. Writing about this club to William Luther White on 11 September 1967, Tolkien said:

> The club met in T.-L.'s rooms in University College; its procedure was that at each meeting members should read aloud, unpublished compositions. These were supposed to be open to immediate criticism. . . . The club soon died . . . but C.S.L. and I at least survived. Its name was then transferred (by C.S.L.) to the undetermined and unelected circle of friends who gathered about C.S.L., and met in his rooms in Magdalen. Although our habit was to read aloud compositions of various kinds . . . this association and its habit would in fact have come into being at that time, whether the original short-lived club had ever existed or not.[24]

The foundations of The Inklings were in place. Lewis's brother, Warnie, attended the occasional meeting when he was home from the Army, and his diary, *Brothers and Friends*, is a major source of information about the group. Hugo Dyson came over from Reading as often as he could, and Lewis's great and dear friend, Owen Barfield, was often there from London. He and Lewis were coming to the end of their Great War discussion about this time.

On 4 February 1933, Lewis wrote excitedly to Arthur Greeves: 'Since term began I have had a delightful time reading a children's story which Tolkien has just written.'[25] It was *The Hobbit* (1937), the first work by an Inkling to become a classic. From there, Lewis and Tolkien went on to plan a joint project. They were dissatisfied with much of what they found in stories, and according to Tolkien, 'L. [Lewis] said to me one day: "Tollers, there is too little of what we really like in stories. I am afraid we shall have to try to write some ourselves." We agreed that he should try "space-travel", and I should try "time-travel".'[26] They had in mind stories that were 'mythopoeic'—having the quality of Myth—but disguised as thrillers. Tolkien wrote 'The Lost Road', the story of a journey back through time, and Lewis wrote *Out of the Silent Planet* (1938).

Lewis saw this as an opportunity to put into effect one of the things that was to be a hallmark of his writing. It is a 'Supposal'—suppose there are rational creatures on other planets that are unfallen? Suppose we meet them?

'I like the whole interplanetary idea', he said, 'as a *mythology* and simply wished to conquer for my own (Christian) pt. of view what has always hitherto been used by the opposite side.'[27] The result was his novel *Out of the Silent Planet* (1938), in which the adventurers from Earth discover on Malacandra (Mars) three races of beings who have never Fallen, and are not in need of redemption because they are obedient to Maleldil (God). When some of his readers failed to see what he was 'getting at', he concluded that 'any amount of theology can now be smuggled into people's minds under cover of romance without their knowing it.'[28]

At this point, I feel I must mention again the great change in Lewis that I attribute to his conversion. But Lewis had always been brilliant, as an atheist as well as a Christian. Before his conversion he could write well, and he was more ambitious then than at any time in his life. But apart from two early volumes of verse, nothing happened. I believe the whole thing can be summed up in five words: *Lewis had nothing to say*. It really does appear that when Lewis cared more about God than being a writer, God *gave* him things to say. I use the word 'gave' advisedly, but I think God *gave* Lewis and Tolkien—sub-creators both—the books we still celebrate. 'Of one thing I am sure', said Lewis, 'All seven of my Narnia books, and my three science fiction books, began with seeing pictures in my head.'[29]

While Lewis was still writing *Out of the Silent Planet*, Tolkien began his masterpiece, *The Lord of the Rings*, which was read and discussed during many meetings of The Inklings. This work, and that of Lewis, cannot be separated from one of Tolkien's most important literary theories—that of 'sub-creation', which he mentioned in his lecture 'On Fairy Stories,' given in 1939. According to Tolkien, while Man was disgraced by the Fall and for a long time estranged from God, he is not wholly lost or changed from his original nature. He retains the likeness of his Maker. Man shows that he is made in the image and likeness of the Maker when, acting in a 'derivative mode',[30] he writes stories which reflect the eternal Beauty and Wisdom. Imagination is 'the power of giving to ideal creations the inner consistency of reality.'[31] When Man draws things from the Primary World and creates a Secondary World, he is acting as a 'sub-creator'.[32] His sub-creations may have several effects. Man needs to be freed from the drab blur of triteness, familiarity, and possessiveness which impair his sight, and such stories help him recover 'a clear view'[33] of Creation. Another effect is the 'Consolation of the Happy Ending' or *Eucatastrophe*.[34] Such stories do not deny the existence of sorrow and failure, but they provide 'a sudden glimpse of the underlying reality or truth'.[35] After all, the Gospel or *Evangelium* contains 'a story of a larger kind which embraces all the essence of fairy-stories'.[36] In God's kingdom we must not imagine that the presence of the greatest depresses the small. The *Evangelium* has not destroyed stories, but hallowed them, especially those with the 'happy ending'.[37]

Lewis was to make the theory of 'sub-creation' his own. And to this he would add his important distinction between Fantasy and Imagination. Fantasy, when directed onto something which purports to be 'real life' is 'compensatory', and 'we run to it from the disappointments and humiliations of the real world. It sends us back to the real world undivinely discontented. For it is all flattery to the ego.'[38] *Imagination*, on the other hand, takes us right out of ourselves—to Middle-earth, to Malacandra, to Narnia—and affords a view of reality from many angles.

Shortly after Tolkien gave his talk on 'Fairy-Stories', England was in the Second World War. This caused a huge upheaval in Oxford. Most of the Inklings had served in the First War, but they could not be sure they would be left alone this time. Indeed, Warnie Lewis was recalled to active service in 1939. Now, in retrospect, it is clear that the war years were the Inklings' golden age. They were meeting every Thursday or Friday evening during term-time in Lewis's College rooms. Those who joined during the war years included Lord David Cecil, lecturer in English at New College; James Dundas-Grant, commander of the Oxford University Naval Division; Adam Fox, dean of Divinity at Magdalen; Colin Hardie, Classical tutor at Magdalen; R. E. 'Humphrey' Havard, Lewis's doctor; R. B. McCallum of Pembroke College; Father Gervase Mathew OP of Blackfriars; C. E. Stevens, historian at Magdalen; Charles Wrenn, lecturer in English Language; Christopher Tolkien (son of JRRT) and John Wain, both students at the time. It would take a large volume to do credit to all these men. Even if their works are not as long-lasting as those of Lewis and Tolkien, that does not mean they were less important in the long run. In any event, they were certainly important to the Inklings.

Of the new members, the one who had the greatest influence on the group was Charles Williams, an employee of Oxford University Press, who in 1939 was evacuated with the Press to Oxford. Lewis was a fervent admirer of Williams's 'theological thrillers', beginning with *The Place of the Lion*. Williams was 53 at the time, and all but one of his seven 'thrillers' had been published. 'In appearance', said Lewis, 'he was tall, slim, and straight as a boy, though grey-haired. His face we thought ugly: I am not sure that the word "monkey" has not been murmured in this context. But the moment he spoke it became, as was also said, like the face of an angel—not a feminine angel in the debased tradition of some religious art, but a masculine angel, a spirit burning with intelligence and charity.'[39]

Charles Williams arrived in time to hear Lewis read aloud to the group a book he'd been asked to write on *The Problem of Pain*, the first straight theological book he wrote as a Christian. As early as 1933, Lewis had made it clear that he would write and talk only about those things which unified Christians—'Mere Christianity'. In a Preface he wrote to the French translation of *The Problem of Pain*, Lewis spelled it out: 'Since my conversion', he said, 'it has seemed my particular task to tell the outside world what all Christians believe. Controversy I leave to others: that is the business of theologians. I think that you and I, the laity, simple soldiers of the Faith, will best serve the cause of reconciliation not so much by contributing to such debates, but by our prayers, and by sharing all that can already be shared of Christian life.'[40] Lewis said many times that he was not qualified to discuss 'points of high Theology or . . . ecclesiastical history',[41] and it seems to me that those interested in ecumenism have much to learn from the Inklings. Divided about equally between Catholics and Protestants, they probably shared as much as fellow Christians can share.

Warnie was in the army when Williams joined the group, and when his brother wrote to him on 11 November 1939 he described a typical meeting. 'On Thursday', he said, 'we had a meeting of the Inklings. . . . We dined at the Eastgate. I have never in my life seen Dyson so exuberant—"a roaring cataract of nonsense". The bill of fare afterwards consisted of a section of the new Hobbit book from Tolkien, a nativity play from Williams (unusually intelligible for him, and approved by all) and a chapter out of the book on the Problem of Pain from me. It so happened . . . that the subject matter of the three readings formed almost a logical sequence, and produced a really first rate evening's talk of the usual wide-ranging kind—"from grave to gay, from lively to severe".[42]

Before returning to 'the new Hobbit book', I should mention that Tolkien was by no means as enthusiastic about Charles Williams as Lewis. Some of his writings, such as his Arthurian poems, were difficult. When I asked Dr. Havard, Lewis's doctor and a member of the group, if he understood them, he said, 'I don't even understand his *prose*!' In a letter written years later, Tolkien said, 'I knew Charles Williams only as a friend of C.S.L. . . . We liked one another and enjoyed talking . . . but we had nothing to say to one another at deeper (or higher) levels. . . . I had read or heard a good deal of his work, but found it wholly alien, and sometimes very distasteful, occasionally ridiculous. . . . Lewis was bowled over. But Lewis was a very impressionable man, and this was abetted by his great generosity and capacity for friendship.'[43]

The permanent *core* of the Inklings was not as large as it appears when you add those who came to meetings occasionally. Lewis dedicated *The Problem of Pain* to 'The Inklings', and when Dom Bede Griffiths asked who they were, Lewis replied: 'Williams, Dyson of Reading, & my brother (Anglicans) and Tolkien and my doctor, Havard (your Church) are the "Inklings" to whom my *Problem of Pain* was dedicated. We meet on Friday evenings in my rooms: theoretically to talk about literature, but in fact nearly always to talk about something better. What I owe to them all is incalculable. Dyson and Tolkien were the immediate human causes of my own conversion. Is any pleasure on earth as great as a circle of Christian friends by a good fire?'[44]

'The new Hobbit book' from Tolkien was their name for what became *The Lord of the Rings*. This great work was to take Tolkien fourteen years to write, and we are able to follow much of its progress in the letters he wrote to his son Christopher, when he was in the Air Force during the war. Before quoting a letter of 31 May 1944, I should explain that a work by Lewis first called 'Who Goes Home?' was published the following year as *The Great Divorce*. And the book his brother, Warnie, was writing on Louis XIV was published in 1953 as *The Splendid Century*. 'The Inklings meeting', wrote Tolkien,

> 'was very enjoyable. Hugo was there: rather tired-looking, but reasonably noisy. The chief entertainment was provided by a chapter of Warnie Lewis's book on the times of Louis XIV (very good I thought it); and some excerpts from C.S.L.'s 'Who Goes Home?'—a book on Hell, which I suggested should have been called rather 'Hugo's Home'. . . . The rest of my time . . . has been occupied by the desperate attempt to bring 'The Ring' to a suitable pause, the capture of Frodo by the Orcs in the passes of Mordor, before I am obliged to break off by examining. By sitting up all hours, I managed it: and read the last 2 chapters (*Shelob's Lair* and *The Choices of Master Samwise*) to C.S.L. on Monday morning. He approved with unusual fervour, and was actually affected to tears by the last chapter, so it seems to be keeping up.'[45]

Lewis and Tolkien were often asked what 'influence' they had on one another. Once, in conversation with Tolkien, he realized I was under the impression that what he was reading aloud to Lewis in the early 1930s was *The Lord of the Rings*. He explained that what Lewis had been listening to—very patiently—for several years was not that story at all, but all the material that made up the Appendices to the *Ring*. He went on to say that he might never have got around to it, but 'You know what a *boy* Jack Lewis was! He *had* to have a story, and that story—*The Lord of the Rings*—was written to keep him quiet!' At first I thought he was just being kind to me, but I have since seen much the same in some of his letters. And now there has come to light confirmation of this from Lewis. In a letter to Francis Anderson of 23 September 1963, Lewis said:

> I don't think Tolkien influenced me, and I am certain I didn't influence him. That is, didn't influence *what* he wrote. My continual encouragement, carried to the point of nagging, influenced him v. much to write at all with that gravity and at that length. In other words I acted as a midwife not as a father.[46]

Besides Christopher Tolkien, the other young member of the Inklings was John Wain, the novelist and biographer of Dr. Johnson, who came up to Oxford in 1944. He had Lewis as his tutor. Eventually he was invited to the Inklings meetings and in his autobiography he left a picture of what the Thursday evening meetings in Lewis's rooms were like. 'I can see the room so clearly now', said Wain,

> the electric fire pumping heat into the dank air, the faded screen that broke some of the keener draughts, the enamel beer-jug on the table, the well-worn sofa and armchairs, and the men drifting in . . . leaving overcoats and hats in any corner and coming over to warm their hands before finding a chair. There was no fixed etiquette, but the rudimentary honours would be done partly by Lewis and partly by his brother, W. H. Lewis, a man who stays in my memory as the most courteous I have ever met—not with mere politeness, but with a genial, self-forgetful considerateness that was as instinctive to him as breathing. Sometimes, when the less vital members of the circle were in a big majority, the evening would fall flat; but the best of them were as good as anything I shall live to see. . . . In a very dead period of Oxford's history, Lewis and his friends provided a stir of life: here, one felt, were some scholars and teachers who were not merely 'day-labouring out life's age', but *building* something.[47]

We must not think of the Inklings as anything like a 'mutual admiration society' or men hungry for professional advancement. They were, first and foremost, Christians, who had in common something that was far more important than their jobs or their other interests. Nowhere is this better put than in the definition Lewis gave of Friendship in *The Four Loves*: 'In this kind of love', he said, '"Do you love me?" means "Do you see the same truth?"—Or at least, "Do you *care about* the same truth?"[48]

Besides the Thursday evening meetings in Lewis's rooms in Magdalen College, the Inklings met every Tuesday morning in the back parlour of the

Eagle and Child pub, or the 'Bird and Baby', as it is known. These meetings were not confined to term-time, but went on all during the year. A number of the Inklings were usually found there from about 11.30 a.m. to 1.00 p.m. Lewis and Tolkien and a few others usually went to both kinds of meetings, those in Magdalen and those in the pub, but there were some who went only to the meetings in the Bird and Baby. Friends such as George Sayer and Roger Lancelyn Green dropped in to both the evening meetings and those in the pub when they were visiting Oxford. Probably none of the Inklings loved pubs and beer as much as Lewis. Once when he was described in a newspaper as 'Ascetic Mr C. S. Lewis' Tolkien wrote to his son Christopher: 'Ascetic Mr Lewis – !!! I ask you! He put away three pints in a very short session we had this morning, and said he was "going short for Lent".'[49] Those who have no experience of an English pub cannot imagine how very different they are from American bars. Lewis loved the friendly, warm atmosphere of a pub, and he told me that if they served milk—which he liked—in pubs he could easily become a lactomaniac. Lewis loved huge quantities of weak liquids—especially tea and beer—and he was once described as 'a great bladder of a man'.

Those thrilling Thursday evenings in Lewis's College rooms ended in 1949. Warnie recorded in his diary on Thursday, 27 October 1949: 'Dined with J at College. . . . No one turned up after dinner, which was just as well, as J has a bad cold and wanted to go to bed early.'[50] On Thursday, 10 November 1949, he wrote, 'No Inklings tonight, so dined at "home".'[51] This upsets so many people that I rush to point out that the Tuesday morning Inklings continued!

But it is sad even so. The story of the Thursday evening meetings is such a pleasant one that, like Jill in *The Last Battle*, we too feel like saying, 'Oh, I do hope we can soon settle the Ape and get back to those good, ordinary times. And then I hope they'll go on for ever and ever and ever.'[52]

The matter is too complicated to explore at the end of a talk. I am inclined to think that the ending of the evening meetings owed more than anything to the fact that the Inklings were older. And, unusual for men not far from retirement, *busier*. Mrs Tolkien was suffering a great deal from arthritis, and Tolkien—and his family—felt he should spend more time at home. Lewis's own home life was in crisis. Some of you will know that when he went to war in 1917 he promised his friend, Paddy Moore, that if he died he—Lewis—would look after his mother. Mrs Moore had been his care since 1919, and by 1949 she was 77 years old and an invalid. Lewis spent nearly every available minute at home looking after the woman he now called his 'mother'.

Lewis was physically exhausted, and when he wrote to his friend Don Giovanni Calabria of Verona on 14 January 1949, the exhaustion and a sense of futility shows through. 'As for my own work', he told Don Giovanni,

> I would not wish to deceive you with vain hope. I am now in my fiftieth year. I feel my zeal for writing, and whatever talent I originally possessed, to be decreasing; nor (I believe) do I please my readers as I used to. I labour under many difficulties. My house is unquiet and devastated by women's quarrels. . . . My aged mother, worn out by long infirmity, is my daily care. Pray for me, Father, that I ever bear in mind that profoundly true maxim: 'if you wish to bring others to peace, keep thyself in peace'.[53]

Besides his care of Mrs Moore, Lewis was worried about his beloved brother, Warnie, who in February 1949 had a serious bout of alcoholism and was in hospital for several weeks. It was almost certainly at about this time, when Lewis's spirits were very low, that he began dreaming of lions. 'At first', he said about the inspiration for *The Lion, the Witch and the Wardrobe*, 'I had very little idea how the story would go. But then suddenly Aslan came bounding into it. I think I had been having a good many dreams of lions about that time.'[54]

Now that the Inklings were meeting on Tuesday mornings, they seem to have re-vivified by it being the only activity of the week, and a regular gathering was larger than the gatherings in Magdalen College. *The Lion, the Witch and the Wardrobe* was completed in 1949, and Lewis had made a start on *Prince Caspian*. Roger Lancelyn Green remembered the proofs of *The Lion, the Witch and the Wardrobe* being handed around in the Bird and Baby on 22 June 1950. Roger Lancelyn Green had earlier remembered running into Tolkien shortly after Lewis had completed *The Lion, the Witch and the Wardrobe*. 'I hear you've been reading Jack's children's story', said Tolkien. 'It really won't do, you know! I mean to say: "*Nymphs and their Ways, The Love-Life of a Faun*". Doesn't he know what he's talking about?'[55]

I, for one, do not find this upsetting. Tolkien didn't like a lot of things! Lewis didn't like a lot of things! You don't like a lot of things! Tolkien didn't like Lewis's mixing of various mythologies, and he was often unhappy with Lewis's theological audacities. Despite the fact that Tolkien didn't like the Narnian stories himself, Mrs Tolkien sent copies to their grandson.

In 1967 Tolkien and I had several visits from William Ready, who had written *The Tolkien Relation* (1968). I remember a sort of post-mortem meeting with Tolkien after Ready left Oxford. Tolkien was confused by Ready's statement that *The Lord of the Rings* had an 'ecclesiastical dimension'. Tolkien didn't like the sound of that, and he told me that his main objection to the Narnian stories was that the Christian elements were 'too obvious'. I suggested that perhaps the Christian elements in *The Lord of the Rings* weren't obvious enough. He thought that was possibly true. But it was this conversation which led me to think hard about the 'freedom' Tolkien and Lewis enjoyed in their creations. Both had to do some deliberate inventing and linking of scenes, but their stories were *given* to them, and one has to accept that.

In conclusion, the weekly morning sessions of the Inklings not only went on, but they gathered pace. At meetings at the Bird and Baby in 1954, proofs of *The Lord of the Rings* were being shown round. After Lewis left for Cambridge in 1955, meetings were changed to Monday mornings, to allow Lewis to get an afternoon train to Cambridge. When, unfortunately, the landlord of the Bird and Baby opened up the little parlour, once the exclusive reserve of the Inklings, to the public, the Inklings moved across St Giles' to the Lamb and Flag. I went to a number of meetings with Lewis there, and usually at the end of the meeting Dr Havard would drive Lewis, Jim Dundas-Grant, and myself to The Trout for lunch by the river. I'd never seen Lewis happier. These lasted right up to his death in November 1963. When I returned to Oxford in 1964, and was asked by Warnie to edit his brother's writings, I joined a few of the Inklings for the morning meetings. Increasingly there were excuses why one or more of them couldn't be there. The epitaph was spoken by R. B. Macallum, Master of Pembroke College, who at a meeting in 1964 said, 'Let's face it. Without Jack we can't go on. When the sun goes out there's no more light in the solar system.'

Notes

1. C. S. Lewis, *All My Road Before Me: The Diary of C. S. Lewis 1922–1927*, ed. Walter Hooper (London: HarperCollins, 1991), 392–3.
2. C. S. Lewis, *Surprised by Joy: The Shape of My Early Life* (London: Bles, 1955), ch. XIV, 204–205.
3. C. S. Lewis, *Collected Letters: Volume I: Family Letters 1905–1931*, ed. Walter Hooper (London: HarperCollins, 2000), 701.
4. Lewis, *Surprised by Joy*, ch. XIV, 215.
5. Letter to Walter Hooper, 30 November 1954, in *C. S. Lewis, Collected Letters: Volume III: Narnia, Cambridge and Joy*, ed. Walter Hooper (London: HarperCollins, 2006), 535.
6. George Weigel, *Witness to Hope: The Biography of Pope John Paul II 1920–2005* (London: HarperCollins, 1999), 136.

7. John 12:24.

8. C. S. Lewis, *Collected Letters: Volume I*, 838.

9. C. S. Lewis, *Collected Letters: Volume I*, 880.

10. C. S. Lewis, *Collected Letters: Volume I*, 917–918.

11. C. S. Lewis, *Collected Letters: Volume II: Books, Broadcasts and War 1931–1949*, ed. Walter Hooper (London: HarperCollins, 2004), 17.

12. Entry of 18 February 1933, W. H. Lewis, *Brothers and Friends: The Diaries of Major Warren Hamilton Lewis*, ed. Clyde S. Kilby and Marjorie Lamp Mead (San Francisco: Harper & Row, 1982), 97.

13. See the biography of Hugo Dyson in Walter Hooper, *C. S. Lewis: A Companion and Guide* (London: HarperCollins, 1996), 651–652.

14. C. S. Lewis, *Collected Letters: Volume I*, 976–977.

15. Lewis, *Surprised by Joy*, ch. XI, 161.

16. 'Reason', *Collected Poems of C. S. Lewis*, ed. Walter Hooper (London: HarperCollins, 1994), 95.

17. Letter to T. S. Eliot, 2 June 1931, in *C. S. Lewis, Collected Letters: Volume III*, 1523.

18. C. S. Lewis and E. M. W. Tillyard, *The Personal Heresy: A Controversy* (London: Oxford University Press, 1939), 2.

19. Lewis and Tillyard, *The Personal Heresy*, 11.

20. Lewis and Tillyard, *The Personal Heresy*, 26–27.

21. C. S. Lewis, *An Experiment in Criticism* (Cambridge: Cambridge University Press, 1961), ch. XI, 137.

22. C. S. Lewis, *Collected Letters: Volume II*, 16.

23. Roger Lancelyn Green and Walter Hooper, *C. S. Lewis: A Biography* (London: Collins, 1974; HarperCollins, revised and expanded edition, 2002), ch. 6, 170.

24. *The Letters of J. R. R. Tolkien*, ed. Humphrey Carpenter, with Christopher Tolkien (London: Allen & Unwin, 1981), 388.

25. C. S. Lewis, *Collected Letters: Volume II*, 96.

26. Letter to Charlotte and Denis Plimmer, 9 February 1967, in *The Letters of J. R. R. Tolkien*, 378.

27. Letter to Roger Lancelyn Green, 28 December 1938, in *C. S. Lewis, Collected Letters: Volume II*, 236–237.

28. Letter to Sister Penelope, 9 August 1939, in *C. S. Lewis, Collected Letters: Volume II*, 262.

29. C. S. Lewis, 'It All Began with a Picture . . .', *Of This and Other Worlds*, ed. Walter Hooper (London: Fount, 1984; HarperCollins, 2000), 64.

30. J. R. R. Tolkien, 'On Fairy-Stories', in *idem, The Monsters and the Critics and Other Essays*, ed. Christopher Tolkien (London: Allen & Unwin, 1983), 145.

31. Tolkien, 'On Fairy-Stories', 138.

32. Tolkien, 'On Fairy-Stories', 144.

33. Tolkien, 'On Fairy-Stories', 146.

34. Tolkien, 'On Fairy-Stories', 153.

35. Tolkien, 'On Fairy-Stories', 155.
36. Tolkien, 'On Fairy-Stories', 155.
37. Tolkien, 'On Fairy-Stories', 156.
38. C. S. Lewis, 'On Three Ways of Writing for Children', in *idem*, *Of This and Other Worlds*, ed. Walter Hooper (London: Collins, 1982; Fount, 2000), 50.
39. *Essays Presented to Charles Williams*, ed. C. S. Lewis (London: Oxford University Press, 1947), ix.
40. Walter Hooper, *C. S. Lewis: A Companion and Guide* (London: HarperCollins, 1996), 297.
41. C. S. Lewis, *Mere Christianity* (London: Bles, 1952), vi.
42. *C. S. Lewis, Collected Letters: Volume II*, 288–289.
43. Letter to Dick Plotz, 12 September 1965, in *The Letters of J. R. R. Tolkien*, 361–362.
44. Letter of 21 December 1941, in *C. S. Lewis, Collected Letters: Volume II*, 501.
45. Letter to Christopher Tolkien, 31 May 1944, in *The Letters of J. R. R. Tolkien*, 83.
46. *C. S. Lewis, Collected Letters: Volume III*, 1458.
47. John Wain, *Sprightly Running: Part of an Autobiography* (London: Macmillan, 1962), ch. V, 184–185.
48. C. S. Lewis, *The Four Loves* (London: Geoffrey Bles), ch. IV, 78.
49. Letter of 1 March 1944, in *The Letters of J. R. R. Tolkien*, 68.
50. W. H. Lewis, *Brothers and Friends*, 230.
51. W. H. Lewis, *Brothers and Friends*, 231.
52. C. S. Lewis, *The Last Battle* (London: Bodley Head, 1956), ch. VIII, 92.
53. *C. S. Lewis, Collected Letters: Volume II*, 905–906.
54. Lewis, 'It All Began with a Picture . . .', *Of This and Other Worlds*, 64.
55. Green and Hooper, *C. S. Lewis: A Biography*, ch. 11, 307.

17

Lewis and/or Barfield

Owen Barfield

THERE ARE TWO kinds of inaccuracies to which references to me in books about Lewis are subject: One of these is the attribution to me of opinions or views that in fact I don't hold and never have held; the other is the attribution to Lewis of opinions or views not explicitly expressed by him, but with the assertion that he held them, supported by quotations from my books.[1] I don't think we need to concern ourselves much with the first class, because, although I may find it rather irritating when I read in an article about Lewis by somebody whose name I can't now recall: 'He does not, like Barfield, hold that God evolves' (now as far as I know, I don't hold, and certainly never *said*, 'God evolves'), yet for students of Lewis it is not particularly important. But the other kind, the attribution to Lewis of opinions or views, which attribution is then supported by quotations from me, that I think is of some interest or should be of some interest to students of Lewis.

First of all, I think I must make a few historical and personal, or historically personal, observations, because it is quite clear that many people who write about Lewis are under a false impression concerning the duration of intimate or philosophical exchanges between Lewis and myself. I think that comes about because there was a short period in our lives when there was a continuous and intense interchange of philosophical opinions between us. It is referred to by Lewis, as most of you probably know, in *Surprised by Joy* as the 'Great War'. Some of you may have read Lionel Adey's little book *C. S. Lewis's 'Great War' with Owen Barfield.*

But all that took place and really had been finished before Lewis's conversion. That, I think, is where people tend to make a mistake. They often assume that the same kind of discursive interchange must have continued throughout our joint lives. That was not so. After Lewis's conversion, we rarely touched on philosophy or metaphysics in our exchanges and, I think I can say, never did we touch at any length on theology. What we did do was just enjoy ourselves. We read a good many books together and talked about the kind of things one talks about. Actually, in the last three or four years of his life, I rarely saw him alone. There were usually three of us: Lewis and me and our mutual friend A. C. Harwood, who died ten years ago. The feeling was, especially between those two, that the thing to do was to enjoy the time as a holiday, rather than have any serious conversation. I confess that I felt a certain amount of distress when I perceived that we never could have any sort of philosophical/ metaphysical interchange of the old kind, because I felt it might have been fruitful. I had the feeling sometimes, when we were enjoying ourselves, *C'est magnifique mais ce n'est pas la guerre.*[2] One particular occasion I do remember vividly, which I don't think I've ever mentioned to anybody. You know that Lewis and I, with other friends, used to go on walking tours in the spring for a few days. Well, Lewis and I, or sometimes Lewis and one of his other friends, would in addition go on what you might call mini walking tours. That might be at any time of the year. In fact, we'd stay away for one night or take the weekend and stay two nights. On such a mini walking tour alone with Lewis, I remember staying at Wallingford. I think it was very late in the year.

It was shortly after his conversion. Just before we went to bed, I tried, you might say, to go on from where we had left off. What I wanted to do was to see what relation there was between his 'stance' after his conversion and the kind of opinions he held before it, and also to see how far we were still in accord. As soon as the conversation took that direction, he broke it off sharply. I don't think I ever heard him speak with such emotion. He simply refused to talk at that sort of depth at all. I remember his saying, and again with more emotion than I ever heard him express: 'I can't *bear* it!' And I do remember also feeling deeply distressed—indeed agitated—on that occasion. He went off to bed, and I went out (it was after dark) for a walk, like Prospero 'to still my beating mind'. I had the feeling something was broken. So, thereafter, broadly speaking, anything Lewis knew about my ideas and opinions he got only from my books, not from conversation with me. He—it's fair to say and I think right to say—thought highly of some of those books. When he read *Saving the Appearances*, he called it a 'stunner'; *Worlds Apart*, when it first came out, he said he found so exciting that he was in danger of reading it too quickly; and shortly before his death, when he was confined to his bed, he wrote to me that the two things that consoled him most were reading that book, *Worlds Apart*, and the *Iliad*. So you see he knew how to couple in a flattering way.

The point I want to get to is that Lewis—regarded as subject matter for research—had a certain advantage there, because he developed; he changed and continued to change. He developed to a considerable extent after his conversion; whereas I have never changed at all. As I have often said, I have the feeling, when I write a book, that I always write the same book over and over again, though perhaps in a different context or from a different approach. But Lewis did change; he had this big change, his conversion, and there were also changes after it in his presentation of Christianity, in his—again I use a favourite American word—stance. That view is confirmed by no less an authority than Walter Hooper, who says in his Preface to the book *Christian Reflections* something that I was struck by and that made me think:

> I beg the reader to note that [the essay] 'Christianity and Culture' came fairly early in Lewis's theological corpus. It might best be considered an early step in his spiritual pilgrimage—but certainly not his arrival. Here, instead of spirit progressively irradiating and transforming soul, he seems to envisage a relation between them in strict terms of 'either-or', with soul as Calvin's 'nature' and spirit as his 'grace', and spirit beginning exactly where soul leaves off. Later on he dealt much more profoundly with the relation between soul and spirit in such things as the essay on 'Transposition' and *The Four Loves*.[3]

I think I had better take that a little further. But first of all, let me emphasize once again that fact, that he changed—if you like, he grew and I failed to grow—but, at any rate, he changed his views, whereas I didn't. That is one of the outstanding, underlying differences between us. I am going to summarize the other differences a little later, but that is the big difference. It often is the case that thinking people change substantially. There is an earlier Wittgenstein and a later Wittgenstein; there is an earlier Heidegger and a later Heidegger, an earlier D. H. Lawrence and a later D. H. Lawrence; but there's no earlier Barfield and later Barfield. He always says the same old thing. And that meant that Lewis had a certain advantage of me. On the other hand, it makes it more difficult to represent what his views were. He has been described by one writer as 'a hard man to pin down'. I find two more difficulties in trying to arrive at what Lewis's real outlook, real opinion was. First, so much of his theology you got from books or broadcasts was deliberately made very simple. *Mere Christianity* is the obvious example. It is very easy, and probably a mistake, to read into them a complete statement of Lewis's theological position, and yet one tends to do so—at least I find myself tending to do so. The other thing is that, in trying to arrive at what Lewis's views on life were, you have, on the one hand, what I call his *theological* utterances and, on the other, his *literary* utterances. Some of the latter, some of the utterances in his literature, whether fictional or critical, do seem to be relevant to that stance. They are certainly assumed to be so by a good many of those who put themselves forward as his—what? exegetes? exponents?

Partly for those reasons, Lewis and Barfield are sometimes confused with each other. I don't mean their persons, of course; I mean their opinions. Because they have been sometimes taken to interpenetrate, in a way that was not the case. I'll try to give an example of that. In—I don't know how to describe it; it was sent to me by my friend Raymond Tripp, of the University of Denver—'Introduction: Jung and the Evolution of Consciousness'—I don't know whether it is part of a book or whether it has been published,[4] but it is mainly about Lewis—after some preliminary remarks, there are four or five pages expounding Barfield. Then the author goes on to say, 'By moving on to the work of C. S. Lewis, a lifelong friend and intellectual opponent of Barfield's, we can find very similar ideas about the evolution of consciousness at work.' That, I think, and as I shall try to show, is decidedly questionable. He adds, 'I offer these remarks on Lewis to provide a context in relation to Jung for his own statements regarding the history of consciousness. Lewis is a hard man to pin down metaphysically, but it cannot be denied that he possessed a keen sense of mental evolution even though his position on historicism in general is not easily determined.' Against 'historicism' there is a note, and the note refers to Lewis's essay called 'Historicism' (reprinted both in *Christian Reflections*, 1967, and in *Fern-seed and Elephants*, 1975, both edited by Walter Hooper) and says that Lewis's most teasing discussion on the value of history is to be found in that essay. Well, if you read the essay on 'Historicism' (and see my essay 'C. S. Lewis and Historicism'[5]), you will find that, so far from suggesting that he had a firm view of mental evolution, or anything like an evolution of consciousness, the whole point of the essay is to deny that there is such a thing as an evolution of consciousness or if there is, that we can ever know anything about it.

Tripp goes on to deal with *The Discarded Image* (1964), which has those fascinating chapters on the mediaeval outlook, and which does seem to suggest that Lewis saw not merely the structure of ideas but the actual consciousness of people as something which had evolved. That book, though not published until after Lewis's death, was based on the lectures he gave early in his career at Oxford, and it contains a wonderful description of mediaeval man's environment, as mediaeval man saw it, or as he thought about it, as contrasted with our own. But then, and this is not referred to by Tripp, in the Epilogue you read this: 'I have made no serious effort to hide the fact that the old Model delights me as I believe it delighted our ancestors. Few constructions of the imagination seem to me to have combined splendour, sobriety, and coherence in the same degree. It is possible that some readers have long been itching to remind me that it had a serious defect; it was not true. I agree. It was not true.'[6] You see, he uses the word *model*, which to my mind makes it clear that what he was thinking about was not the sort of thing that I have always tried to write about, an evolution of consciousness, that is, a change not only in the ideas people have formed about the world, but a change in the very world they experience. He is thinking of change in a structure of ideas *about* an unchanging world; he is talking about changing thoughts, not about changing perception. A little later, he continues: 'It would . . . be subtly misleading to say, "The medievals thought the universe to be like that, but we know it to be like this". Part of what we know is that we cannot, in the old sense, "know what the universe is like" and that no model we can build will be, in that old sense, "like" it.'[7] That, I think, is really the voice of Lewis when contrasting former views of the world with later, or Christian, ones: you cannot possibly know what the universe is like. That is Lewis himself speaking.

One more example. In the book *The Longing for a Form: Essays on the Fiction of C. S. Lewis*, edited by Peter Schakel (a very fine collection it is), there is an essay by Father Edward G. Zogby, who is Assistant Professor of Religious Studies at Le Moyne College, in Syracuse. I found it a profoundly interesting essay. What he maintains is that Lewis's experience of the world and of life was essentially based on polarity. He goes on to say that he lived this polarity, a polarity between reason on the one hand and imagination on the other. I think he's right in saying that Lewis lived the polarity, but I don't think he's right in saying that it was part of his system of ideas. In fact, I know it wasn't; for I tried more than once to expound the concept of polarity to him, and he more or less laughed me out of court. Zogby uses his first three or four pages expounding Barfield; and then he goes on to say things like this (in his essay called 'Triadic Patterns in Lewis's Life and Thought'): 'The triadic pattern in Lewis's life and autobiographies is *delight: pain: fruit*; in his social criticism— *tradition* (Tao): *anti-tradition* (being outside of the Tao): *the Tao realized* in the individual person; in his theology—*begetting* (*zoe*): *making* (*bios*): *participation* in the life of the Trinity.'[8] I can't think that Lewis would have been easy with having attributed to him this concept of participation in the life of the Trinity, and I think the reason Father Zogby can attribute that concept to him is really because he made that mistake I began by pointing out: attributing to Lewis ideas, or, at any rate, emphases, that he finds in my books. He himself is obviously impressed by the concept of polarity as being what Coleridge called 'the universal law of polarity', extending through the whole of being. But, as I say, when I tried to propound that to Lewis, it was quite alien to his whole mental structure.

Here, then, are examples of the kinds of illusion some people are under as to the relation between what Lewis thought and what I thought and think. I doubt very much indeed, as I said, that Lewis would have been happy with the notion of participation in the life of the Trinity. It is just the kind of thing that that conversation at Wallingford that never materialized might have led to. Lewis, or so it seems to me, in his theological utterances always emphasized the chasm between Creator and creature, rather than anything in the nature of participation.

I hope I've said enough to show that among those commentators on Lewis who take Barfield into their consideration, those who stress the differences sometimes do so by attributing to Barfield ideas or opinions he never held. Those who stress the affinity are apt to do so by attributing to Lewis ideas or opinions that they find in Barfield. That's why I felt that I must, to fulfill the purpose of this piece, emphasize the differences or disagreements between Lewis and myself, though there are all sorts of reasons why I should be happier to emphasize only the agreements. Of course, there was plenty we agreed on, it hardly needs to be said—particularly, I suppose, on the superficiality and confused thinking which characterize the atmosphere of 'secular humanism', and which is very much the prevailing atmosphere. We both were very particularly aware of the silliness, the triviality of the average intellectual life of the time, and the confused thinking it was based on. And it was a delight to me to watch the way Lewis's brilliant intellect and absolute honesty of mind just cut through all that, like a red-hot knife going through butter, in some of his writings, for instance, *The Abolition of Man*.

I will try to enumerate or summarize some of the differences which were undoubtedly there and which, as I have said, I feel are perhaps insufficiently realized by a good many of those who write about Lewis, bringing in Barfield. Barfield never held, and does not hold now, that 'God evolves'. He does hold that the relation of man to God is something that evolves, continuously evolves. I think if you had asked Lewis whether he felt the same, he would definitely have said 'No', and that leads to another difference, partly connected with it. The very use of the word *man*, if one speaks of the relation of man to God, and does so in terms of evolution or its possibility, implies that one conceives of humanity as a whole constituting an entity, a real being. Now whatever 'literary Lewis' has said, 'theological Lewis' always writes of the individual man, the individual soul. If he used the word *humanity* at all, I think it is clear that he thought of it simply as a numerical aggregate of individual souls. So that anything in the nature of evolution or progress or improvement can occur only in the life of some one soul between birth and death. There Barfield differs from him; he thinks that man, humanity as a whole, is a spiritual reality and, as I said, that it has been evolving and will continue to evolve. Incidentally, this exclusive emphasis on individual soul, or individual spirit, as the only reality, is something which appeared earlier in Lewis's life, which was there even before his conversion, and was part of his makeup. It is there in the kind of thing that interested him and the kind of thing that didn't. He was not ever interested in collectivity of any sort. It wasn't real to him. He was not interested in races, civilizations as a whole, nations and the differences between them, societies, groups—still less in movements of any sort. He always came back to the individual soul; a movement might be there in the background, but it was of no particular importance—for instance, the Renaissance. He could not take the Renaissance really seriously; in his *English Literature in the Sixteenth Century,* he argued that there is no such thing as the Renaissance; and I think if you had talked with him about the Reformation, you would have found that he regarded the movement of the Reformation as of quite minimal importance compared with the personal relationship of, say, Martin Luther to God. I have already mentioned his essay on historicism. Yet there *is* some evidence—a good deal of evidence, in fact—that what I am calling 'literary Lewis' did think there was such a thing as the evolution of consciousness, as distinct from the history of ideas. There are hints of that in *The Pilgrim's Regress, The Allegory of Love,* in some of his *Studies in Medieval and Renaissance Literature,* and, as I pointed out, in *The Discarded Image.* Yet I think it is true to say, and I have tried so to indicate, that theological Lewis would have nothing of the sort. There does seem to be a rather evident dichotomy between Lewis's two personalities, those two outlooks—that of literary Lewis and that of theological Lewis.

Both those concepts, of man, of humanity—of man as distinguishable from, but of course not separable from, a mere aggregate of separate souls—and the idea of evolution—of man's relationship to God—are relevant to the further concept of revelation. The English word *revelation,* of course, can mean either what in Latin would be called *revelatio,* that is, a continuing process, or *revelatum,* which means that which has been revealed. I think it is true to say that Lewis took the word in its second meaning only. He considered, and I am thinking of 'theological Lewis' now, that revelation had occurred once and for all in the past and that it is finished—whereas to my mind revelation is to be a continuing process. Then we come to the church. What do we mean by 'Christian'? 'Theological Lewis' seems to propose that it means membership, not necessarily of the Anglican Church, but at least of some organized body which shares his own view of what is meant by revelation. Barfield would include all who accept the Incarnation, and then the Resurrection, of Christ as the central point of human evolution. And that has all sorts of consequences. It means, for instance, that one feels many of the heretics (of course, not all of them)—for example, some of the Gnostics, some of the neo-Platonists, Cathars, Knights Templar, Rosicrucians—to have been more truly Christian than most (again, of course, not all) of their orthodox contemporaries. The interesting thing here is that 'literary Lewis' knew more of the details, the literature, of those heretical figures than Barfield. But 'literary Lewis' was not interested in their truth value, because that is not a literary issue. And theological Lewis refused to consider it because they have been stigmatized as heretics by the church in its ecumenical councils and otherwise. One could go on at some length enumerating and refining the differences, but one has to stop somewhere. I think another one, perhaps in a way the most important, is difference of opinion regarding the religious value of *knowledge* as opposed to *belief.* Another one is the issue of hierarchy. Lewis seems to have accepted it as a necessary basis of healthy social structure, including in it a hierarchical relationship between man and woman. Whereas Barfield thinks that the hierarchical structure of society was a phase in its evolution, which is presently disappearing.

Perhaps all these differences may be summed up or may stem from that central issue, whether the relationship between man and God is or is not an evolving one, evolving from a relationship of subjection to one of, let us say, cooperation and freedom. Whatever the source is, the differences between Barfield and 'theological Lewis' are wide enough to make me often feel uneasy while reading such Christian apologetics as *Mere Christianity,* some of the *Letters to Malcolm,* and *Reflections on the Psalms.* This is especially the case when the topic is sin; as it frequently is, naturally enough, when the main topic is the relationship between God and man. For Lewis, it seems to have been almost a synonym for disobedience. I remember a letter from Lewis's Cambridge days that he wrote to Harwood, the friend I have already referred to. They had evidently been having some correspondence or conversation on the differences and agreements between them. I don't think I ever saw either of their letters, but Harwood, a good deal later on, printed somewhere an article in which he quoted from Lewis's reply. And I remember the sentence he quoted: 'I was not born to be free; I was born to adore and obey.' Harwood, in that article, said that, although he agreed with all else that Lewis said, that was the point where he had to part company from him. And here, I am on Harwood's side. That way of putting it sounds to me more like the voice of what is sometimes called Yahwism, than it is like anything I find in St. Paul's Epistles, or indeed in the New Testament as a whole.

There were two things on which Lewis and I were certainly agreed: one, that the virtual disappearance from the general consciousness of the very idea of sin is perhaps the most threatening of all the signs of the times; and two, that the relationship between God and man is, in the last resort, expressible only in metaphor. But there, somehow, the agreement seems to end, because the *choice* of metaphor, the tendency to emphasize one particular kind of metaphor, at the expense of others, must be taken as positively revealing; since that is, after all, the whole function of metaphor. In Lewis's choices of metaphor—again I say *theological* Lewis's choices of metaphor—I find something that I cannot feel is auspicious for the future either of the church or of humanity as a whole. What to name it? The effort makes me uneasy, but I can only call it a kind of 'devotional reductionism'. I hope you see what I mean. Perhaps I can epitomize it best in this way: When I have sinned, as I frequently do, though perhaps not in a particularly spectacular or interesting way, I do not feel at all like a naughty child who has disobeyed a kind parent and grieved him, or like a dog that has failed to come to heel when called; I feel like a trustee who has committed a breach of trust.

And there I think I had better stop and leave you to make the best you can of it all.

Notes

1. This talk was given on 19 November 1985. An unrevised version has previously been published in *Owen Barfield on C. S. Lewis*, ed. G. B. Tennyson (Middleton, CT: Wesleyan University Press, 1989; and London: Barfield Press, 2011).
2. 'It is magnificent, but it is not war.'
3. C. S. Lewis, *Christian Reflections*, ed. Walter Hooper (London: Geoffrey Bles, 1967), xii.
4. This was a lecture by Raymond B. Tripp, Jr., delivered to the Colorado Jung Society on 26 September 1978.
5. *Owen Barfield on C. S. Lewis*, 67–81.
6. C. S. Lewis, *The Discarded Image: An Introduction to Medieval and Renaissance Literature* (Cambridge: Cambridge University Press, 1964), 216.
7. Lewis, *The Discarded Image*, 218.
8. Edward G. Zogby, S. J., 'Triadic Patterns in Lewis's Life and Thought', in *The Longing for a Form: Essays on the Fiction of C. S. Lewis*, ed. Peter J. Schakel, (Kent, OH: Kent State University Press, 1977), 20–39; quote at 24–25.

18

Brothers and Friends: The Diaries of W. H. Lewis

John Wain

I WAS HAVING dinner in an Oxford college a year or so ago and the conversation happened to turn on the Lewis circle, and some chap said, 'W. H. Lewis was a bore.' I said to him, 'How well did you know W. H. Lewis?' and he said, 'Ah I never met him.'[1] And obviously in saying that W. H. Lewis was a bore, the man was simply parroting what somebody else had parroted from somebody else, who had parroted it from somebody else. I didn't bother to argue with him, but merely briefly informed him that the person who had told him that W. H. Lewis was a bore was a fool and a liar, and passed on to the next topic. In fact, W. H. Lewis was a delightful man with a very well-stocked mind, tolerant, generous, imaginative, with a great sensibility, very sensitive to music, very sensitive to visual impressions, deeply read, very gifted in verbal expression. He wrote extremely well and was a very interesting person to talk to, a good listener, unobtrusive, not concerned to push his own point of view, and—in some ways typical of a man who was spending the second half of his life in retirement in a milieu which is not his own milieu and which his advancement does not depend on in any way—he was simply interested in having good conversation and meeting interesting people and hearing what they had to say and occasionally, when called on, putting his own opinions in but never pushing them. I found him a totally delightful person, and if there existed in the world anybody who found W. H. Lewis boring, I can only say that that is a very sad comment on that person.

Now I in fact made the acquaintance of W. H. Lewis within ten minutes of making acquaintance with C. S. Lewis, because my dates as an undergraduate are strange ones. They're 1943 to 1946; 1943 was when the war really began to bite. People no longer got any kind of reservation for being students and so on, but just went straight into the war. When I presented myself for my medical in March 1943, I was put into grade four, from which they were not taking any men at all, because I had things wrong with my eyes, which I always have had. I had not expected that, but when I was faced with the fact that I was not going to be required for military service in the war, I thought I might as well get on with it and have my undergraduate life. So my dates are 1943 to 1946, and St John's is my college, but the tutor in English at St John's, Gavin Bone, had died in 1942, and they were sending such few men as there were doing English out of site. I don't know who it was who decided that I was to be sent to C. S. Lewis, but it was certainly a very good turn for me because it was a major thing in my life to be taught by him. He was so good as to say that he enjoyed our weekly tutorials, and I became a friend of his, and he invited me to go to the meetings of the outfit which they occasionally jokingly referred to as the Inklings. The Inklings has become a rather sullen label fixed on them; in those days, they just referred to themselves that way in a casual way. It wasn't the sort of heavy iron lid that's been screwed down on them in just about every way now. If only I could get one person in the world to see the difference between the casualness with which those men took their discussions and the awful solemnity in which it's all taken now, I would have done one thing in my life. But they just said, 'Oh, you know, the Inklings are meeting tonight.'

I used to go to these meetings for a bit until I went off to get a job in Reading. I sometimes came over from Reading for them, too, because I used to enjoy them very much, without ever really being what I would call an inner circle member of the Inklings, because I didn't come from the original vintage or the original foundational beliefs of the Inklings, and I never was there in the presence of the person who really was the genius of that circle, namely Williams, though I had greatly admired Williams and had been to his lectures.

So I went along to see C. S. Lewis in order to be told what to do and what to read and so on, and he received me in that Staircase 3, New Buildings, Magdalen, a great adventure. He was a famous man, but of course to any freshman coming to Oxford from the most provincial of the provinces, as I was, your tutor at Oxford is somebody very august. You always start off by thinking that anyone who's an Oxford don must be somebody very tremendous, and it takes a little time to realize that a great many people who are Oxford dons are actually quite ordinary. But anyway, it's right that you should start out feeling that they must be super-human. So I just felt like anyone else. You remember that the first time you knocked on the door of your tutor and went in to talk to him, you thought, 'This is going to be wonderful', and it usually was. I went in and there was this burly, red-faced man—we all know what he looked and sounded like—and we got going, and he was telling me what to read. We started with the seventeenth century, and for three years we worked at such a brisk pace that I've been trying to slow down ever since. You know Lewis's rooms in Magdalen: There was a sort of big sitting room which was lined with books, then there was a little inner study, and then there was his bedroom. And after about ten minutes, the door of the inner sitting room opened and a man appeared who seemed like somebody almost got up to represent C. S. Lewis at a fancy dress ball, except that he had a heavy moustache. I'd never even heard that Lewis had a brother, but the two of them were so absolutely alike that it really was only the moustache, and (if they happened to stand together) the fact that the brother was a little bit taller, that distinguished them. W. H. Lewis, for it was he, emerged from the inner room with a slight limp, and C. S. Lewis said to him, 'Has your leg come on again Warnie?' and Warnie replied, 'No I've just bumped it against the confounded table.' Those are the first words I ever heard him utter, and what shook me again was that the two of them had exactly the same voice. It was physically the same timbre, the same pitch, and of course the identical accent, because they had both had the same education. To hear the two of them was absolutely uncanny.

Anyhow, I got used to that, because Warnie used to spend a lot of time lurking in that inner room, and sometimes Jack would ask him a question. I mean, when Warnie came round to get something while he was doing secretarial work, Jack would ask him, 'What should I recommend him to read in the eighteenth century, eighteenth century satire or something, Warnie?' and Warnie would say, 'Well there's so and so and so and so', and he would always take a pleasure in putting in his suggestions, because of course he was an extremely well read man, certainly in certain periods. He didn't know as much about the Middle Ages as C. S. Lewis, but he knew a great deal about eighteenth- and nineteenth-century literature—and of course in the field he had chosen to study, namely seventeenth-century France, he knew more than Jack Lewis did, and indeed, I suppose, more than anybody except a professional scholar in that field would know.

So that was my first meeting with him. Later, when I began to go to meetings of this outfit, I used to see him quite often and I became very fond of him. He stood out in that circle. He was in some ways very similar to the others and in some ways different. He was similar in that he was bookish, loved to read, loved to talk about what he read, and fitted very, very naturally into that circle. On the other hand, there were certain differences: his professional life, which of course had been military, was over. He had served. He had entered the army via Sandhurst around 1912 or 1913, whenever it was, and had served throughout the 1914–18 war in I suppose the service corps.

He was mainly concerned with the bringing up of supplies and the regiment transport, which I'm quite sure he did very effectively. I'm also quite sure that inasmuch as he was in any positions of danger, he was very brave and cool in those positions. Anyhow, he served all the way through the 1914–18 war, and he then remained in the army until about 1933, after which he became a half-pay officer and threw in his lot with his brother. The two of them had always been very close, and Warnie spent virtually the rest of his life helping Jack with the immense load of correspondence. As C. S. Lewis gradually became a world figure, the load of correspondence that reached him became more and more impossible for somebody with his simple habits and lack of a huge infrastructure to answer, and W. H. Lewis took that over. He had no secretarial skills—he didn't do shorthand and so on—but he sat at the typewriter many hours a week and did the job.

As I said, W. H. Lewis was around at Inklings meetings, and he was like the others in some ways, and in other ways he was totally unlike them, because they were all men who to some extent depended for their livelihood on being intelligent about what they'd read, and to him it was just a great pleasure to read and a great pleasure to think about what he read. He liked good conversation, but he wasn't there to push his point of view, and unless you actually asked him what he thought, he very rarely came out with anything. And that, perhaps, might have given rise to the grotesque travesty of whoever it was that said he was a bore. I mean, if it's being a bore to be unobtrusive, then he was, and it's a very proud title if that's what it means. I daresay there are people in Oxford whose definition of a bore is somebody who's unobtrusive, but none of us would fall into that.

Now W. H. Lewis I remember as being gentle, humorous, tolerant, and his persona was that of a totally unambitious man. I say 'his persona' because I don't know whether anybody really is totally unambitious. I don't know to what extent any of us has a persona, by which I mean—and I'm using the word in its strict sense—the mask of the Roman actor, which was also to some extent an amplifier. His persona was that of the totally unambitious man, and I think he was unambitious in a worldly sense. He certainly wasn't after money. He wasn't after position. He wasn't after anybody giving him a job.

I remember having a talk with him just after I gave up my lectureship. I used to be a university lecturer, and thirty years ago I gave it up in order to give my life to writing. I mentioned this to W. H. Lewis in the pub along the road here, and he said, 'Oh well, well . . . you've given up your security then haven't you?' and I said, 'Yes I have, but you know, you can have security all your life and at the end of it you'll look back and think that you've lived your entire life and done nothing.' And he said, 'Well I've lived my entire life and done nothing. I feel perfectly contented about it.' I mean that was to some extent a persona, because he really hadn't done nothing: he'd served a perfectly honourable career in the army and so forth. But this was the front that he gave to the world: 'You see, I am a quiet man who sits in the corner. I've done nothing all my life, and I'm very happy about it.' And that, of course, was what differentiated him from C. S. Lewis, who was aggressive and, although obviously not ambitious in any worldly way, out to impress: C. S. Lewis was somebody who went for targets, attacked heresies, attacked opponents, came out. I mean there was a gladiatorial side to him that there wasn't at all in Warren Hamilton Lewis. He had his opinions, and they were quite deeply rooted and quite strongly felt; but he did not come out and clout and lay about it like C. S. Lewis, and that tended to make the two of them seem very different when you got to know them. But in the first few minutes when you met them, of course, they seemed uncannily similar, and I often wondered whether W. H. Lewis's decision to hold onto his moustache was not simply so that you could tell them apart.

Now the outline of his life, as I say, is that he served in the army. After the war of 1914–18 ended, he remained in France for some time. Now, I've never researched what he did. He once said to me, 'Yes, I spent a year or two in Paris on a sinecure.' I don't know whether it really was a sinecure, but that, again, would be his way, you see, to describe it as a sinecure. Anyhow, he had become very accustomed to French life, and then, as everybody knows, he did a tour of duty in China, in Shanghai, and of course his being a very travelled man was another thing that set them apart. You see one of the things that I always find mildly surprising about C. S. Lewis is that he was very content to take everything just from books. He was a man incredibly orientated towards the printed word, and that was enough for him. For example, fervent Christian though he was and passionate mediaevalist though he was, he never bothered to travel and look at the Italian cathedrals, or even take the relatively short and easy journey to the great cathedrals of northern France. He never bothered. Year after year went by and he never even bothered to go . . . I don't believe he ever looked at Chartres, except perhaps quite late—but certainly years and years and years went by in which he became a great authority on these things and never bothered to go to the places. He'd got it all from the printed page, which, now that I look at it, seems to me quite surprising in some ways: he was a literary man who was so totally literary that I find it quite surprising.

Now W. H. Lewis fell in love with France while on French soil, and (as you know of course) he wrote a great many books about French social history and in particular about his passion, the seventeenth century. Two books that he wrote, *The Splendid Century*[2] and *The Sunset of the Splendid Century*,[3]

became quite well known in their day, and were read by many general readers. But whereas he shared in French life to a great extent, and spent a lot of
time in France, C. S. Lewis got back from France immediately after his war
experience. To him, France simply meant the trenches and being wounded
and all the rest of it, as it did to all the other Tommies. And so when he returned, he was quite happy to stay where he was, and he never again crossed
the Channel during the years I knew him. His only travels were the occasional walking tour in southwestern England, and of course the occasional
visit to Ireland.

W. H. Lewis, as I say, was not so much like that. He was more sensitive to
where he was. I think that C. S. Lewis tended to be more of a pure intellectual, and to be rather indifferent to his actual surroundings, as witnessed to
by the constant debates that kept coming up during his working life as a tutor
at Magdalen. Every so often he'd be offered a chair. (You have to remember
that the academic world was very, very much smaller then. The colossal ex-
pansion of the academic world in the 1960s has altered everybody's perspective. The universities of this country now number God knows how many, but
in those days they numbered about six, and the departments were smaller
and the jobs were fewer, and to have a chair then really was something.) Now
Lewis would occasionally be offered a chair. He was offered one in Birmingham. I mean, he wasn't offered it explicitly: He was told that he would be a
strong candidate if he put in, which is the academic way of offering you a job.
And he thought very carefully about going to live in Birmingham. At other
times (more understandably, in my opinion), he thought carefully about
whether to accept a job in Belfast. But in fact he never did leave Oxford until
it came to him to go to Cambridge.

One thing in which the Lewis brothers were very similar is their tremendous talent for writing. I think C. S. Lewis is the best writer of expository
prose that modern England has to show. Setting aside his fiction and his romances and so on (which have many things to be said for them), and just
thinking at the moment of his many works of exposition and criticism, I
think that they could not be improved on. He sets out his subject matter absolutely perfectly, and his style is perfect from one sentence to the next. It's
always rhythmical, cogent, economical, memorable. The words are right, the
rhythms are right. The words are in their right order, the images are right,
there is no clumsy sentence anywhere. It's absolutely superb prose. Now
W. H. Lewis is exactly the same. In his less ambitious way, there is no clum-
sily written sentence anywhere in his work. He had the same gift.

One of the things I remember most about C. S. Lewis is that, as with
other people I have known in my life—Philip Larkin, was one—everything

he said had a certain spice of wit. I don't mean, of course, that he was one of those tiresome people who talk in epigrams; but I do mean that he was so witty by nature that each remark, rather than being a witty remark in itself, tended to be put in a form that was flavoured with wit, if you see what I mean. For example, quite late in his life I went to see him one day at The Kilns, and I am very bad about finding my way anywhere. I have bad eye-sight and a bad sense of direction, and frequently, when visiting a house I've been going to for twenty-five years, I actually go to the house next door and knock on the door. I do things like that, and so I was wandering about in Kiln Lane and thought, 'Now which of these rather large, impersonal houses, is it?' And I blundered about for a bit, and finally found myself outside the back door of some house. I knocked on this back door, and it was instantly opened by C. S. Lewis, who must have been standing just inside. He whipped the door open and I said, 'Oh, I'm not making a mistake then?' 'If you are, I'm making a worse one.' I don't think of that as a great epigram, but that was how he talked in every sentence—he never said anything that wasn't, as it were, spiced in that way with wit. Now Warren, in a gentler way, was very like that.

Now I have here his lovely edition, dated 1966, of the first volume of let-ters of Lewis that ever came out. W. H. Lewis, of course, wrote the memoir as well as editing them, and you will remember how beautifully that was done, sometimes with humour, sometimes (when the subject called for it) with a sombre quality. All of you will know the utterly horrifying description in *Surprised by Joy* of that dreadful prep school they went to, where the head-master was actually insane and was a maniacal sadist. It's worse than any-thing in Dickens. Those pages upset me: any description of cruelty to chil-dren makes me feel ill. I have to avoid the pages in which Jack Lewis describes the behaviour of this fiend of a man. It shows . . . I don't know what it shows, but I do know that if it had not been a boarding school, if the children had gone home at the end of each day and told the parents what was happening at school, they wouldn't have been allowed to go the next day, and it would have closed down. But because they went to school for month after month and then dispersed to their distant homes—and as you know children, when they get home, like to pretend that everything's all right at school and all that—it went on year after year, and it's one of the many reasons why board-ing schools really are a bad idea. But these poor little devils went through things that are much worse than anything in Dickens, because this man ac-tually was a maniac, and you remember the terrible description in *Surprised by Joy* of how he used to flog them, and particularly the ones that he had a particular hatred against. Well, of course, W. H. Lewis has to deal with that in the memoir, and he deals with it very reticently, but in a chillingly reticent way. He writes:

> In the Christmas term of that year [1908], Jack followed me at the school referred to in *Surprised by Joy* as 'Belsen'. As he has made very clear, he hated the place, but he escaped its worst brutalities: he amused the headmaster, who even made something of a pet of him, so far as was possible for such a man.

> Jack's letters and diaries of the time convey little of the full depressing story of this school and its headmaster. In 1901 a boy had been treated so brutally that his father brought a High Court action: this was settled out of court, but it confirmed local suspicions, and the school went downhill rapidly. In 1910 the headmaster wrote to my father [—well that's not very rapid, 1901 to '10, you know] that he was 'giving up school work', which meant deliverance for Jack: in fact the school collapsed, the house was sold, and its proprietor retired to a country living. [He was a clergyman.] There, his behaviour towards his choir and churchwardens was such that he was put under restraint and certified insane: he died in 1912, soon afterwards. With his uncanny flair for making the wrong decision, my father had given us helpless children into the hands of a madman.[4]

I find that a very moving sentence. It's chilling, but it's good writing, isn't it? And of course all of the writing in this beautiful little memoir is superb. Mark the living portrait of their father:

> The highlight of our year was the annual seaside holiday. Children of today, accustomed as they are to be driven casually to the coast on any fine Sunday afternoon, can hardly imagine the excitement, the bustle and glory of preparation that these holidays entailed, the unique moment of arrival. Of many such holidays, two pictures remain in my memory. The first is of my father's gloomy detachment. He would sometimes come down for the week-end, but he never stayed with his wife and children throughout this summer holiday. Urgent business was his excuse—he was a solicitor—and he may also have felt that eleven months of our company every year was more than enough. It may have gone deeper than that. I never met a man more wedded to a dull routine, or less capable of extracting enjoyment from life. A night spent out of his own home was a penance to him: a holiday he loathed,

having not the faintest conception of how to amuse himself. I can still
see him on his occasional visits to the seaside, walking moodily up and
down the beach, hands in trouser pockets, eyes on the ground, every
now and then giving a heart-rending yawn and pulling out his watch.[5]

Oh, beautiful stuff; and you see, the writing is as good as C. S. Lewis's writing. This is what I'm trying to say.

And then, of course, the immensely moving description of the situation with
Mrs Moore. It might just help one or two of you if I reminded you that because
L and M come together in the alphabet, when Jack Lewis was a cadet just about
to go into the First World War, he roomed with another bloke called Moore. They
were friends, and this chap Moore said, 'If anything happens to me, will you
look after my mother?' Jack Lewis said he would, and since he was the kind of
chap who kept his word, even if it took the next fifty years, he did. I never met
Mrs Moore—it was a very rare person who was admitted to that actual ménage,
and I certainly wasn't in *that* circle—but I remember how she'd ring up in the
middle of a tutorial, and he would be very patient with her, and she was obviously grumbling on the other end of the line, and he'd say, 'Did you have a good
night dear? Oh so sorry, so sorry.' Well, obviously she was talking about her illnesses and all that sort of thing. It made me decide that when I get to be very old
and feeble, I'm not going to talk about my illnesses. Anyway, she, though no
doubt a very worthy woman in her own way, was to some extent a penance to all
of them, and W. H. Lewis quite obviously detested her. 'The thing most puzzling to myself and to Jack's friends', he writes, 'was Mrs Moore's extreme un-
suitability as a companion for him.'[6] You can feel him reining himself in.

> She was a woman of very limited mind, and notably domineering and
> possessive by temperament. She cut down to a minimum his visits to
> his father, interfered constantly with his work, and imposed upon him
> a heavy burden of minor domestic tasks. In twenty years I never saw a
> book in her hands; her conversation was chiefly about herself, and was
> otherwise a matter of ill-informed dogmatism: her mind was of a type
> that he found barely tolerable elsewhere. The whole business had to be
> concealed from my father of course, which widened the rift between
> him and Jack; and since an allowance calculated to suit a bachelor
> living in college was by no means enough for a householder, Jack
> found himself miserably poor. Nevertheless he continued in this re-
> strictive and distracting servitude for many of his most fruitful years,
> suffering the worries and expense of repeated moves, until in 1930 we
> all settled at The Kilns, Headington Quarry.[7]

Of course, mind you, when you say of somebody that their conversation is chiefly about themselves or is 'otherwise a matter of ill-informed dogmatism',[8] and that in twenty years you never saw a book in their hands, that only puts them in the same position as 75 percent of the human race. But anyway, it certainly did not make her a suitable companion for Lewis.

It is of course documented everywhere what a difficult time they had. You see, the household, which consisted of Mrs Moore and Mrs Moore's daughter and . . . I don't know, a few strays . . . was a difficult one. In 1966, after it's all over, he talks in his diary about an evening in Oxford:

> It was too cold to sit outside, but we found a pleasant little bar facing into a very beautiful sunset and a stretch of smooth river, its surface broken only by the occasional passage of a duck or a moorhen. In the middle distance, moored, was the largest cruiser I've ever seen so high up the river.[9]

Of course he had a motorboat for years, and was interested in motorboating.

> The whole mis en scene [sic] filled me with nostalgia—thoughts of Parkin here, with Victor and the *Bosphorus* [that was his boat], and idle, pleasant chat by the riverside. Twilight crept over us on our way home, and with it white mist began to smoke up from the river putting me in mind of a melancholy last evening on board my boat in September with the thoughts of next day's return to all the horrors of The Kilns— the spite, envy, hatred, malice and all uncharitableness, the thousandth repetition of the pointless story, the pervading discomfort. And yet how I would leap at the chance to return to those bad days for the bright patches which made them tolerable—public works, or a walk with Tykes, Inklings, Bird and Baby mornings, and even at the end of the boating season, the distant prospect of the winter walking tour.[10]

A few sentences which encapsulate many years of a life, then.

I used to think that C. S. Lewis was rather like Samuel Johnson: the scholarship, the piety, the conviviality, the liking to be in a group of men enjoying themselves, eating and drinking and being happy together—all that is very Johnsonian. So is the gift for economical phrasing: some of Lewis's remarks are almost worthy of Johnson. And one curious resemblance to Johnson is that Johnson, of course, had a household that was full of people that he looked after—usually peevish, rather ill old people who quarrelled with one another and fell out and made the place a misery. And when somebody said to him, 'Why do you have all these people in your house?' he said, 'Well who'd have them if I didn't?' with perfect Christianity. If he didn't have them, they'd be on the pavement—that is what it's supposed to be about, isn't it? Lewis was very like Johnson in that way. Johnson used to have to brace himself sometimes before he went into his house in Gough Square because he knew the hubbub; they'd be having rows, and they'd appeal to him to settle their foolish, peevish, silly quarrels, and he used to have to sort of take a deep breath and get himself into his own house. Now, Warren quotes a bit from Jack Lewis, writing to some lady:

> I have lived most of it (my private life) in a house which was hardly ever at peace for 24 hours, amid senseless wranglings, lyings, backbitings, follies and *scares*. I never went home without a feeling of terror as to what appalling situation might have developed in my absence. Only now that it is over do I begin to realize quite how bad it was.[11]

W. H. Lewis, as I said, suffered it and detested Mrs Moore, but there is also a very moving passage, after her death, in which he speaks quite spontaneously of her good points and her kindnesses. Minto, as they called her, died of influenza: 'And so ends the mysterious self imposed slavery in which J has lived for at least thirty years. How it began, I suppose I shall never know but the dramatic suddenness of the "when", I shall never forget.'[12] His final summing up is in fact as charitable as it can be.

Now W. H. Lewis was a man immensely sensitive. He was immensely sensitive to visual impressions, to music, to literature. My goodness, he was a lovely critic. His opinions on literature, though they were tersely expressed, were lovely. He says somewhere, 'I'm reading *War and Peace*. It's a book that puts all other war novels completely in the shade.' He continues: 'Where the anti-war novelists of the 1920s tell you how horrible war is to look at, this tells you what war feels like',[13] and that is a powerful sentence, I think. The beautiful thing about him was that he didn't care whether you accepted his point of view: he just had his own point of view. I remember him saying to me that he didn't like *The Ancient Mariner*, which is a poem I've always loved very much. He didn't like outré, romantic poetry at all, you see. He liked eighteenth-century literature. He loved Wordsworth, and of course Wordsworth was an eighteenth-century poet in many ways, but he didn't like very far out romantic poetry. He said he didn't like *The Ancient Mariner*, and I was staggered as a young chap. I had never met anybody who didn't like *The Ancient Mariner*, and I said to him, 'What? What do you mean? It's an absolutely perfect specimen of poetry.' And he said, 'Yes, it's a perfect specimen of the kind of poetry I don't like.' There's no arguing with that.

One of the many interesting topics about these two old boys was the fact that they were Irish boys—before partition, when an Ulsterman was just an Irishman like any other Irishman—and yet were taken very early and 'brainwashed', as it were, into being members of the English upper middle class. They never seemed to have had any kind of second thoughts about that, but fully accepted it. They fought and put their lives on the line for England, and fully identified with the whole English thing. They were very interested in Ireland, and loved going there, but oddly enough, I don't ever remember any political comments about it from them in all the years. They once went on a little tour by ship from Belfast, docking at certain points, but it was really just a tour of the coastline of Ireland. It only took a few days (they never had many elaborate holidays), and they landed at Waterford. The reason I'm telling you this is that W. H. Lewis had an almost Wordsworthian sense of the atmosphere that comes off a landscape. One of the gifts that makes Wordsworth a very great poet is that there is a kind of vibration that comes off any setting that Wordsworth can get and put into words. It could be the Lake District, the countryside, or London. He could be going over Westminster Bridge and you could see, 'Dear God! The very houses seem asleep; And all that mighty heart is lying still!'[14]—and it was just as much of an epiphany as he would get in the mountains.

Now W. H. Lewis had a touch of that feeling. They landed, and they went inland at Waterford.

> On the merely physical side, it was most depressing country. I have never seen any place so enclosed before: wherever you go, the grey road is flanked by old stone walls, and banks on the top of which grow thick hedges, the whole over hung by heavy motionless foliage on old trees and lidded with a grey brown sky. [What a lovely way to put it, 'lidded with a grey . . .'.] After a time the longing for any sort of escape from these everlasting tunnels became acute, and one almost fancied it to be accompanied by a sensation of choking from trying to breathe air from which the oxygen was exhausted. The natives . . . [this is one Irishman discussing other Irishmen] were as depressing as their landscape: during the whole morning I did not see anyone of any age or of either sex who was not definitely ugly: even the children look more like goblins than earthborns. . . . I wonder can it be possible that a country which has an eight hundred year record of cruelty and misery has the power of emanating a nervous disquiet? Certainly I felt something of the sort, and would much dislike to see this place again.[15]

The man is vibrating all the time. It's wonderful stuff.

Well, I shall begin to phase down in a minute because we must think of our comforts and go to the pub, but since we're going to the Eagle and Child, I would like to say a few words about that. They used to go to the Eagle and Child, because it was handy for the Taylorian Institution. The great days of that circle, of course, were during the war, and during the war a lot of lectures were held in the Taylorian Institute. The English Faculty was not as big as it is now, and they used to lecture either in college halls or in the Taylorian. Now, Charles Williams who, as an employee of the Oxford University Press, did not have a college, used to lecture in the Taylorian, where I went to hear him. Tolkien used to give his weekly lecture on *Beowulf* at the same time, also in the Taylorian. I once complained to Lewis that I was supposed to go to Tolkien's lectures on *Beowulf*, but always wanted to go and hear Charles Williams, who was an electrifying lecturer: 'It's very inconvenient, you know', I said, 'that Charles Williams and Tolkien lecture at eleven o'clock on a Tuesday, both of them.' And he said, 'Yes, well, it's so they can be free at twelve o'clock to go to the Eagle and Child.' So I used sometimes to go and hear Tolkien lecture on *Beowulf* and deny myself the excitement of going to hear Charles Williams lecture on Milton or Shakespeare or whatever. He was a wonderful lecturer. Tolkien, on the other hand . . . well, his greatest friends would not say that Tolkien was a good lecturer. You could never hear what he was saying much. He had a set of notes that he used year after year, which was his stock in trade; and he would come in and say, 'Well, we're getting more and more behind', and then he would sort of mumble on a bit, and out would come certain formal phrases which were fair and recognizable, and then he'd go back and you couldn't make any of it out. But come twelve o'clock, of course, they would get up to the Eagle and Child, and obviously it was Lewis who was behind that.

It might be worth clarifying another matter. Williams was a good pub drinking man. During all his years in London he had obviously had a pub lunch every day, and his daily lunch remained beer and sandwiches. C. S. Lewis, too, liked pubs: he liked draught beer, and he liked ordinary men, and indeed suffered from the absurd delusion that he was one himself. Tolkien was not that kind of chap at all. Tolkien didn't really like going to pubs. He would nervously go in and have half a pint of beer, but he didn't like it. Now, at the Eagle and Child, kept by Charlie Blagrove, there was a little back room. The whole layout of the pub was much smaller, then, and behind a door there was a room which was really a sitting room for the family, but if you asked them, they would let you use it as a special favour. I sometimes used it myself when I was with friends, perhaps ones who'd come from a distance, and we'd really have something to talk about. I'd say to the landlord, 'Could we have the inside room this evening?' and he'd go, 'Oh all right', and he'd get me a drink and I'd go in there. Now, Tolkien went behind the backs of the other Inklings and asked the landlord if they could have the inside room on Tuesdays. Lewis confided to me that this had spoilt it for him, because he liked the feeling of meeting in an open tavern. If you go in there now, it's all been ripped out and made open plan, and there's a rather fancy wooden plaque which says, 'In this room the Inklings . . .'. Well, what it actually ought to say is, 'In this space J. R. R. Tolkien ruined C. S. Lewis's Tuesday lunchtime drinks.'

The landlord in those days was Charlie Blagrove. He was a very interesting character. He was one of the last men in Oxford to have a cape round his shoulders and sit in the road on a horse-drawn cab. His father had been a cab driver with a horse-drawn cab, which he took over; and when that went under, he got the licence of the Eagle and Child. He was a delightful man. C. S. Lewis was very fond of him, and in fact had a little snapshot of him up in his rooms in Magdalen. Curiously, Charlie Blagrove was very similar in appearance to C. S. and W. H. Lewis. When you saw C. S. Lewis on one side of the bar ordering a pint, and Charlie Blagrove on the other serving it, you felt like you'd gone round the other way—they were the same kind of florid, burly, man.

One day, years later, I went into the pub, and Mrs Blagrove said that he'd died. 'I knew it was coming', she said, 'but I never thought it would come like this, eight o'clock on a Sunday.' At about that time, W. H. Lewis was writing the following in his diary:

> I was sitting in the study this evening when Paxford came in with a very sad piece of news: Charles Blagrove, landlord of the 'Bird and Baby', died very suddenly on Sunday. He was I think about 63, and had been complaining of shortness of breath for some time, but I had no idea that there was anything seriously wrong. With him I lose not only a publican, but a friend, and an irreplaceable one, for he had endless stories of an Oxford which is as dead as Dr. Johnson's: the past Oxford of the turn of the century. Through his father, also a publican, his tales went back to an Oxford in which it was not uncommon for undergrads. to *fight* a landlord for a pint of beer: both would strip to the waist, have a mill in the backyard, and then the battered undergrad. would throw down a sovereign and depart. Many stories he had too of his father— literally—throwing people out of his pub. Charles himself was a big, clean shaven, burly, smartly dressed fellow, with "horsey man" written all over him [You might say just the same about C. S. Lewis.]; He had

begun in life as a cab driver, and from that graduated to a hansom. And was never tired of repeating that any man who had 18/- a week before 1914 was far better off than his son is today. His was the Oxford of undergraduates who made nothing of giving a couple of new suits to cab drivers because the fit was not exact: of leisurely country drives to Godstow and such places. Of lavish tips for taking what he used to call 'fancy goods' to secluded spots: of people who would hire his cab and ask to be taken 'somewhere where they could find a fight': of the Bullingdon Club, of rags, dinners, that general reckless extravagance and panache which prevailed when the security of the upper classes was still absolute, and England ruled the world. . . . The loss to ourselves will be severe; even if the new landlord tolerates Tuesday mornings, things can never be the same again. Poor dear Blagrove, he had long dreamed of retiring to a little country pub somewhere, and I like to think that perhaps in some form he has his wish; for is there not wine in the next world? God rest his soul.[16]

I feel about W. H. Lewis much as he felt about Charlie Blagrove, that is to say, true admiration, the feeling of love for a simple man. When I say that, I know of course that no human being is simple. The human being is a complex animal, but let us say that both Blagrove and W. H. Lewis were people who came on, or preferred to present themselves, as simple, uncomplicated men. And I think, just as he thought of Blagrove, that perhaps he has his wish.

Notes

1. This talk was given on 28 January 1986.
2. W. H. Lewis, *The Splendid Century: Some Aspects of French Life in the Reign of Louis XIV* (London: Eyre & Spottiswoode, 1953).
3. W. H. Lewis, *The Sunset of the Splendid Century: The Life and Times of Louis Auguste de Bourbon duc du Maine, 1670–1736* (London: Eyre & Spottiswoode, 1955).
4. W. H. Lewis (ed.), *Letters of C. S. Lewis* (London: Geoffrey Bles, 1966), 3–4.
5. Lewis, *Letters of C. S. Lewis*, 1–2.
6. Lewis, *Letters of C. S. Lewis*, 12.
7. Lewis, *Letters of C. S. Lewis*, 12–13.
8. Lewis, *Letters of C. S. Lewis*, 12.
9. W. H. Lewis, *Brothers and Friends: The Diaries of Major Warren Hamilton Lewis*, ed. Clyde S. Kilby and Marjorie Lamp Mead (San Francisco: Harper & Row, 1982), 264–265.
10. Lewis, *Brothers and Friends*, 265.

11. Mary Van Deusen, letter of 18 April 1951; quoted in Lewis, *Brothers and Friends*, 265.

12. Lewis, *Brothers and Friends*, 236.

13. Paraphrasing Lewis, *Brothers and Friends*, 98.

14. William Wordsworth, 'Composed upon Westminster Bridge, September 3, 1802' (sonnet).

15. Lewis, *Brothers and Friends*, 111–112.

16. Lewis, *Brothers and Friends*, 220–221.

19

Nevill Coghill and C. S. Lewis: Two Irishmen at Oxford

John Wain

WELL, LADIES AND gentlemen, what I'm going to say tonight will inevitably seem to some of you a series of footnotes rather than a commentary on matters of central interest to you about Lewis.[1] I'm sure that a lot of the people who belong to the C. S. Lewis Society, which must necessarily have a wide range, are interested in a field quite distinct from the one I'm interested in. They assimilate Lewis to some extent to Tolkien and *The Lord of the Rings*, they follow particularly the Lewis of the romances and the science fiction stories, taking him back to George MacDonald and the other writers of romance (Addison and so on) whom that circle admired so much. That has never been the side that particularly appeals to me. It's a limitation in me that romance is the kind of literature I appreciate least. I'm personally more at home with imaginative literature that concerns itself with the world I recognize about me. I've never been much of a reader of romance, and therefore of course I'm not good at telling good ones from bad ones. I know that Lewis's children's stories seem to me very charming: they are good examples of narrative, and they're very beautifully done, and I can read them, which I can't do with Tolkien. I can't get on with *The Lord of the Rings* at all. I know that's a statement about me, but it's just a fact. When I used to be present at the meetings of that circle on a Thursday night, and Tolkien turned up with a bulge in his side pocket that said he'd got a wad of manuscript, I used to feel, oh, that the evening was in ruins and I was going to have to sit through it. It is not that side of C. S. Lewis I'm interested in.

I'm much more fascinated by his scholarly work, which I think brilliantly done and presented, although it is marred by special pleading and therefore open, by the very highest standards, to certain very stringent criticisms. Nevertheless, it is a brilliant body of work; hardly anyone else could have produced anything to rival it. Lewis has the great gift of exposition: he can make anything interesting. He handles with such cogency and crystal clarity topics that the modern reader approaches with very great trepidation, expecting not to be interested—the immensely complex and difficult religious controversies of the sixteenth century in his Oxford History of English Literature volume, for example—that you find you have enjoyed reading about it. This is a wonderful gift, and of course to be taught by him was a wonderful privilege.

However, tonight I want to talk not about one but about two men, both of whom were crucial in my education (if that's what it was), and I want to talk about both of them as men and as minds. These two men are C. S. Lewis and Nevill Coghill, both members of the English Faculty from the 1920s onward.

Perhaps the year 1955 would make a convenient starting point. In that year, a number of things happened which are memorable to me. It was the year in which I gave up my university post and became a professional writer, earning my living by writing, which is what I've done ever since. It was also the year in which Lewis brought out his autobiographical book *Surprised by Joy.*[2] I don't think that it is a very successful book, all things considered. It is offered as an account of his conversion, but I don't think it is a very successful account of his conversion. A religious conversion is a very difficult thing to write about, and Lewis, I think, is not really successful in making one experience from the inside that conversion. The key passage in which he sets out to spend the day at Whipsnade, not a Christian, and comes back in the evening a Christian, frankly, is a failure. It doesn't come off. Still, Lewis had such a well-stocked mind and wrote so well that it was impossible for him not to write a book with many interesting and arresting and amusing passages, and I read that book with very great interest in the year that it came out.

Although I was in fairly constant touch with Lewis himself, I wanted, of course, to read what he'd written about himself. Many things pulled me up, but one thing in particular pulled me up in reading *Surprised by Joy.* He's talking about being at Oxford briefly just before going off to fight in the first World War. The same kind of thing happened in both wars: a young man would find himself briefly at the university while being sorted out for military service, and then he would go off and do his military service, and then (provided he survived) he would be back at the university after being demobilized. Well, during Lewis's first period, he says the college was almost empty (of course the shutdown was much more complete in 1914–18 than it was in 1939–45), that there were only two other fellows there or something, one of whom was a Sinn-Feiner who would not fight for England. That sentence—'a Sinn-Feiner who would not fight for England'[3]—struck me: how strange that Lewis should offer no comment of any kind on that. Presumably this chap, being an Irishman, didn't feel that he ought to defend England, because he saw England as the oppressor; and the fact that Lewis merely notes this and passes on—a man of the same generation and the same background, also an Irishman—is strange. He doesn't even say, 'I'd thought it through and I'd decided I wasn't a Sinn-Feiner'; he simply brushes it aside, without even giving this man a whole sentence.

This made me think about Lewis's Irish background and his Irishness as I never had done. I had known Lewis for three years while he was teaching me, and then for ten years as a friend, and I'd never thought about Ireland in connection with him or talked to him about Ireland, although I knew as an intellectual fact that he was a northern Irishman.

A useful intellectual backdrop to this question in relation to Lewis and his fellow Irishman Nevill Coghill is Louis MacNeice's book on W. B. Yeats. Mac-Neice was an Irishman of virtually the same generation as Lewis and Coghill, and another one of these very Anglicised Irish men of letters. They now talk about MacNeice as an Irish poet. During his lifetime, nobody ever thought of him very much as an Irish poet. In fact, when he wrote his book on Yeats, he more or less had to bring forward the whole subject of what it was like to be an Irishman writing and living in England, and he did so very, very interestingly. That is the reason why, as a backdrop to Lewis and Coghill, I would like to quote from MacNeice's book *The Poetry of W. B. Yeats*:

It is notoriously dangerous to generalize about Ireland, but there are certain things which I can point out, either because they are patent facts or because I myself have experienced them. Like Yeats, I was brought up in an Irish middle-class Protestant family. I allow for the difference that he spent his childhood in the primitive west, whereas I spent mine in the industrial north.

Among the patent facts are the facts of size. Geographically Ireland is considerably smaller than England; in respect of population it is very much smaller indeed. And other things within the country are smaller than their English counterparts. Incomes are smaller, fields are smaller, cottages are smaller. The large English meadow, like the large English country meal, is a rarity in Ireland. The farmers are mainly small farmers; consequently there is a lesser proportion of hired agricultural labourers. These characteristic smallnesses, while uniting the country against England, which is regarded as essentially big, divide it against itself. As in Spain, there is a very intense local feeling; a man from the next parish is a foreigner.

Other patent facts are the facts of landscape and climate. Climate cannot be stressed too strongly. I sympathize with Bernard Shaw, who wrote in his Introduction to *John Bull's Other Island*: 'There is no Irish race any more than there is an English race or a Yankee race. There *is* an Irish climate, which will stamp an immigrant more deeply and durably in two years, apparently, than the English climate will in two hundred.' This climate affects the landscape. An Irish landscape is capable of pantomimic transformation scenes; one moment it will be desolate, dead, unrelieved monotone, the next it will be an indescribably shifting pattern of prismatic light. The light effects of Ireland make other landscapes seem stodgy; on the other hand, few countries can produce anything more depressing than Ireland in her grey moments. Yeats' best-known landscapes were Sligo and Galway, and he deliberately set out to match his verse to them. I do not think it fanciful to maintain that he succeeded, that there is something palpably in common between the subtle colour and movement of his verse and that western landscape which is at the same time delicate and strong.

It is harder to predicate characteristics of the Irish themselves than of their country. I would risk the stock generalization that the Irish are born partisans. Whatever they are supporting, they support it violently and—usually—bitterly. This violence is as common in the north as in the south. With it there goes a vigour of speech and a colour of phrasing uncommon across the water.[4]

You can say that again.

Well, *Surprised by Joy* talks about growing up in Ireland and going for walks out of Belfast as a young man, and Lewis writes about it in very similar terms, with so much knowledge and so much love.

Hitherto my feelings for nature had been too narrowly romantic. I attended almost entirely to what I thought awe-inspiring, or wild, or eerie, and above all to distance. Hence mountains and clouds are my especial delight; the sky was, and still is, to me one of the principal elements in any landscape, and long before I had seen them all named and sorted out in *Modern Painters* [Ruskin's—one of his favourite books], I was very attentive to the different qualities, and different heights, of the cirrus, the cumulus, and the raincloud. As for the Earth, the country I grew up in had everything to encourage a romantic bent, had indeed done so ever since I first looked at the unattainable

Green Hills through the nursery window. For the reader who knows those parts it will be enough to say that my main haunt was the Holywood Hills—the irregular polygon you would have described if you drew a line from Stormont to Comber, from Comber to Newtownards, from Newtownards to Scrabo, from Scrabo to Craigantlet, from Craigantlet to Holywood, and thence through Knocknagonney [sic] back to Stormont. How to suggest it all to a foreigner I hardly know.[5]

Suddenly we're foreigners, because he's talking about home now.

First of all, it is by Southern English standards bleak. The woods, for we have a few, are of small trees, rowan and birch and small fir. The fields are small, divided by ditches with ragged sea-nipped hedges on top of them. There is a good deal of gorse and many outcroppings of rock. Small abandoned quarries, filled with cold-looking water, are surprisingly numerous. There is nearly always a wind whistling through the grass. Where you see a man ploughing there will be gulls following him and pecking at the furrow. There are no field-paths or rights of way, but that does not matter for everyone knows you—or if they do not know you, they know your kind and understand that you will shut gates and not walk over crops. Mushrooms are still felt to be common property, like the air. The soil has none of the rich chocolate or ochre you find in parts of England: it is pale. . . . But the grass is soft, rich, and sweet and the cottages, always whitewashed and single storeyed and roofed with blue slate, light up the whole landscape.

Although these hills are not very high, the expanse seen from them is huge and various. Stand at the north-eastern extremity where the slopes go steeply down to Holywood. Beneath you is the whole expanse of the Lough. The Antrim coast twists sharply to the north and out of sight; green, and humble in comparison, Down curves away southward. Between the two the Lough merges into the sea, and if you look carefully on a good day you can even see Scotland, phantom-like on the horizon. Now come further to the south and west. Take your stand at the isolated cottage which is visible from my father's house and overlooks our whole suburb, and which everyone calls The Shepherd's Hut, though we are not really a shepherd country. You are still looking down on the Lough, but its mouth and the sea are now hidden by the shoulder you have just come from, and it might (for all you see) be a landlocked lake. And here we come to one of those great contrasts which have bitten deeply into my mind—Niflheim and Asgard, Britain and Logres, Handramit and Harandra, air and ether, the low world and the high. Your horizon from here is the Antrim Mountains, probably a uniform mass of greyish blue, though if it is a sunny day you may just trace on the Cave Hill the distinction between the green slopes that climb two-thirds of the way to the summit and the cliff wall that perpendicularly accomplishes the rest. That is one beauty; and here where you stand is another, quite different and even more dearly loved—sunlight and grass and dew, crowing cocks and gaggling ducks. In between them, on the flat floor of the Valley at your feet, a forest of factory chimneys, gantries and giant cranes rising out of a welter of mist, lies Belfast. Noises come up from it continually, whining and screeching of trams, clatter of horse traffic on uneven sets, and, dominating all else, the continual throb and stammer of the great shipyards. And because we have heard this all our lives it does not, for us, violate the peace of the hill-top; rather, it emphasises it, enriches the contrast, sharpens the dualism.[6]

That description is so lovingly, so meticulously, so carefully written, that it is clear that he really wants you to see that landscape, and if possible, to share his love of it. It can't really matter much to him whether a lot of English foreigners know what it's like there, but it does matter. He really is lost in it, and he's very, very keen to tell us what it's like—and of course this is another Irish characteristic, isn't it? In the end, an Irishman speaks of Ireland with that particular passion: 'I am of Ireland, and the holy land of Ireland.'[7]

In *Surprised by Joy*, Lewis describes going to discussion classes just after the end of the First World War, run by a don called George Gordon. The nicest and most intelligent man in the class, he writes, was a Christian named Nevill Coghill.[8] So the two of them knew each other from those days, and they both had similar backgrounds and were in similar positions. They were both Irishmen with an English public school education followed by the trenches which, thank goodness, both survived. In the early-mid 1920s, they both read English. English was virtually a new subject, and people who were on the lookout for jobs tended to come from other disciplines. A lot of the early English dons at Oxford were people who had been very well schooled in something else. I can't help feeling that the subject was rather enriched by that. Lewis, of course, had been through Greats, and got a First both in Mods and in Greats. He had also won the Chancellor's Essay Prize and a few other things, and he'd decided that he'd read the English School because, although he didn't particularly want to teach in the English School, he thought it might be a job. So to have that string to his bow, he read the English School in a year, and got a First. He was, of course, very well-read already, and really all he had to do was get up his Anglo-Saxon and the history of the language and make sure he was *au fait* with the set texts in Shakespeare and so on. Nevill Coghill came from a slightly different direction. He had read history, and (like Lewis) thought he'd better have the English School behind him if he wanted to get a job. He, too, read the English school in a year and got a First. They then both became members of the English faculty, and were friends—not, I think, very close friends, because they were temperamentally quite dissimilar, but Nevill used to come along sometimes to these gatherings on a Thursday night, and certainly they were always very friendly and had regard for each other.

Nevill Coghill and Lewis functioned against the background of a very research-oriented English School. That English School was suspicious of purely literary study, and preferred hard facts and exact scholarship. Of course it was an establishment that could never do anything to Lewis. There was nothing they could do to Lewis because Lewis could always beat them at their own game. I mean Lewis was so learned and he knew the classics and so on so well and he knew so many things about mediaeval theology and all the rest of it that they didn't know that he could make rings round them; the most sort of traditional anti-literary literary scholar could never make any dent on Lewis, but I'm afraid they rather got together on Nevill Coghill. They rather gave him a bad time, or perhaps would have done if his naturally sunny temperament would have been daunted by it. Nevill Coghill had an entirely different approach. He brought in something very, very valuable. He was a don, he was committed to his work, he taught his pupils and so on, but at the same time he brought with him an air of the wider world. He was interested in theatre and music; many of his friends were from that world, and he was a man who naturally moved in a wider world. He knew the major continental cities. He travelled about and saw the masterpieces of architecture and painting, and he went to the great opera houses as naturally as he breathed. Because he had one foot in that world, he also, for instance, approached Shakespeare's work as something that was meant to be played—and if you want to know how it works, you subject it to the strains of rehearsal and performance. He worked with the Oxford University Dramatic Society to put on an annual production, testing his critical theories by seeing how they worked in production. Some of his more conservative colleagues barely tolerated it. They thought it was all a lot of fooling about with greasepaint, and generally displayed that academic dislike of theatricals which is really the old puritan dislike of the theatre in a new guise. Nichol Smith, the Merton Professor, wouldn't even go and see Nevill's production of *Two Gentlemen of Verona* in Turkish costume when his own daughter was in it. You see, Nevill was very looked down on, and unfairly so. Here was a man totally disciplined, totally dedicated. His approach to Shakespeare was a total approach. He was very scholarly, but he also wanted to get it off the page. He used to come to Stratford with a gang of us when we had to put up with any kind of conditions during the war and stay in terrible, sleazy lodgings just so that we could see as many plays as we could. You can't imagine Lewis doing that. He was very approachable and very human, but he wouldn't have done that, because that kind of thing didn't matter to him in that way.

Nevill had a natural grace. It was a beautiful quality of gentleness and humour and kindliness and hospitality, and he was very, very easy to get along with, but he wasn't a pushover, I mean he wasn't flaccid. If you said something that contradicted one of his dearly held convictions he would come back at you, but he was always in every way courteous: 'He never yet no villainy ne'er said. In all his life unto no manner wight.'[9] I believe his love of Chaucer came partly out of that. He found the embodiment in Chaucer's poetry of qualities that he himself had. His beautiful little book *The Poet Chaucer*, now unjustly out of print, has a passage about comedy towards the end, in which he talks about Chaucer's vision, a new and perennial comic vision loved and shared by Shakespeare.

> These two poets see and show a whole society in being, united by common purposes and moving towards a happy end in a dominant mood of easy goodwill (roguery notwithstanding) where the whole is made up of diversities, and the individual a part of it in virtue of being so fully himself. Common sense and fantasy, wit and pathos, ride side by side and make the ordinary and the normal unique, touching, funny and memorable. And in both poets romantic love is the core of the comedy.

> Both writers seem to lack the 'moral purpose' so palpable in Ben Jonson and other corrective writers of comedy, in whom satire and self-assurance predominate over good nature and modesty. Chaucer and Shakespeare seem more concerned with a 'happy' than with a 'moral' ending for comedy. Happy endings they certainly do create, and the happiness is transferred from the characters in their stories to the reader and spectator. It may well be that the creation of their kind of happiness is, in the long run, more moral than all that the moralists can do.[10]

That is his basic position—very thought-out, very solid, and very much shown in detail in his own critical writing.

Now someone like that around is a tremendous asset, and Nevill spread a great deal of light and happiness and illumination in his life. He taught me as much as Lewis did, and it's an interesting side light on the way Oxford University works that Nevill Coghill never got a penny for teaching me anything, since he was not employed to teach me anything. I got to know him by acting in one of his productions, and then knew him for the rest of his life. I used to sit around with him having a drink and so on, and I just so much enjoyed talking to him and being with him. Being produced by him in a Shakespeare play was a wonderful experience, because you went through it scene by scene and brought it to life. No literary teaching could ever be quite as good as that.

I especially remember the year that we did *Measure for Measure*, and I was Claudio and Richard Burton was Angelo. Burton wasn't a newcomer to acting like the rest of us, because he'd been in a little travelling theatre company before he came up to the university. He brought, not only his gifts, but also a bit of experience to it. But he did what Nevill told him like the rest of us, and learnt, like the rest of us, Nevill's vision of the play, which I remember he put on as what he called a romantic Christian melodrama. Well, they were good days, because one was in contact with a mind very, very rare, at a time when one's own mind was malleable, and I was just very grateful for it. I think the only thing I can say in conclusion is that coming here from the most provincial of the provinces and really not knowing anything about how to compare anything from outside, I was getting into middle life before it struck me that what Oxford had actually given me was something enormously valuable, namely an Irish education.

Notes

1. This talk was given on 24 January 1989.
2. C. S. Lewis, *Surprised by Joy* (London: Geoffrey Bles, 1955).
3. Lewis, *Surprised by Joy*, 177.
4. Louis MacNeice, *The Poetry of W. B. Yeats* (London: Oxford University Press, 1941), 44–45.
5. Lewis, *Surprised by Joy*, 146.
6. Lewis, *Surprised by Joy*, 146–148.
7. From the poem 'I Am of Ireland' by William Butler Yeats.
8. Lewis, *Surprised by Joy*, 201.
9. From *The Canterbury Tales* by Geoffrey Chaucer.
10. Nevill Coghill, *The Poet Chaucer* (London: Oxford University Press, 1949), 175.

Afterword:
A Brief History of the Oxford
C. S. Lewis Society

Michael Ward

IN THE FOREWORD to this volume, Greg and Suzanne Wolfe have described how, with the help of Walter Hooper, they came to found the Oxford University C. S. Lewis Society in 1982. In this Afterword, I will give a brief account of the history of the Society since its founding. Space does not allow for completeness, and I have made little attempt to go beyond the limits of my own memories and perspectives. Fuller details are available upon consultation of the Society's archives in the Bodleian Library, Oxford, and at the Wade Center, Wheaton College, Illinois.

University clubs and societies at Oxford are very various. The Oxford Union[1] and the Boat Club[2] are nationally and internationally known; few among the other two hundred or so have a profile beyond Oxford's city limits. Many have music or drama as their *raison d'être*. Some, like the Conservative Association, OICCU,[3] and Students for Life, exist for a political or religious or moral end. Others, such as the Vietnamese Society, the Ukrainian Society, and the Mexican Society, reflect the increasingly global nature of the University. Still others, such as the Tea Appreciation Society and the Quidditch Club, are deliberately frivolous and tend to be short-lived. When I was an undergraduate, it was the Winnie-the-Pooh Society and the Tiddlywinks Club that occupied that category at the Freshers' Fair.

I made the acquaintance of the Lewis Society in the Michaelmas Term of 1987 and have had the pleasure of being involved with it in various capacities ever since, first as an ordinary member, then as an officer for several years in the 1990s, and now as Senior Member (Faculty Supervisor). The Senior Member back at the founding in 1982 was Fr Peter Bide, then a Canon of Christ Church, and it was because of his college affiliation that the Society first met in Christ Church (or 'the House'—Aedes Christi—as it is known in Oxford parlance). After Bide retired, the link with Christ Church was gone and a new Senior Member was found in Fr William Oddie, then a Fellow of St Cross College and Librarian at Pusey House.[4] Since 1983 therefore, the Society has met at Pusey House, in the Frederic Hood Room, a characterful chamber overlooking St Giles', and conveniently close to both the Eagle and Child and the Lamb and Flag public houses. These pubs were among the favourites of the Inklings (the 'Bird and Baby' still trades off the association very heavily), and the Society has found them appropriate places in which to entertain speakers before meetings and to repair to afterwards for conversation over a pint.

Meetings take place every Tuesday evening during Full Term. In other words, there are normally twenty-four meetings per year. Usually, the format of the evening is an address by an invited speaker, followed by questions and discussion. The final meeting of each Michaelmas Term is traditionally a Christmas party at The Kilns, Lewis's Oxford home, now run as a residential study centre by the Lewis Foundation. The final meeting of each Trinity Term is a walk to a pub such as The Perch at Binsey, The Trout at Godstow, or The King's Arms at Sandford-upon-Thames. Other meetings over the years have included film viewings (for example, the documentary *Through Joy and Beyond*), theatre trips (*Shadowlands* at the Oxford Playhouse, for instance), and 'Please Bring a Book' evenings, at which members recover the lost art of reading aloud in public—and not just favourite passages from works by the Inklings, but from any writings whatsoever.

Lewis would presumably be a little surprised if he knew of the existence of an Oxford Society dedicated to discussions of his works and of his intellectual world. However, he had no aversion to participating in similar sorts of societies himself. He was 'an vnworthie member'[5] of the Oxford Dante Society and addressed it on a couple of occasions in the 1940s.[6] He read a paper on Scott to the Edinburgh Sir Walter Scott Club at their annual meeting in 1956. In principle, then, Lewis acknowledged the value of groups meeting to discuss writers and works of particular interest, however much he might have doubted its importance in relation to his own literary legacy. But that need not trouble us. Lewis knew full well that a writer is not necessarily the best, and is never a perfect, judge of his own work.

One assumes he would have approved of our determination as a Society to focus not only on his own corpus, but also on that of his fellow Inklings, friends such as Dorothy L. Sayers, and certain intellectual forebears such as G. K. Chesterton and George MacDonald. Perhaps chief among the reasons for the longevity and liveliness of the Oxford Lewis Society is that, despite its name, it is not a single-issue group. 'Lewis' really serves as an umbrella term that covers an array of authors and a range of concerns. This breadth of interest is itself characteristic of Lewis, who laboured in several different fields (literature, theology, philosophy), did so in a great variety of literary genres, and made it a point of honour to count among his close friends and acquaintances people from whom he had significant differences: the traditionalist Catholic Tolkien, the anthroposophist Barfield, the Baha'i-leaning and Unitarian Greeves, the Hindu-inclined Griffiths, the atheist Eddison. Lewis's dedicatory epigraph to Barfield in *The Allegory of Love*—'Opposition is true friendship'—reflects his continual quest for and genuine enjoyment of rational disagreement. The Lewis Society has tried to emulate this example. Though the Christian faith that was central to his life and writings naturally plays a large part in our discussions, the Society does not proselytize, not all members are Christians, and those who do subscribe to the Christian faith come from diverse denominational backgrounds.

'Diversity' is something of a buzzword these days. 'Unity' is its balancing quality, which we tend to hear less about. Any successful organism, including a university society, needs both unity and diversity, both a centripetal and a centrifugal dynamic, firm convictions and broad sympathies. Many people know of Lewis's firm convictions, his tendency towards 'bow-wow dogmatism', as he self-mockingly called it. George Watson, Lewis's erstwhile colleague at Magdalene College, Cambridge, once informed the Society of his capacity for being 'endlessly counter-suggestible'; and Tolkien famously wrote of how impressionable Lewis could be—indeed, too impressionable, Tolkien thought. Lewis's habits of mind covered the waterfront, so to speak, from blunt simplisms to the subtlest chiaroscuro sensitivity. Speakers at the Society likewise cover the bases: from devout partisanship, to friendly though critical engagement, to actual hostility and a priori disagreement. The uncritical friends and the friendly critics are perhaps to be expected among speakers to a Society of this kind, but opponents and sceptics are welcome too: John Beversluis, Philip Pullman, A. N. Wilson, and others, have purposefully been invited to address the group in order that we should hear from all quarters. On one memorable evening, which I learnt of but did not witness, the guest speaker maintained with unblinking seriousness and against all objections, that Lewis was very definitely now an occupant of hell. One can imagine how Lewis would have admired the pluck of the speaker on that occasion—a lion thrown to the Daniels. It puts one in mind of his own desire to take the fight to his opponents, as in his 1940 address to the Oxford Pacifist Society under the title 'Why I Am Not a Pacifist'.

Like Dr Johnson, Lewis would often, in certain moods, 'talk for victory'. He was in his element as president of the Oxford Socratic Club,[7] 'snuffing the imminent battle and saying "Aha!" at the sound of the trumpet'.[8] That club, alas, is no longer in existence, but I like to think that the Oxford Lewis Society perpetuates some of its spirit, on occasion. We have never, I believe, staged a formal debate, but we have at least allowed for the expression of unfashionable or unpopular views. Lord Longford and Lord Alton have been among our fierier, more campaigning speakers, and have subjected themselves, naturally enough, to vigorous questioning at the conclusion of their talks. Since Lewis's day, the general ethos of the University has become—I think it would be fair to say—less combative, more inclusive. Disputation tends now to be avoided rather than deliberately practised as an art form, and so these more provocative meetings are a refreshing reminder of the sorts of encounter that were a staple of the Socratic Club.

Lewis would have ascribed much of our modern pusillanimity in public debate to 'scepticism about reason', for in a radically subjectivist age, reason cannot be considered to be corporately binding. He identified subjectivism as a tendency of the twentieth-century mind in an essay entitled 'Modern Man and his Categories of Thought' (1946). The essay remained largely unknown until it was read aloud at the very first meeting of the Oxford Lewis Society back in 1982, thus inaugurating a tradition of airing previously unpublished work. There have been other notable examples. They include Dr Michael Piret's presentation of 'The Tragi-Comicall Briefe Reigne of Lewis the Bald' (Lewis's humorous verdict on his unsuccessful tenure as vice-president of Magdalen College)[9] and Professor Don King's recitation of forty-five newly discovered poems by Joy Davidman, a stunning sonnet sequence[10] that radically alters our understanding of the nature of her relationship with Lewis and significantly raises her profile as a twentieth-century poetic voice.

Piret's and King's editorial labours have yet to see the light of day beyond the walls of the Frederic Hood Room. However, the Society has been responsible for publications of its own on a couple of occasions. To mark the twentieth anniversary of Lewis's death, the Society published a *jeu d'esprit* between Owen Barfield and Lewis entitled *A Cretaceous Perambulator (The Re-examination of)*; and in 1990 it printed a hundred copies of another work of wit, *Mark vs. Tristram: Correspondence between C. S. Lewis and Owen Barfield*, complete with illustrations by Pauline Baynes.

There have been other, larger-scale undertakings, too. To commemorate the centenary of Lewis's birth in 1998, the Society raised over five thousand pounds for the installation of a stone plaque in Addison's Walk at Magdalen College. The plaque bears the text of his poem 'What the Bird Said Early in the Year' and was unveiled by the president of Magdalen, Mr Anthony Smith, after a special service of Evensong in the college chapel, at which the lessons were read by Lady Freud (who, as June Flewett, had been an evacuee at The Kilns during the Second World War) and Laurence Harwood, Lewis's godson.

In another venture marking Lewis's centenary in 1998, the Society organized eight afternoon lectures, endorsed and advertised in the English Faculty's official lecture list, and hosted by Regent's Park College. The Society president responsible for arranging this lecture series was Andrew Cuneo (now an Orthodox priest), still the only person ever to have completed a doctorate at Oxford on the writings of C. S. Lewis.[11]

In the first decade of the twenty-first century, the Society began to be led by Judith and Brendan Wolfe (no relation to the founding Wolfes), the co-editors, with Roger White, of the present volume. Their scholarly seriousness and practical energy have taken the Society's operations to a new level. In 2009, they organized a revival of the Donald Swann opera based on Lewis's *Perelandra*, which had not been publicly performed since the 1960s. (Swann himself addressed the Society in 1986.) It received two public performances, one in Keble Chapel and one in the Sheldonian Theatre. This operatic revival was accompanied by a two-day international colloquium, held at St Stephen's House, on the subject of Lewis's novel. Proceedings of the colloquium were published as *C. S. Lewis's Perelandra: Reshaping the Image of the Cosmos* (Kent State University Press, 2013).

Judith and Brendan Wolfe also founded the *Journal of Inklings Studies*, a peer-reviewed scholarly journal, indexed in the MLA. It began life in 2004 as the *Chronicle of the Oxford University C. S. Lewis Society* and in 2011 became the *Journal of Inklings Studies* when the Society forged an official collaboration with the Owen Barfield Literary Estate, the Charles Williams Society and, more recently, the G. K. Chesterton Library.

The Wolfes' accomplishments on behalf of the Lewis Society have also included the publication of a festschrift for Walter Hooper, Lewis's editor and biographer. Hooper has played an absolutely invaluable part in the founding and continuing success of the Society, and this was recognized in the year of his eightieth birthday with the publication of *C. S. Lewis and the Church: Essays in Honour of Walter Hooper* (T. & T. Clark, 2011).

Other books to have been officially launched at meetings of the Lewis Society include Deborah Higgens's *Anglo-Saxon Community in J. R. R. Tolkien's Lord of the Rings* (Oloris Publishing, 2014), Alister McGrath's *The Intellectual World of C. S. Lewis* (Wiley-Blackwell, 2013), and my own *Planet Narnia: The Seven Heavens in the Imagination of C. S. Lewis* (Oxford University Press, 2008).

As this brief history draws to a close, some reflections on the present volume are in order. Divided as it is into 'Essays' and 'Memoirs', the book you hold in your hands gives a fair impression of the Society's two main preoccupations over the years. On the one hand, the group exists to examine and dissect, to explore and analyse in scholarly fashion the ideas found in Lewis's works and in the works of his circle. On the other hand, the Society likes simply spending time with these writers, enjoying their personalities and histories, appreciating their peculiar qualities and gifts as unique individuals.

The essayists included in these pages are representative of a huge number of scholars who have addressed the Society over the years. They include (in no particular order): Priscilla Tolkien, John Lucas, Tony Nuttall, Tony Cockshut, John Kiteley, Mary Midgeley, John Finnis, Peter Van Inwagen, Heather O'Donoghue, Judith Priestman, Santha Bhattacharji, Simon Horobin, Tim Mawson, Diane Purkiss, Beatrice Groves, Humphrey Carpenter, Brian Sibley, Colin Duriez, Aidan Mackey, Stratford Caldecott, John Garth, Stuart Lee, Barbara Reynolds, James Brabazon, Jill Paton Walsh, Christopher Dean, Jerry Root, Lyle Dorsett, Joe Ricke, Diana Glyer, Stan Mattson, Chris Mitchell, Philip Ryken, Graham Leonard, Donald Allchin, Mark Edwards, Richard Harries, Keith Ward, Liz Carmichael, Andrew Linzey, John Webster, Douglas Hedley, Tom Weinandy, Jerome Bertram, Charles Taliaferro, and Stephen Prickett.

And the memoirists, likewise, represent just a small sample of those who have shared their reflections and personally-acquainted perspectives upon Lewis and his friends. They include Fr John Tolkien, Karl Leyser, Rachel Trickett, Nan Dunbar, Harry Blamires, Basil Mitchell, Lord David Cecil, Douglas Gresham, John Heath-Stubbs, Francis Warner, Martin Lings, Martin Moynihan, Eric Stanley, Emrys Jones, Simon Barrington-Ward, George Watson, David Bleakley, Laurence Harwood, Ruth Spalding, and Mary Rogers.

On the fiftieth anniversary of Lewis's death, 22 November 2013, a memorial to him was unveiled in Poets' Corner, Westminster Abbey. The Oxford Lewis Society, which helped raise a substantial portion of the funds involved, was well represented at the thanksgiving service on that occasion and at the colloquium hosted by the Abbey's educational Institute the day before. As this account has shown, I hope, the Society has played no small part in maintaining and developing the conditions within which such a permanent, national memorial could be conceived and realized. Its role continues.

Notes

1. Officially, the 'Oxford Union Society'. Founded in 1823 as a small debating club, the Union has grown into a multimillion pound operation, complete with an extensive range of buildings in the centre of Oxford and a permanent staff. Lewis was a member of the Union. From its library in 1924 he borrowed Alexander's *Space, Time and Deity* and learnt of the distinction between 'Contemplation' and 'Enjoyment', that 'indispensable tool of thought', as he later described it.

2. The Oxford University Boat Club was founded in 1829 and continues to achieve worldwide attention in 'the boat race', the annual competition on the River Thames against a rival eight from Cambridge.

3. Oxford Inter-Collegiate Christian Union.

4. Fr Oddie was followed as Senior Member by successive Principals of Pusey House, Fr Philip Ursell and Fr Jonathan Baker. From 2013 to 2014, the Senior Member was Dr Judith Wolfe, Fellow of St John's College (now of St Andrews).

5. Letter to E. R. Eddison (7 February 1943). Cf. letter to his brother (18 February 1940); and Dorothy L. Sayers (5 January 1949).

6. Lewis read 'Dante's Similes' to the Oxford Dante Society on 13 February 1940 and 'Imagery in the Last Eleven Cantos of Dante's *Comedy*' on 9 November 1948.

7. The Socratic Club was founded by Stella Aldwinckle in 1941 and remained in existence till 1972. Lewis was president from its foundation until his move to Cambridge in 1955.

8. Austin Farrer, 'The Christian Apologist', in *Light on C. S. Lewis*, ed. Jocelyn Gibb (London: Geoffrey Bles, 1965), 25.

9. Planned for publication as a Magdalen Occasional Paper. The Revd Dr Michael Piret, Dean of Divinity at Magdalen, is a former president of the Oxford C. S. Lewis Society.

10. (Grand Rapids, MI: Eerdmans, 2015). Don W. King is Professor of English at Montreat College, North Carolina.

11. Cuneo, Andrew P. 'Selected Literary Letters of C. S. Lewis', D.Phil. diss., University of Oxford, 2001.

Index

Note: Works by Inklings are indexed under title; other literary works are indexed under author; locators followed by the letter 'n' refer to notes.